Madame Audrey's Guide to Mostly Cheap But Good Reference Books for Small and Rural Libraries

AUDREY LEWIS

AMERICAN LIBRARY ASSOCIATION

Chicago and London

1998

While extensive effort has gone into ensuring the reliability of information appearing in this book, the publisher makes no warranty, express or implied, on the accuracy or reliability of the information, and does not assume and hereby disclaims any liability to any person for any loss or damage caused by errors or omissions in this publication.

Project editor: Eloise L. Kinney

Cover and text design: Lesiak Design

Composition by the dotted i in Garamond using QuarkXPress 3.32

Printed on 50-pound White Offset, a pH-neutral stock, and bound in 10-point coated cover stock by Data Reproductions

The paper used in this publication meets the minimum requirements of American National Standard for Information Sciences—Permanence of Paper for Printed Library Materials, ANSI Z39.48-1992. ∞

Library of Congress Cataloging-in-Publication Data
Lewis, Audrey.
    Madame Audrey's guide to mostly cheap but good reference books for
small and rural libraries / Audrey Lewis.
        p.   cm.
    ISBN 0-8389-0733-4
    1. Reference books—Bibliography.   2. Small libraries—United
States—Book lists.   3. Rural libraries—United States—Book lists.
    I. Title
    Z1035.1.L59   1998
    011'.02—dc21   98-30767

Printed in the United States of America.

02 01 00 99 98   5 4 3 2 1

Contents

DISCARDED

ix

CONTENTS

Introduction

The introduction to a reference work or bibliography is supposed to give the user the scope and purpose of the work itself. How can I best describe the potpourri of clever compendiums, awesome atlases, delightful dictionaries, excellent encyclopedias, and helpful handbooks that are gathered here for the express purpose of enabling you, the librarian, to astonish and amaze your patrons?

Purpose

First, let me explain the purpose of the book. It is designed to be used mainly by small and rural libraries that do not subscribe to a wealth of reviewing media nor are able to attend many bibliographic classes or workshops. Staff of rural libraries have limited time in which to choose helpful reference materials. The purpose of this book is to help staff of small, busy libraries by picking out some of the basic materials available and telling library workers about the features they offer.

Scope

As to scope, this book covers the whole range of reference books offered by a library, with one or two exceptions, encyclopedias being the most obvious. I should explain that I did not take the Dewey schedules and fit books into them. Rather, I chose good books and arranged them in rough Dewey order. I have included some older titles to help the balance of subjects, but, in most cases, if there was not a new, well-reviewed, relatively inexpensive title available in a topic, that topic is not "covered."

Cost

I have tried to keep the cost of the books below $200 each, with a relatively small number of titles going over the $100 mark. Time was when a list of inexpensive reference books could come in at under $50 apiece. That time is past.

Arrangement

As mentioned above, the books are arranged in "rough Dewey order." This means that I followed the order where it was handy and deviated from it where I felt the subject matter or treatment warranted it (e.g., some historical atlases are placed with the main topic, such as "Civil War," rather than in the "Historical Atlas" section). Within each Dewey section (100s, 200s, and so forth), the books are arranged under subject categories and then alphabetical by author and then title under these subjects.

I have starred (★) certain titles that I feel are especially good in their particular fields.

Content

For each book listed, the following information is given where known: author, title, publisher, publication date, number of pages, features, LC number, ISBN number, and price. This information is followed by a short summary of information about the book taken from reviews or experience. I tend to be quantitative in many of my annotations. I have tried to tell librarians if a book has four hundred color photos, twelve maps, and a five-page bibliography. Money does not come easily to many of my fellow librarians, and I want to make sure they know what they are getting.

Sources

Where did these titles come from? Where did I get my "material"? For the most part, I scanned the pages of *American Reference Books Annual (ARBA),* from 1994 to 1997, and *Library Journal,* from 1995 to May 1997, and picked out books and subjects I thought most likely to be most useful in rounding out the reference or the circulating nonfiction collections of a small or rural library. I then read the reviews and wrote a short annotation abstracting the information found therein. For the older titles I have included, I went to older editions of this list, which I had published for the White Pine Library Cooperative.

So . . . what is this list? It is a list of quick reference sources, all of which have been well received and reviewed in a qualified source, that should be considered for purchase by small and rural libraries beefing up their collections. I hope that it will be of use to selection staff in medium-sized libraries and students of reference.

Well . . . what are you waiting for? Go spend a little money on books!

MADAME AUDREY

000s
Generalities

One could easily define the 000s as all of the things for which Melvil Dewey could not find a place elsewhere, such as computers, sign language, and newspapers! As a matter of fact, Dewey was not even around when many of the 000s as we know them were invented or discovered!

Some genuine "general works" are in this category, such as books about obtaining information, famous firsts, world records, and lists of associations.

Information on books and book collecting is a valuable part of this section. Prices, tips on collecting, and how to set up a home library are covered in the books chosen here.

Books on computers, technology, and the Internet have been included, even though it's possible some of them will probably be easily outdated. For this area, readers and selectors would do well to check current reviewing media when possible and to be on the lookout for updated editions of the listed materials.

Books on uncovering information and collections of trivia or unrelated facts make up an important part of a library's collection of "general works." As with books of quotations, one can never have too many books of trivia.

Books

Carter, John, ed. *ABC for Book Collectors*. Edited and revised by Nicolas Barker. 7th ed. Oak Knoll Books, 1995. 224p.   LC 94-29934   1-884718-05-1 $25

> A glossary of terms for book collectors, this defines more than four hundred fifty words in entries consisting of a few sentences to one thousand words. There is a British bias, but U.S. cognates are given. It also contains a four-page table of abbreviations.

Wagner, Patricia J., ed. *The Bloomsbury Review Booklover's Guide: A Collection of Tips, Techniques, Anecdotes, Controversies and Suggestions for the Home Library.* Bloomsbury Review, 1996. 280p. illus. index.   0-9631589-3-7 $21.95

> How do you transform a "bunch of books into a library that works"? By using this book. There are sections on checking the physical state of your books with lots of information on mold, pests, and storage. There is a discussion on the process of actually buying books (who needs help for that?) and material on cataloging, restoration, and online services. Aimed at the "home librarian," this could also be used by staff of small libraries.

Zempel, Edward N. and Linda A. Verkler, eds. *Book Prices: Used and Rare, 1996.* Spoon River, 1996. 798p.   0-930358-14-7 $72

> Questions are often asked about the value of old books. *American Book Prices Current* (Bancroft Parkman, annual) and *Bookman's Price Index* (Gale Research, semiannual) are the classics, but both are expensive. *Book Prices* helps fill a need for this information in small libraries. It gives much of the same material from British and American book dealers' catalogs at a fraction of the price of *Bookman's Price Index* (around $280 a volume).

Computers and Computer Technology

Dillon, Patrick M. and David C. Leonard. *Multimedia Technology from A to Z.* Oryx, 1994. 256p. bibliog.   LC 94-37853   0-89774-892-1 $25 paper

> The vocabulary of multimedia is, to say the least, confusing to the layperson because it deals with many technologies in one. This dictionary is one of the best available, with a wide range and attention to detail. The entries are well written, and a good bibliography adds to its value.

Freedman, Alan. *The Computer Glossary: The Complete Illustrated Dictionary.* 7th ed. AMACOM, 1995. 574p. illus.   LC 94-37624   0-8144-0127-9 $39.95 with disk

> This dictionary has a topics section that contains basic vocabulary for each aspect of the computer industry and is very helpful in finding a particular term. There are many useful and amusing drawings and photographs. Definitions are by acronym, so one has to think in those terms rather than in words.

Hansen, Brad. *The Dictionary of Multimedia: Terms and Acronyms.* Franklin, Beedle, 1997. 343p.   LC 96-9368   1-887902-18-X; 1-887902-14-7 $26.95; $16.95

> HTML, CGI, URL—when will it all end? Probably not in our lifetime, so get a copy of this timely handbook to one area of "computerspeak" and learn the meaning of more than two thousand terms. It includes a great list of other sources and a good section for web developers.

Hordeski, Michael F. *The McGraw-Hill Illustrated Dictionary of Personal Computers*. 4th ed. McGraw-Hill, 1995. 568p. illus.   0-07-0304092; 0-07030410-6 $32.95; $24.95 paper

> The terms here are those that would be found by the average computer user in reading books and periodicals. The cross-references are good, but the book assumes some familiarity with computers, and it is not for the total novice.

Spencer, Donald D. *The Large Print Computer Dictionary*. Camelot Publishing, 1995. 196p. illus.   LC 94-32000   0-89218-242-3 $24.95 paper

> This dictionary for the visually impaired is printed in eighteen-point Times Roman. Twelve hundred words are defined for "the average, non-technical computer user." It may go out-of-date quickly, but it would be good for libraries with patrons who use large-print materials.

Spencer, Donald D. *Personal Computer Dictionary*. Camelot Publishing, 1995. 184p. illus.   LC 94-23064   0-89218-223-7 $19.95 paper

> Unlike his *Illustrated Computer Dictionary* (below), Spencer has here produced a work that will serve more experienced users as well as beginners in the field. Fourteen hundred terms represent almost all areas of computer studies. Excellent diagrams help explain terms, and the language is clear and relatively jargon free. Recommended for anyone who uses computers.

Spencer, Donald D. *Spencer's Illustrated Computer Dictionary*. Camelot Publishing, 1995. 237p. illus.   LC 94-33107   0-89218-220-2 $24.95 paper

> For the person who knows practically nothing about computers, this offers clear and precise definitions. Biographies and historical terms are offered for the student. Coverage in some areas is spotty, and this is not a work for the advanced user. It is perfect for the beginner who wants a start in the right direction.

The Internet

Comer, Douglas E. *The Internet Book: Everything You Need to Know about Computer Networking and How the Internet Works*. Prentice-Hall, 1995. 312p.   LC 94-22316 0-13-151565-9 $25.95 paper

> What the title promises, it gives. This is a treatise on how the Internet works rather than on tools for its use. A nuts-and-bolts description of how the whole thing operates.

Hahn, Harley. *The Internet Yellow Pages*. 3d ed. Osborne/McGraw-Hill, 1996. 812p. illus. index.   0-07-882182-7 $29.95 paper

> This wide-ranging book has more than five thousand listings and plenty of personality. Each listing has a brief, humorous annotation. Because it is a true "yellow pages," the entries are arranged by subjects and cover all

types of sources, such as FTP, Gopher, TELNET, and World Wide Web sites. There are listservs, newsgroups, and chats. There is a detailed table of contents. The overshy might be aware that there are listings for alternative news groups and frank discussions of sex.

Ihnatko, Andy. *Cyberspeak: An Online Dictionary*. Random, 1996. 218p.
LC 96-42055   0-679-77095-X $12.95 paper

> Did someone once say that the computer would rid us of our need for paper? One has only to count the books written about computers to see the error of this theory. The author himself admits that the term *cyber* attached to a product usually means fast money for the producer of the item! Nonetheless . . . this is a good start for newbies among a library's clientele who want to learn the ins and outs of cyberspeak.

★ Maloy, Timothy K. *The Internet Research Guide: A Concise, Friendly, and Practical Handbook for Anyone Researching in the Wide World of Cyberspace*. Allworth, 1996. 208p.   LC 95-83010   1-880559-45-5 $18.95 paper

> Worried by the web? Have nightmares about the 'Net? Try this book written by an experienced 'Net author and learn how to evaluate service providers, how to find a user-friendly browser, and how to locate various types of information. The author is realistic and discusses the Internet's strengths and weaknesses and what kind of material one is likely to find thereon. Recommended for all libraries.

Morse, David. *CyberDictionary: Your Guide to the Wired World*. Knowledge Exchange, 1996. 300p. bibliog.   1-888232-04-8 $17.95

> This clearly written dictionary gives definitions of more than nine hundred words, phrases, and acronyms on the Internet and its background. Sidebars add to this work's browsability. Appendixes list associations and agencies involved in the "information superhighway," and there is a long bibliography of sources.

★ Smith, Darren L., ed. *Web Site Source Book*. Omnigraphics, 1996. 522p.
LC 96-658735   0-7808-0095-8 $65 paper

> More than seventy-one hundred web sites are arranged in alphabetical order and organized in fifty subject areas. Each entry gives full directory information for each organization or company represented. Directories such as these are excellent for those who fear "surfing," are not skilled in the use of search engines, or are starting out and just want to know what's on the web.

Tauber, Daniel A., Brenda Kienan and J. Tarin Towers. *Surfing the Internet with Netscape Communicator 4*. Sybex, 1996. 496p.   0-7821-2055-5 $24.99 paper

> Because, at this point, Netscape is still a popular Internet browser, a guide is needed for those who are technically impaired. The authors come to the rescue with good, clear explanations of the ups, downs, ins, and outs of Netscape Communicator 4.

Turlington, Shannon R. *Walking the World Wide Web: Your Personal Guide to the Best of the Web.* 2d ed. Ventana, 1996. 650p.   LC 94-40638   1-56604-298-4 $39.95 paper with CD-ROM

> The reviewer called this "easily one of the best introductions on the most significant development in computing." The text is available in CD and paper format. The CD-ROM allows the user to connect to the Internet and interact with a hypertext version of the book.

Government Documents

Bailey, William G. *Guide to Popular U.S. Government Publications.* 3d ed. Libraries Unlimited, 1993. 289p. index.   1-56308-031-1 $42

> The author deals with popular publications, or those devoted to topics of interest to the general public. Although the number of free publications has been cut considerably from "the old days," many free and inexpensive documents are still available to the public. This is one of the best guides of the type. The user is led to such sources as *U.S. Government Information* (U.S. GPO, semiannual) to help keep abreast of current titles. This is good for small libraries that want to boost their collections with documents.

Miscellaneous Information

Ash, Russell. *The Top Ten of Everything, 1997.* 8th ed. Dorling Kindersley, 1996. 256p. photogs. index.   LC 96-14203   0-7894-1083-4; 0-7894-1264-0 $24.95; $16.95

> Taken from governmental and research organizations as well as specialists in each field, this volume gives the top ten in many fields of human and natural endeavor. Both reference and circulating collections can use a copy of this title.

★ Berkman, Robert I. *Find It Fast: How to Uncover Expert Information on Any Subject.* 3d ed., rev. and updated. HarperCollins, 1994. 384p. index.   LC 93-50922 0-06-273294-3 $13 paper

> This useful book helps researchers unlock the doors to libraries and their resources as well as instructing them in the use of subject experts on various topics. The final section discusses some sample searches. For those who need "facts, data, answers or advice."

Bernstein, Peter and Christopher Ma. *The Practical Guide to Practically Everything:. The Ultimate Consumer Manual, 1997.* Random, 1996. 963p. illus. index. 0-679-75492-X $13.95 paper

> Two *U.S. News and World Report* editors have gathered a compilation of everyday "necessary" information on such topics as finance, health, education, computers, housing, travel, entertainment, and sports. It is well organized and well written. Much of the information can be found elsewhere, but small libraries and home libraries will find it useful and concise.

Madigan, Carol Orsag and Ann Elmwood. *Life's Big Instruction Book: The Almanac of Indispensable Information*. Warner, 1995. 912p. illus. index. LC 94-26523 0-446-51757-7 $29.95

> Books that try to be all things to all people seldom succeed, but this one succeeds better than some. The authors are part of *The Book of Lists* (Little, Brown, 1995) editorial team, so they have some experience in the information biz. Full of general, instructive consumer advice and coping techniques, this book will find a niche in most libraries.

Firsts

★ Kane, Joseph. *Famous First Facts: A Record of First Happenings, Discoveries and Inventions in American History*. 4th rev. ed. H. W. Wilson, 1981. 1350p. LC 81-3395 0-8242-0661-4 $80

> The grandaddy of all the "first" books. Still useful and chock-full of facts. The first time something happened is described in a short entry with dates and persons involved. Note, however, that these are American firsts.

Parliamentary Procedure

★ Robert, Henry M. *Robert's Rules of Order*. Fleming H. Revell Co., 1993. 192p. 0-8007-8160-6 $5.99 paper

> This famous rule book is a compendium of parliamentary law for societies, conventions, and other assemblies. There are many editions.

Communications

Weiner, Richard. *Webster's New World Dictionary of Media and Communications*. Rev. ed. Macmillan, 1996. 676p. LC 96-1249 0-02-860611-6 $39.95

> The first edition of this book was named a *Library Journal* Best Reference Book of the Year for 1990. The updates in this edition show new vocabulary in communications and give information on the Internet and its use in communications. A work of large scope, this defines approximately thirty-five thousand terms, including slang. This is a good work in the field for most libraries.

100s

Philosophy and Psychology

Although philosophy is a subject that usually does not get much of a work-out in small public libraries (or large public libraries, for that matter), a basic dictionary or one-volume encyclopedia on the subject is a must for a well-rounded reference collection. Listed here are various dictionaries of philosophies and historical material on those philosophies. It is important to choose works that include information on Eastern as well as Western traditions.

The occult and astrology have always been topics of high interest to adults and young people. The usual information on witches and the supernatural is included, but this seems to be a prime era for publishing on vampires. Two of the best-reviewed selections are included here.

Works on psychology need to reflect some history of the discipline as well as up-to-date information on facts, terms, and theories in the field.

Dictionaries of Philosophy

★ Audi, Robert, ed. *The Cambridge Dictionary of Philosophy*. Cambridge University Press, 1995. 910p. index.   LC 95-13775   0-521-40224-7; 0-521-48328-X $89.95; $27.95 paper

> This book fills the need for a comprehensive one-volume source on philosophy. Three hundred eighty-one scholars have contributed more than four thousand signed entries that are up-to-date and authoritative. Philosophers and all fields and subfields of philosophy are covered, as are non-Western philosophy and related subjects.

Blackburn, Simon. *The Oxford Dictionary of Philosophy*. Oxford University Press, 1994. 408p.   LC 94-8832   0-19-211694-0 $39.95

> This compact dictionary brings the study of philosophy into the current era with five hundred biographies, including twentieth-century figures and recent concerns such as bioethics, abortion, and feminism. Twenty-five hundred entries cover a wide range of topics in an objective and concise manner.

Honderich, Ted, ed. *The Oxford Companion to Philosophy*. Oxford University Press, 1995. 500p. bibliog. maps. index.   LC 94-36914   0-19-866132-0 $49.95

> Accurate and informative entries in this work include brief bibliographies. Along with the expected entries (historical figures, systems of philosophy, appropriate terms), are an excellent index, a chronology, and good maps.

Mautner, Thomas, ed. *A Dictionary of Philosophy*. Blackwell Publications, 1995. 482p.   LC 95-21625   0-631-18459-7 $29.95

> Unlike *The Cambridge Dictionary of Philosophy* and *The Oxford Companion to Philosophy* (above), this work is limited to Western philosophy. Unique to this work is a summing up of their ideas by many current thinkers. There is overlap in all of these books, but all treat some things the others don't. Larger collections may want to own more than one.

History of Philosophy

Kenny, Anthony, ed. *The Oxford History of Western Philosophy*. Oxford University Press, 1994. 390p. illus. maps. index.   LC 94-9858   0-19-824278-6 $45

> Western philosophy is covered in five chapters dealing with ancient, medieval, and Continental philosophy and philosophers from Descartes to Kant and Mill to Wittgenstein. The history of political philosophy is in a sixth chapter. This material and its presentation presumes some knowledge of philosophy on the part of the user.

★ McAllister, Linda L. *Hypatia's Daughters: Fifteen Hundred Years of Women Philosophers*. Indiana University, 1996. 336p. index.   LC 95-45598   0-253-33057-2; 0-253-21060-7 $49.95; $22.50 paper

> This book provides the first overview of the roles of women in the history of Western philosophy. Among the women discussed here are Hypatia, Hildegard of Bingen, Princess Elisabeth, Sor Juana, Mary Wollstonecraft, Hannah Arendt, and Angela Davis. Recommended for philosophy students and lay readers alike.

★ Schuhmacher, Stephen and Gert Woerner, eds. *The Encyclopedia of Eastern Philosophy and Religion: Buddhism * Hinduism * Taoism * Zen*. Shambhala, 1994. 468p. illus.   0-87773-980-3 $25 paper

> Definitions are clearly and concisely written in this dictionary of the four major traditions of Eastern philosophy. Each article begins with an indication of the tradition to which it belongs. The phrases and names are transliterated from the original Eastern language. Good for those new to Eastern studies and for small libraries.

The Supernatural

★ Guiley, Rosemary Ellen. *The Encyclopedia of Witches and Witchcraft.* Facts on File, 1990. 432p. illus.   LC 89-11776   0-8160-1793-X $45

> This detailed history of witchcraft covers the subject from ancient times to more recent developments and interest. Guiley holds no truck with the view of witches as devil worshippers. Information on modern personalities is included.

Guiley, Rosemary Ellen with J. B. Macabre. *The Complete Vampire Companion: Legend and Lore of the Living Dead.* Macmillan, 1994. 240p. illus. bibliog. index. LC 94-10737   0-671-85024-5 $16 paper

> Somewhat more tongue-in-cheek than the usual reference tome, this work covers such topics as varieties of vampires, vocabulary, prevention and extinction, haunts of vampires, and much more. The section entitled "The Entertaining Vampire" covers the movies, books, music, and so forth devoted to the species. There is a twenty-three-page bibliography, a nine-page filmography, a list of organizations, and a calendar of dates (presumably for those whose thirst is not sated by *Chase's Calendar of Events—see* under "Events").

Litvinoff, Sarah, ed. *The Illustrated Guide to the Supernatural.* Macmillan, 1986. 160p. illus. biblog.   LC 86-11928   0-8161-8904-8 $25

> Not a comprehensive work, this is a useful introduction to the topic. Each of 145 terms on the supernatural is handled in layperson's language. Litvinoff was coeditor for *Man, Myth and Magic* (Marshall Cavendish, 1994), but there is no duplication in text or illustration.

Melton, J. Gordon. *The Vampire Book: The Encyclopedia of the Undead.* Gale, 1994. 852p. illus. index.   0-8103-9553-3; 0-8103-2295-1 $39.95; $16.95 paper

> Just when you thought it was safe to walk down that dark alley, here comes J. Gordon Melton with twice the information on vampires as the Guiley and Macabre work (above). The almost four hundred entries are arranged in alphabetical order, and entries range from two hundred to three thousand words. Most have a brief bibliography. Special features include a chronology, more than one hundred illustrations, a filmography, and a list of fan clubs. Patrons of public libraries will find both of these works useful and entertaining. They will be good for reference or circulating collections.

Spencer, John and Anne Spencer. *The Encyclopedia of Ghosts and Spirits.* Headline Book Publishing/Trafalgar Square, 1993. 416p. illus. bibliog. index.   0-7472-0508-6; 0-7472-3800-6 $39.95; $13.95 paper

> First divided by type of occurrence, three hundred substantiated ghost stories are covered here. Each event has the name or source of the information. An introduction explains real-life ghost-hunting techniques. There is

a good bibliography, and the book itself is a great read. Recommended for libraries where stories of the supernatural are popular as well as for those who want it as a reference tool.

Astrology

Lewis, James R. *The Astrology Encyclopedia*. Gale/Visible Ink, 1994. 550p. illus. bibliog. index.   0-8103-8900-2; 0-8103-9460-X $45.00; $19.95 paper

> Business and agricultural astrology are two of the fields covered in this excellent work written by an expert in alternative religions. The 780 entries are intended to help students of astrology but also to help the skeptic understand the topic. Simple sun-sign astrology (see your local newspaper) is given little credence here, but there is an emphasis on natal astrology, which deals with individuals. An excellent work for any library.

★ Parker, Derek and Julia Parker. *The New Compleat Astrologer: The Practical Encyclopedia of Astrological Science: New Twenty-first Century Edition*. Completely revised, updated, and expanded. Random House Value, 1990. 288p. illus. bibliog. index.   0-517-69700-9 $15.99

> If you have astrology buffs, this is another fine reference book for you! And them! The *American Reference Books Annual* (Libraries Unlimited, 1990) calls it "graphically stunning" and a "landmark in astrological compilation"! And all for around sixteen bucks. The book covers history of astrology, the zodiac, science and astrology, how to interpret aspects and progressions, and any other topic an astrologer could wish for.

Psychology

Chaplin, J. *Dictionary of Psychology*. 2d rev. ed. Dell, 1985. 528p.   0-440-31925-0 $6.99 paper

> This handy paperback lists terms of common use in the fields of psychology, psychiatry, and psychobiology. Somewhat limited in scope, this will be a good starting point for the layperson to use before turning to more technical works.

Corsini, Raymond J. and Alan Auerbach. *Concise Encyclopedia of Psychology*. 2d ed. Wiley, 1996. 1200p. bibliog. index.   0-471-13159-8 $135

> A condensation of the acclaimed four-volume *Encyclopedia of Psychology* (Wiley, 1994), this work is accessible for lay readers. Many well-known experts in current psychology have contributed to it, and a wide range of topics are covered. Articles are cross-referenced, and an appendix of brief bios of one thousand psychologists completes the book.

Dreams

Fontana, David. *The Secret Language of Dreams: A Visual Key to Dreams and Their Meanings.* Chronicle Books, 1994. 176p. illus. index.   LC 93-48583   0-8118-0791-6; 0-8118-0728-2 $29.95; $17.95 paper

> Fontana, a psychologist with a great deal of experience in the field, opens *The Secret Language of Dreams* with three introductions: one, a historical outline of dream analysis; two, the meanings of dreams from a scientific point of view; and three, the inner language or grammar of dreams. The larger part of the book is given over to a discussion of dream symbols and their meanings.

Lewis, James R. *The Dream Encyclopedia.* Gale, 1995. 416p. illus.   LC 95-10759 0-7876-0155-1 $49.95 paper

> Recommended for libraries that need popular materials on dreams, this work includes definitions of more than 250 dream topics. There is a brief overview on sleep and dream research, a section on the interpretation of dreams, and a list of resources, such as organizations that study dreams and sleep.

Parker, Julia and Derek Parker. *Parker's Complete Book of Dreams.* Dorling Kindersley, 1995. 208p. illus.   LC 94-27918   1-56458-855-6 $24.95

> This attractive and useful dream book has information on the history and theories of dream meanings. The reader is given advice on how to recall dreams and record them for further study and thought.

200s
Religion

The field of religion is a wide one that encompasses the whole of mankind. A dictionary or encyclopedia of religious theory is an important purchase.

Materials on the Bible are important for small or large libraries. Such materials may include dictionaries, atlases, and concordances. Biographical information and commentary on the Bible are also important.

Works on various belief systems should make up a part of any library collection. Materials on denominations and cults of Christianity will be useful as will materials on Jewish history and observance and other religions of the world. Again, dictionaries, atlases, and handbooks will make up the bulk of these materials.

World mythology is another popular topic for literate adults and students. Because many literary allusions are based on mythology and the stories of myth are taught on all levels, from elementary school to college, it is important to have the great mythological traditions—such as classical, northern European, Asian, Egyptian, and New World—represented in your collections.

Dictionaries of Religion

Pye, Michael, ed. *The Continuum Dictionary of Religion*. Continuum, 1994. 336p. bibliog.   LC 93-36623   0-8264-0639-4 $34.95

A seven-member board of experts and forty-three contributors have ensured that this book approaches all religions with equal reverence. Five thousand entries give information on deities, beliefs, theology, practices, and schools of thought. The definitions are clear, and the book is truly worldwide in coverage. This is an excellent addition to any reference collection.

Religion in America

Queen, Edward L., Stephen R. Prothero and Gardiner H. Shattuck. *The Encyclopedia of American Religious History*. 2 vols. Facts on File, 1995. 704p. illus. index. LC 95-2487   0-8160-2406-5 $99

For libraries that cannot afford the three-volume *Encyclopedia of the American Religious Experience* (Macmillan Library Reference, 1987), this work does a good job of portraying the diversity of religious experience in American history. Articles of varying length deal with Buddhism, Islam, Judaism, Christianity, and other religions and also cover people, denominations, religious movements, and issues. Reviewers called the book "well-researched and authoritative."

The Bible

★ Achtemeier, Paul J. *HarperCollins Bible Dictionary*. HarperCollins, 1996. 1178p. illus. maps. index.   LC 96-25424   0-06-060037-3 $40

> One hundred eighty members of the Society of Biblical Literature—Protestant, Catholic, and Jewish—took part in the compilation of this all-new objective dictionary that emphasizes current knowledge and discoveries. Good illustrations and maps make this a reference bargain.

Bimson, John J., ed. *Baker Encyclopedia of Bible Places: Towns and Cities * Countries and States * Archaeology and Topography*. Baker Book House, 1995. 320p. illus. maps. index.   0-8010-1093-4 $29.99

> A good index makes the information in this book readily accessible to its users—laypeople interested in biblical topics. It is full of color photos, diagrams of ancient buildings, and maps. Reviews suggest that this would be a good choice for travelers to the Middle East. It is easily read and filled with facts on the culture and geography of the world of the Bible.

★ Mays, James L. *Harper's Bible Commentary*. Harper, 1988. 132p. illus. maps. index.   LC 88-45148   0-06-065541-0 $40

> This commentary on ideas and events in the Bible serves as a companion to *HarperCollins Bible Dictionary* (above). Recommended for academic and public libraries, this work represents mainstream Bible scholarship.

Moyter, J. Alec and Gordon J. Wenham. *New Bible Commentary*. 4th ed. InterVarsity Press, 1994. 1304p. illus. maps.   LC 94-4076   0-8308-1442-6 $39.99

> Discussion of each book of the Bible is begun with information on its authors and setting, an outline of contents, and a bibliography. The easy reading style of the chapter breakdowns makes the book accessible to all audiences. Comments are based on the New International Version of the Bible. Bible events are discussed and illuminated with maps, timelines, family trees, and diagrams.

Porter, J. R. *The Illustrated Guide to the Bible*. Oxford University Press, 1995. 288p. illus. maps. index.   0-19-521159-6 $35

> This outstanding guide takes the reader "from creation to the end of the world," with beautiful illustrations and an excellent, neutral text. Arranged by books of the Bible, it shows how culture and, indeed, all walks of life

have been influenced by the Bible. An excellent addition to inexpensive works in this field.

★ *Who's Who in the Bible*. Reader's Digest/Random, 1994. 480p. illus.   LC 94-17591 0-89577-618-9 $32

> Incorporating biblical criticism, this book presents more than five hundred personalities, with faults and virtues alike. Articles on people from the Old Testament, the New Testament, and the Apocrypha are illuminated by four hundred color illustrations. User-friendly, this work is excellent for the general reader.

Bible Concordances

★ Cruden, Alex, ed. *Cruden's Complete Concordance*. Dugan Publishers, 1986. 0-932453-68-6 $29.95

> Look up the word or idea you want and find Bible quotations with chapter-and-verse citations. Check *Books in Print* (Bowker, annual) for various editions of this classic concordance. There is usually a wide range of prices.

Strong, James. *The New Strong's Exhaustive Concordance of the Bible*. 2d ed. Nelson, 1990.   0-8407-5442-6 $29.99

> This is the most complete concordance to the King James version of the Bible, and it features a "Key Verse Comparison Chart," which lists more than eighteen hundred verses of the Bible as they appear in six modern versions.

Bible Atlases

Aharoni, Yohanan and Michael Avi-Yonah. *The Macmillan Bible Atlas*. 3d rev. ed. Macmillan, 1993. 224p. illus. index.   LC 92-27895   0-02-500605-3 $35

> New information from recent archaeological excavations has been added to this revision of a 1977 title. Each map, in a period from 3,000 B.C.E. to 200 C.E., is supplemented with references to Bible sources. Some of the maps cover events that may not have been mentioned in the Bible but took place in a relevant time period. Excellent text and photographs add to the value of each map.

★ Wiseman, David, J. J. Bimson and D. R. Wood. *New Bible Atlas*. Intervarsity, 1994. 132p. illus. bibliog. maps. index.   0-8308-1443-4 $21.99

> With a total of more than eighty maps, this book has more than comparable Bible atlases. Two-thirds of the good, clear maps are in color. The Holy Land and environs are covered in terms of history, topography, archaeology, travel routes, and so forth. Excellent value for scholars and casual students alike.

Christian Theology

Erickson, Millard J. *Concise Dictionary of Christian Theology.* Baker Book House, 1994. 192p.   0-8010-3029-3 $8.99 paper

> Theological terms, movements, church history terms, biblical terms, events, figures, and groups are all covered here with short (one- to three-sentence) definitions. The work is unbiased, mentioning only if a term arises from one denomination. The price is certainly right.

★ Livingstone, E. A. and F. L. Cross. *The Oxford Dictionary of the Christian Church.* 3d ed. Oxford University Press, 1997. 1824p. bibliog.   0-19-211655-X $125

> This is the classic one-volume dictionary on the practices, doctrines, and figures of the Christian church. There is new information on what former editions might have thought of as "fringe Christianity" and many doctrinal revisions. By the same token, more Evangelical figures are included in the ranks of historical biography. Almost five hundred contributors have added their scholarship to this edition, and many bibliographies have been updated.

Christian Biography

Douglas, J. D., ed. *Twentieth-Century Dictionary of Christian Biography.* Baker Book House, 1995. 439p.   LC 95-91   0-8010-3031-5 $24.99

> This work contains biographical sketches of "ministers, theologians, missionaries, lawyers, social reformers, educators, historians, scientists, writers and so forth" who had an impact on Christianity and whose lives were lived in the present century. Basic facts are given, and an evaluation of the person's impact on his or her time is made. This biographical dictionary is a good source that can give short answers on important persons in this area.

Denominations

★ Bedell, Ken, ed. *Yearbook of American and Canadian Churches, 1996.* Abingdon, 1996. 312p.   0-687-05589-X $29.95 paper

> Basic facts and statistics about the many denominations of North America are covered in a concise style. Pertinent addresses and brief historical sketches for each group are included.

Melton, J. Gordon. *Encyclopedic Handbook of Cults in America.* 2d rev. and updated ed. Garland, 1992. 424p. index.   LC 92-11540   0-8153-0502-8; 0-8153-1140-0 $65.00; $18.95 paper

> We've seen their magazine ads, but who exactly are the Rosicrucians? What do followers of the Unification Church believe? Answers to these and many

more questions may be found in this accessible, unbiased work on "cult" religions in the United States.

Catholicism

Broderick, Robert C. *The Catholic Encyclopedia*. Rev. ed. Thomas Nelson, 1990. 613p. illus. 0-8407-3175-2 $19.99 paper

> Thirty-five new articles have been added to the old edition, mostly on topics relating to changes in the Code of Canon Law. The reader can expect clear, well-written articles on traditional Catholicism.

Hellwig, Monika K. and Michael Glazier, eds. *The Modern Catholic Encyclopedia*. Liturgical Press, 1994. 976p. illus. LC 94-21359 0-8146-5495-9 $69.95

> One hundred ninety contributors have written thirteen hundred entries on various aspects of Catholicism. Articles on controversial topics are even-handed, and there is good coverage of general interest topics such as Catholic organization and practice, doctrine, and women in the church. This work has lots of *see also* cross-references to help the reader navigate between related topics.

★ McBrien, Richard P., ed. *The HarperCollins Encyclopedia of Catholicism*. HarperCollins, 1995. 1349p. illus. LC 94-39972 0-06-065338-8 $45

> Highly recommended for academic, public, church, and synagogue libraries, this larger work contains forty-two hundred entries, with twenty-nine longer essays on topics such as God, Christ, marriage, Mary, and the Eucharist. Tables—such as a list of popes, patron saints, statistics, and a time line—enhance the text, as do many black-and-white photographs and drawings. Pronunciation is included, and almost every article has a bibliography. If you are only going to purchase one title in this field, make it this one, although it and *The Modern Catholic Encyclopedia* (above) complement each other well.

Saints

Benedictine Monks of St. Augustine's Abbey, comps. *The Book of Saints: A Dictionary of Servants of God*. Morehouse Publishing, 1993. 605p. illus. index. LC 89-33515 0-8192-1611-9 $24.95 paper

> According to reviewers, this is the "most accurate, up-to-date list of people whose lives of faith and virtue" led to sainthood in the Catholic Church. More than eleven thousand persons are covered in brief entries. Also included is a list of those legendary figures whose feast days have been eliminated from the calendar. Useful for reference librarians are lists of emblems of saints as well as patron saints.

Sandoval, Annette. *The Directory of Saints: A Concise Guide to Patron Saints.* Dutton, 1996. 297p. bibliog. index. LC 95-44252 0-525-94154-1 $18.95

> This is one of the few dictionaries of saints to offer access by field of patronage. Several hundred saints are listed alphabetically by subject, with a short biography for each.

World Religions

Bowker, John. *World Religions: The Great Faiths Explored and Explained.* Dorling Kindersley, 1997. 200p. illus. maps. index. LC 96-38277 0-7894-1439-2 $34.95

> In an innovative attempt to explain religion by means of the art of various cultures, Bowker has produced an excellent reference that uses icons, paintings, or sculptures as starting points from which to discuss various religious concepts.

★ *Eerdmans' Handbook to the World's Religions.* Rev. ed. William B. Eerdmans, 1994. 464p. illus. maps. index. 0-8028-0853-0 $24 paper

> This revised edition is illuminated by the many color photos and illustrations that did not appear in the first edition. Articles—especially on Judaism, Islam, and Christianity—have been revised, and there is a new section on "Religion in Today's World." The work is divided into eight main sections with a "rapid fact-finder" for brief definitions. History, beliefs and practices, divisions, festivals, and pantheons are discussed for the religions covered.

Goring, Rosemary, ed. *Larousse Dictionary of Beliefs and Religions.* Larousse Kingfisher Chambers, 1994. 624p. illus. LC 93-072903 0-7523-5000-5; 0-7523-0000-8 $30.00; $14.95 paper

> Key concepts of various religions are defined here by fifteen contributors in three thousand entries, usually brief. Terms for concepts, rituals, objects, and religious figures are covered. Most entries refer to living religions, although there is some coverage of ancient traditions. Although some inconsistencies exist in the coverage of certain topics, the entries are clear and accurate. Not a first-choice work but one that will complement others.

Harpur, James. *The Atlas of Sacred Places: Meeting Points of Heaven and Earth.* Henry Holt, 1994. 240p. illus. maps. index. LC 94-4597 0-8050-2775-0 $45

> A "valuable reference tool or coffee table book," this work takes the user on a tour of holy places of the world in beautiful color photos and respectful text. Text, maps, and an index-gazetteer add to the usefulness and enjoyment value of the work.

Classical Mythology

Snodgrass, Mary Ellen. *Voyages in Classical Mythology.* ABC-Clio, 1994. 478p.
illus. bibliog. maps. index.   LC 94-21167   0-87436-734-4 $55

> Although a work on voyages would seem to be limiting, this motif is recurrent in most mythologies, and almost every important figure in classic myth is covered here. Travels of forty-four heroes and deities are detailed alphabetically by name of traveler, with info on the hero's background, a travel map, a description, alternate versions, symbolism, and a bibliography.

Judaism

★ Himelstein, Shmuel. *The Jewish Primer.* Facts on File, 1992. 256p. illus. index.
0-8160-2322-0; 0-8160-2849-4 $24.95; $12.95 paper

> Although this excellent introduction to the Jewish faith is in question-and-answer form, an index helps locate specific information. All forms of Judaism are covered, but the emphasis is on Orthodoxy. This is one of the best introductions available.

Isaacs, Ronald H. and Kerry M. Olitzky. *Sacred Celebrations: A Jewish Holiday Handbook.* Ktav Publishing House, 1994. 197p. illus.   LC 94-1391   0-88125-484-3;
0-88125-496-7 $19.95; $12.95 paper

> Every Jewish holiday is explained by words from the scriptures and given a historical background, calendar date, and ways it is celebrated in the synagogue and at home. Prayers and rituals are presented in English, Hebrew, and Hebrew in the English alphabet. Recipes and games are included.

Werblowsky, R. J. Zwi and Geoffrey Wigoder, eds. *The Oxford Dictionary of the Jewish Religion.* Oxford University Press, 1997. 1088p.   LC 96-45517   0-19-508605-8
$95

> This is the most scholarly one-volume reference work available on the Jewish faith, and it includes twenty-four hundred entries on a variety of Jewish traditions and innovations. Articles are in alphabetical order, and there are good cross-references to subject headings.

World Mythology

★ Cotterell, Arthur. *A Dictionary of World Mythology.* Oxford University Press, 1990.
320p.   0-19-217747-8 $11.95 paper

> Arranged by the seven great traditions of mythology (West Asian, South and Central Asian, East Asian, European, American, African, and Oceanic), this work provides more than five hundred brief entries for mythic themes and figures. This interesting and accurate treatment includes an overview article for each tradition.

Goddesses, Heroes, and Shamans: The Young People's Guide to World Mythology.
Larousse Kingfisher Chambers, 1994. 159p. illus. maps. index.   LC 94-01374
1-85697-999-7 $19.95

> Well illustrated and well written, this book has entries for more than five
> hundred characters of myth and legend. Although designed for students,
> this book will be of use to anyone interested in mythology, folklore, and
> comparative religion.

Jordan, Michael. *Encyclopedia of Gods: Over Twenty-five Hundred Deities of the
World.* Facts on File, 1993. 352p. index.   LC 92-46762   0-8160-2909-1 $40

> In compiling this book, the author included deities that "someone with a
> serious interest in mythology would be most likely to want to identify."
> Short entries give culture source, role of deity, genealogy, and attributes.

Mercatante, Anthony S. *Who's Who in Egyptian Mythology.* 2d ed. Scarecrow, 1995.
256p. illus. bibliog.   LC 94-38889   0-8108-2967-3 $32.50

> Because the only changes were in updated bibliography, either the first or
> second edition of this book makes a good place to start a study of the
> deities of ancient Egypt.

Miller, Mary and Karl Taube. *The Gods and Symbols of Ancient Mexico and the
Maya: An Illustrated Dictionary of Mesoamerican Religion.* Thames & Hudson/
Norton, 1993. 240p. illus. bibliog. maps. index.   LC 92-80338   0-500-05068-6
$34.95

> Both the beginning student and the scholar can learn from this study of
> ideas, concepts, and practices in middle-American religion. A good index
> and cross-references are helpful, as are the hundreds of illustrations. The
> bibliography is a useful aid to further study.

★ Willis, Roy, ed. *World Mythology.* Holt, 1996. 320p. illus. index.   LC 93-3045
0-8050-2701-7; 0-8050-2701-7 $45.00; $22.50

> This is one of the few illustrated editions of world myth for adults. Its more
> than five hundred maps, photographs, and pictures describe mythologies
> of the world in an oversize volume. A good introduction, it offers food for
> thought for scholars as well.

300s
Social Sciences

One of the largest and most widely used sections in the library is the social sciences category. This catchall category also holds works specializing in various segments of the population, such as gays and lesbians, women, African Americans, and Hispanics.

Statistical works, such as the *World Almanac, Statesman's Yearbook,* and *Statistical Abstract of the United States,* are an important part of this Dewey category, and they are all musts in any library's reference collection.

Up-to-date information on the many faces of politics and government (government departments and agencies, the military, espionage, political terms, and parties) is included, and legal works for the layperson make up a big part of the 300s. Books on laws in all fifty states, legal forms, the Constitution, copyright, courtroom trials, and legal guides for the average citizen make up the bulk of the law bookshelf.

Information on careers and educational opportunities are another important category in this section. Students (or mature workers) who are looking for career information often start with such titles as *Occupational Outlook Handbook.* A good selection of college guides is a must for the high school students among a library's clientele.

"Folkways"—titles that deal with costumes, anniversaries and holidays, etiquette, and folklore—make up the final part of the social sciences section. Books about events, such as *Chase's Calendar of Events;* handbooks of manners, such as those begun by Amy Vanderbilt or Emily Post; and books of proverbs, folktales, and legends enrich and help us in our daily lives.

Sociology

Marshall, Gordon, ed. *The Concise Oxford Dictionary of Sociology.* Oxford University Press, 1994. 592p.   LC 93-37140   0-19-285237-X $13.95 paper

Thirty sociologists contributed twenty-five hundred articles ranging in length from five lines to two pages. Terms, concepts, and information about deceased sociologists are included as well as related terms in anthropology, economics, philosophy, political science, and psychology. There are hundreds of *see* references to lead readers from one topic to another. British spelling is used in this work.

Mitchell, Susan. *The Official Guide to the Generations*. New Strategist, 1995. 414p. 0-9628092-8-4 $69.95

> With public and private statistics, the author has created tables and charts with short commentary comparing the four generations from those born prior to 1933 to those born in 1976. Such topics as families, education, labor force, income, health, and attitudes are measured.

Death

Quigley, Christine, comp. and ed. *Death Dictionary: Over Fifty-five Hundred Clinical, Legal, Literary and Vernacular Terms*. McFarland, 1994. 207p. LC 93-28817   0-89950-869-3 $29.95

> It comes to us all and it is almost as inevitable as taxes. The author gives brief definitions of death-related terms from the fields of medicine, religion and myth, archaeology and anthropology, mortuary science, law and police science, and slang. Terms and concepts are in English (foreign terms are translated) and Latin. One reviewer complains that the definitions are sometimes too brief and leave one wanting more information or etymology of phrases. *Death Dictionary* has a valuable thesaurus section, listing like words under a subject heading.

Women

Franck, Irene and David Brownstone. *The Women's Desk Reference*. VikingPenguin, 1993. 840p. illus.   LC 93-17515   0-670-84513-2 $29.95

> Women in many different situations will find this book helpful. There are long sections on resources, help, and action for women. Short entries give medical, legal, and political definitions. A handy book for libraries and individuals.

Franck, Irene and David Brownstone. *Women's World: A Timeline of Women in History*. HarperCollins, 1995. 240p. photogs.   LC 94-31298   0-06-273336-2 $20

> Covering the time span from prehistory to the early 1990s, this illustrated book is divided into four different sections—politics, war, and law; religion, education, and everyday life; science, technology, and medicine; and arts and literature. Many interesting sidebars offer contemporary comments on happenings mentioned in the time line.

Gall, Susan, ed. *Women's Firsts*. Gale, 1996. 564p. photogs. bibliog. index.
LC 96-9792   0-7876-0151-9 $44.95

> Broader in scope than *The Book of Women's Firsts* (below), this work arranges its entries in fifteen subject areas including arts, education, religion, and science. Twenty-five hundred firsts are arranged by year and by country, and there is a time line. This is good for school and public library collections.

★ Olsen, Kirstin. *Chronology of Women's History*. Greenwood, 1994. 528p.
bibliog. index.   LC 93-50542   0-313-28803-8 $39.95

> This has the broadest coverage of any women's history. The span is worldwide, from prehistoric times to 1993. Each section highlights women's activity in ten areas: status and daily life; government, the military, and law; literature and the visual arts; performing arts and entertainment; athletics and exploration; activism; business and industry; science and medicine; education and scholarship; and religion. There is an index and a bibliography.

Read, Phyllis J. and Bernard Witlieb. *The Book of Women's Firsts*. Random, 1992.
511p. index.   0-679-40975-0 $24.95

> One thousand women with "breakthrough achievements" are included in this book. There are photo illustrations and short information about each woman, with emphasis on her achievements rather than her personal life. There is an index by subject.

Weatherford, Doris. *American Women's History: An A-to-Z of People, Organizations, Issues and Events*. Prentice-Hall, 1994. 396p. illus.   0-671-85028-8 $18

> Although this work excludes many entertainers, poets, and gender-stereotyped occupations, there is a wealth of information here about women that might not be included elsewhere. There are entries for biography and topics and lots of photos.

Gay and Lesbian Issues

The Gay Almanac: The Most Comprehensive Reference Source Available. Berkley, 1996. 400p. illus. index.   0-425-15300-2 $16.95 paper

The Lesbian Almanac: The Most Comprehensive Reference Source Available. Berkley, 1996. 400p. illus. index.   0-425-15301-0 $16.95 paper

> These resources feature historic time lines, lists of noted gays and lesbians, glossaries, quotations, statistics, and directories. There is also information on AIDS and cultural matters. There is some overlap in history, stats, AIDS coverage, and resources. Information is aimed at the general reader and is easily accessed. Recommended for any library.

Kroll, Gerry, ed. *The Alyson Almanac 1997 Edition: The Gay and Lesbian Fact Book*. Alyson Publications, 1997. 350p. index.   1-55583-390-X $11.95 paper

This is one of the most standard, reliable, and noteworthy sources of information on the gay and lesbian experience. There is information on history, symbols and slang, research on couples, good and bad literature (books, plays, music), biographical sketches, health, polices, laws, and much more. Voting records of members of Congress on gay and lesbian issues are included. There is an excellent subject index.

Black Experience

★ Cowan, Tom, and Jack Maguire. *Timelines of African-American History: Five Hundred Years of Black Achievement.* Perigee Books/Berkley, 1994. 368p. index. LC 94-12771   0-399-52127-5 $15 paper

> African American past is divided into seven time lines, focusing on the years 1492 to 1993. More than fifteen hundred entries show achievement in social, cultural, intellectual, and political areas. Sidebars give information on important events, people, and organizations. A good index adds to the value of this handsome book that will enrich all collections.

Estell, Kenneth. *African America: Portrait of a People.* Visible Ink Press/Gale, 1993. 791p. illus. index.   LC 94-22484   0-8103-9453-7 $18.95

> Eighteen topical chapters, written by thirteen experts in the field, cover subject entries and biographical sketches. In fact, the work is more a biographical dictionary than anything else. Coverage is broad and historical. The emphasis is on persons who have made contributions in the fields of law, the arts, medicine, religions, business, politics, and sports. There are some surprising omissions, but more women are covered here than in many other similar works. The articles are well written and informative.

Mabunda, L. Mpho, ed. *The African-American Almanac.* 7th ed. Gale, 1996. 1450p. illus. bibliog. maps. index.   0-8103-7867-4 $165

> Although costly, this contains many useful pieces of information, such as a list of African American award recipients and a valuable bibliography. The book boasts more than eight hundred maps and illustrations. Chapters are devoted to firsts, history, landmarks, civil rights, organizations, population, employment and income, religion, literature and the arts, science, fashion, and much more. This is a "noteworthy achievement" in the literature of black history and life.

Potter, Joan and Constance Claytor. *African-American Firsts: Famous, Little-Known and Unsung Triumphs of Blacks in America.* Pinto Press, 1994. 352p. illus. bibliog. index.   LC 93-84716   0-9632476-1-1 $14.95 paper

> Those seeking a useful, no-frills reference source on African American firsts should purchase *Black Firsts* (below). *African-American Firsts* is a more "literary" listing of four hundred achievements arranged by subject area. Several paragraphs give information on biographical and historical

details on the person and the "first" involved. This is excellent reading and browsing for adults and young adults.

Smith, Jessie Carney, Casper L. Jordan and Robert L. Johns, eds. *Black Firsts: Two Thousand Years of Extraordinary Achievement.* Gale, 1994. 529p. illus. index. LC 93-44155   0-8103-9490-1 $16.95 paper

Smith, a noted author on black historical topics, has joined with other experts to compile an up-to-date and attractive book of firsts in black history. Three thousand entries range in size from a sentence to a paragraph. Most entries briefly identify the subject and tell about the "first." Users have to go elsewhere for substantial biographical material. There is a calendar of firsts and a fold-out time line.

Smith, Jessie Carney, ed. *Epic Lives: One Hundred Black Women Who Made a Difference.* Gale, 1993. 632p. illus.   LC 93-106495   0-8103-9426-X $18.95 paper

These one hundred biographies of African American women are well written and long. Sources for further information are given, including newspaper and periodical articles. A photograph is included with each biography. For more biographies, see *Notable Black American Women* (Gale, 1991), also edited by Smith. Both are good additions to all collections.

Hispanic Life

Kanellos, Nicolas. *The Hispanic-American Almanac.* Gale, 1993. 780p. illus. bibliog. LC 92-75003   0-8103-7944-9 $99.50

Produced by a team of scholars as a one-stop source for information about "Hispanic life and culture in the United States," this work includes historical, cultural, and biographical material. There are more than four hundred illustrations to complement the text and a glossary of terms. The detailed table of contents will be helpful in finding information. A good bibliography lists resources for further study.

Meier, Matt S. with Conchita Serri and Richard Garcia. *Notable Latino Americans: A Biographical Dictionary.* Greenwood, 1997. 429p. index.   LC 96-27392 0-313-29105-5 $65

Well known as authors of materials on Mexican Americans, Meier, Serri, and Garcia have produced, in this book, an extremely useful compilation of 127 biographies of Hispanic men and women who have made a contribution to society after having been born in the United States of Hispanic descent or having immigrated there. The greater percentage of the people covered here are important in literature, sports, politics, or acting, but other fields are covered as well.

Novas, Himilce. *The Hispanic 100: A Ranking of the Hispanic Men and Women Who Most Influenced American Thought and Culture*. Citadel Press/Carol Publishing Group, 1995. 556p. illus. index.   LC 94-44289   0-8065-1651-8 $24.95

> This dictionary gives information about one hundred Hispanic Americans from all fields of endeavor. The one hundred people are given ranking in order of influence of U.S. culture. Ratings are determined by the person being "a trailblazer," "a legend in their own time or later," and "recognized on a far-reaching or international level." To quote the introduction, "By the year 2000, Latinos will be the largest single minority group in the United States and account for one out of three U.S. citizens." Entries give dates, a photo, and a biography with main events and publications. Written in a clear and readable manner, this is of special use to small libraries, who need inexpensive resources.

Moving and Relocation

Barlow, Diane and Steven Wasserman. *Moving and Relocation Sourcebook: Reference Guide to the One Hundred Largest Metropolitan Areas in the United States*. Omnigraphics, 1992. 724p. maps. index.   LC 91-43714   1-558883-09-6 $180

> Once in awhile, one comes across a reference book that has more than one use, and this is such a book. Aside from its main purpose, which is helping persons who have to move or relocate for a job, this is an excellent reference guide to the metropolitan areas of the United States. For each area, population, housing, cost of living, rate of growth, employment, climate, health care, education, taxes, public safety, local transportation, automobile regulations, recreation, culture, events and media, and cost of housing are covered in some detail, making it easier for the mover to make decisions. The authors supply the reader with maps of the various metropolitan areas, state maps, and lots of statistics and census rankings. A general index helps the reader locate facts.

★ Savageau, David and Geoffrey Loftus. *Places Rated Almanac*. Macmillan, 1996. 0-02861-233-7 $24.95 paper

> Another double-purpose tome such as its neighbor (above), this handy book for those wanting to move or just looking for information about cities in the United States is a guide to the major metropolitan areas, and it packs a lot of facts and opinions into a compact volume. Areas that "affect the quality of life," such as economics, climate, the arts, crime, environment, transportation, and health care, are used to rate each area. There is an overall rating from highest to lowest, plus information about each of the covered areas for each city. Thinking of moving? It will pay you to check this handy book out before you make that move!

World Politics and Statistics

Banks, Arthur S., Alan J. Day and Thomas C. Muller. *Political Handbook of the World, 1997*. 6th ed. CSA Publications, 1997. 1220p.   LC 81-643916   0-933199-12-0 $109.95

> This authoritative work competes with *The Statesman's Yearbook* (below) to provide information on the countries of the world. Included is information on urban centers, languages, and economics. There is some historical background for understanding of current events and chronologies of events.

Cook, Chris, comp. *The Facts on File World Political Almanac*. 3d ed. Facts on File, 1994. 496p. index.   0-8160-2603-3 $40

> Much-needed facts and statistics are provided in this convenient compilation of info about national and world politics since World War II. Most of the information is in the form of statistics or tables. Included are international political organizations, wars, UN operations, terrorism, the nuclear age, and so forth.

Kurian, George Thomas, ed. *The Illustrated Book of World Rankings*. 4th ed. M. E. Sharpe, 1997. 428p. illus. index.   LC 96-46086   1-56324-892-1 $99

> This new edition of the *New Book of World Rankings* rates nations of the world in thirty-two sections and three hundred fields. There are new sections on "Women," "The Environment," and "Global Indexes." The facts presented here are usually up-to-date through 1994 or 1995. This will prove to be a handy title for ranking the nations of the world according to various socioeconomic factors.

★ Reddy, Marlita A., ed. *Statistical Abstract of the World*. Gale, 1994. 1111p. maps. index.   LC 95-640698   0-8103-9199-6 $49.95

> All of the countries of the world are listed here in alphabetical order. For each country, five to six pages of data are organized into forty-two panels. Statistics cover such topics as land area, climate, resources, demographics, health statistics, ethnicity, religion, language, education, and many others. Data are taken mostly from the United Nations, the World Bank, the International Monetary Fund, and the U.S. State Department.

★ World Almanac Book Staff. *World Almanac and Book of Facts, 1997*. World Almanac, 1996.   0-88687-805-5 $19.95 paper with CD-ROM

> A library sage once said that a reference desk could handle 75 percent of its questions with a dictionary, a *World Book,* and an almanac. Requests for information have become somewhat more sophisticated since then, but this almanac is still an essential purchase for libraries. Among the multitude of items it contains are a perpetual calendar, many U.S. and world statistics, an Islamic calendar, flags of the world (in color), and a list of district judges. There is also a miniatlas and a chronology of the year's events. If you have no other book in your reference collection, have this one.

U.S. Statistics and Information

Alampi, Gary, ed. *Gale State Rankings Reporter.* 2d ed. Gale, 1996. 1657p.
0-8103-6412-3 $100

> With information from government and private sources, this book com-
> pares the states of the union in terms of physical characteristics, education,
> culture, jobs, income, economics, government, leisure, and so forth. The
> 3,044 tables show data mainly collected between 1987 and 1993.

★ Kurian, George Thomas. *Datapedia of the United States, 1790–2000: America
Year by Year.* Bernan Press, 1994. 600p. index.   0-89059-012-5 $90

> An update of *Historical Statistics of the United States,* this brings together in
> one source valuable statistics on hundreds of indicators of social, eco-
> nomic, political, and cultural developments. Many graphs and highlights
> sections show significant patterns or shifts.

★ U.S. Bureau of the Census. *Statistical Abstract of the United States, 1995:
National Data Book.* National Technical Information Service, 1995.   0-934213-46-1;
0-934213-47-8 $30.75; $28.00 paper

> This indispensable collection of statistics includes data from many sources,
> government and private. Some retrospective statistics are included.

Politics and Government

Comfort, Nicholas. *Brewer's Politics: A Phrase and Fable Dictionary.* Rev. ed.
Cassell/Sterling, 1995. 704p.   LC 94-165032   0-304-34659-4 $29.95

> This enjoyable and highly browsable dictionary has more than five thou-
> sand entries covering people, parties, treaties, and terms that readers might
> encounter in everyday reading. It is made more valuable by including hu-
> morous and informative quotations about the subjects of the definitions.

Congressional Yearbook 1994, 103rd Congress, 2nd Session. Congressional
Quarterly, 1994. 289p.   1-56802-093-7 $23.95

> With information on the makeup, operations, and legislative actions of
> Congress, this book covers its topics for one session of Congress, so look
> for the most recent one when purchasing. The largest part of the book
> deals with those topics that received the greatest consideration by the leg-
> islature that session. There is information on what is happening in con-
> gressional reform, a glossary of terms, and membership information. An
> excellent and relatively inexpensive source.

Morin, Isobel V. *Women Who Reformed Politics.* Oliver Press, 1994. 160p. illus.
index.   LC 93-46336   1-881508-16-1 $14.95

> Eight American women who made a difference are given detailed biogra-
> phies in this short but insightful work. These women—Abby Kelley Foster,
> Frances Willard, Ida Wells-Barnett, Carrie Chapman Catt, Molly Dewson,

Pauli Murray, Fannie Lou Hamer, and Gloria Steinem—gave their time and efforts to ending mob violence, abolishing slavery, curbing alcohol consumption, improving working conditions, and fighting for women's rights. Most of these issues still have ramifications today. This would be an excellent starting place for a report.

★ National Archives and Records Administration Staff, eds. *United States Government Manual, 1995–96.* Bernan Press, 1995. 904p. index.   0-89059-057-5 $33

The official handbook of the federal government, this has information on all the agencies and their purposes, programs, and officials. There is an index of names, subjects, and agencies.

Preimesberger, Jon, ed. *National Party Conventions, 1831–1992.* Congressional Quarterly, 1995. 301p. photogs.   LC 94-45711   0-87187-856-9 $29.95

Preimesberger, Jon, ed. *Presidential Elections, 1789–1992.* Congressional Quarterly, 1995. 274p. maps.   LC 94-45937   0-87187-857-7 $29.95

These companion volumes give an overview of the complete process of choosing a president. Narratives of conventions, highlight summaries, tables of votes, election laws, a list of presidential and vice-presidential candidates, and the origins of the electoral college are just a few of the features of these books that make them useful for libraries.

★ Safire, William. *Safire's New Political Dictionary: The Definitive Guide to the New Language of Politics.* Random, 1993. 960p. index.   LC 93-14554
0-679-42068-1 $35

William Safire is known as a political analyst, political insider, and wordsmith. He combines all of these talents into this volume, which is a guide to political terms and phrases. The author also goes into the origin of the phrase and some etymology where appropriate. Use caution in consulting this book. It's accessible and readable, and once you pick it up to answer a question, it's hard to put down.

The World Almanac of U.S. Politics, 1995–1997. World Almanac, 1995.
0-88687-774-1; 0-8868-7-773-3 $29.95; $18.95 paper

Even though it has a narrower scope than such titles as the *United States Government Manual* (above) and the *Washington Information Directory* (Congressional Quarterly, 1996), this work is easily accessible and will be of great use to high school and junior college students who are less skilled in research. There are lists of congressional committees, overviews of committee jurisdictions, and biographies. Toll-free and hotline numbers abound. Lots of features, such as "A Typical Day for a Member of Congress," "How a Case Moves through Court," and "How to Write a Member of Congress," will make this must reading for the politically impaired.

Divorce

ABA Staff. *The ABA Guide to Family Law: The Complete and Easy Guide to All the Laws of Marriage, Parenthood, Separation and Divorce.* Times Books/Random, 1996. 192p. maps.   LC 95-52854   0-8129-2791-5 $13 paper

> This handy guide to various domestic relations gives tips and counsel on divorce, child custody, adoption, prenuptial arrangements, cohabitation, and child support.

Engel, Margorie L. *Divorce Help Sourcebook.* Gale, 1994. 350p.   0-8103-9480-4 $17.95 paper

> Step-by-step advice and information are given to persons in the midst of a divorce or contemplating one. Legal, financial, parenting, and health problems are dealt with in a clear and practical manner. A list of sources mentions many books and magazine articles that would be of help to a divorcing person or family.

Sitarz, Daniel. *Divorce Yourself: The National No-Fault Divorce Kit.* 4th ed. Nova, 1998. 334p. bibliog. index.   0-935755-63-2; 0-935755-25-X $24.95 paper; $34.95 paper with CD-ROM

> Because the courts have determined that do-it-yourself legal manuals do not constitute "practicing without a license," we are fortunate to have such books as this one, which makes the user a more informed layperson. It includes explanations of terminology, checklists, advice on various aspects of divorce procedures, and sample forms. There is a summary of divorce laws (with citations) for all fifty states.

Espionage

Lloyd, Mark. *The Guinness Book of Espionage.* Da Capo Press, 1994. 256p. illus. maps. index.   0-306-80584-7 $16.95 paper

> This is a work that attempts to "clarify the veil of secrecy surrounding this multifaceted yet important area of governmental activity." Eight chapters cover early history, World War II, the cold war, and future trends. Historical subjects are profiled, operational terms are discussed, and the role of aircraft in espionage is covered. This has a British perspective, but it will prove useful in American libraries.

Polmar, Norman and Thomas B. Allen. *Spy Book: The Encyclopedia of Espionage.* Random, 1996. 633p. photogs. index.   LC 96-34737   0-679-42514-4 $30

> More than two thousand short entries cover people, agencies, and tools of the espionage trade. The authors are well-known collaborators on topics involving World War II and military intelligence, and they have produced a good and timely book on the topic that includes information taken from former Soviet archives. It is suitable for schools and public libraries.

Volkman, Ernest. *Spies: The Secret Agents Who Changed the Course of History*. Wiley, 1994. 288p. illus. index.   LC 93-13786   0-471-55714-5 $16.95

> Divided into "Moles," "Defectors," "Legends," "Traitors," "Spymasters," "Infamies," and "Mysteries and Curiosities," the forty-four spies uncovered here come to life in entertaining essays on their lives complete with code names and aliases. Good for the general nonfiction collection because of its readability, this will answer many questions on espionage with its good biographical material and glossary of terms.

Career Information

Federal Jobs Digest, eds. *Working for Your Uncle: Complete Guide to Finding a Job with the Federal Government*. Breakthrough, 1993. 824p. index.   0-914327-27-5 $19.95

> A complete guide to finding a federal job, this book identifies job titles and helps the user find the right hiring pathway. There is information on how to find out about job vacancies or tests. Taking the exam, preparing for an interview, and considering an offer are all covered in this handy guide to "working for your Uncle."

★ Hopke, William E., ed. *The Encyclopedia of Careers and Vocational Guidance*. 10th ed. 4 vols. G. Ferguson, 1996. illus. index.   LC 96-20555   0-89434-170-1 $140

> The ninth edition of this valuable work adds seventy-one new career articles, and, for the first time, careers in volumes two to four are arranged in alphabetical order. Volume 1 provides an overview of industry and adds four new categories—environmental science, franchising, museums and cultural centers, and wildlife management. Each specific career article includes a definition, history, nature of the work, requirements, and opportunities. Methods of entry, outlook, earnings, and conditions of work are also covered. Although this title costs more than $100, that is not a bad price to pay for more than five hundred articles with information on more than fifteen hundred occupations.

Krannich, Ronald L. and Caryl Rae Krannich. *Almanac of International Jobs and Careers: A Guide to Over 1001 Employers*. 2d ed. Impact Publications, 1994. 342p. index. bibliog.   LC 94-9323   0-942710-99-1; 0-942710-95-9 $34.95; $19.95

> This is not a book of advice for job seekers, but a guide to identifying organizations that hire for international positions. Types of organizations and types of jobs are covered, and there is a chapter on work permits and the legalities of working overseas. Information on electronic bulletin boards as search tools and a bibliography of further resources are included.

★ U.S. Department of Labor, Bureau of Statistics Staff. *Occupational Outlook Handbook 1996–97 Edition*. Rev. NTC Publishing, 1996. 500p.   0-84424-530-5 $18.95 paper

> A must for all libraries, this provides information on more than eight hundred occupations. There is information on the nature of the work, the train-

ing required, earnings, and working conditions. Trends and job outlook are spotted, and sources of further information (usually organizations) are listed.

Economics

Anderson, Rolf. *Atlas of the American Economy: An Illustrated Guide to Industries and Trends.* Congressional Quarterly, 1995. 176p. illus. index.   LC 94-23105 1-56802-052-X $24.95 paper

> "The Big Picture" covers the U.S. economy as a whole; "The Big Trends" follows. "The Basic Industries" has one-page coverage of seventy industries. The book is colorfully illustrated with graphs and charts that present information that explains industry trends and highlights.

Greenwald, Douglas, ed. *The McGraw-Hill Encyclopedia of Economics.* 2d ed. McGraw-Hill, 1993. 1120p. index.   LC 93-9805   0-07-024410-3 $99.50

> A major revision of Greenwald's 1982 *Encyclopedia of Economics,* this encyclopedia has more than three hundred articles from two to ten pages long. A little more scholarly than Henderson (below), it can be understood by the educated layperson. A bibliography for further study is included with each signed entry.

Henderson, David R., ed. *The Fortune Encyclopedia of Economics.* Warner, 1993. 896p. index.   LC 92-50535   0-446-51637-6 $49.95

> This authoritative work is arranged in fourteen chapters, each containing articles written by experts. Each of these articles has brief information about its author and a bibliography. Occasional editorial boxes discuss topics mentioned in the text. This has a detailed index and would be equally good for circulation or reference.

Income and Cost of Living

Darnay, Arsen J. and Helen S. Fisher. *American Cost of Living Survey.* 2d ed. Gale, 1995. 800p.   LC 93-640936   0-8103-4324-X $149

> Price data is given for six hundred goods and services in 443 U.S. cities. The information is taken from seventy sources, which are listed. There is a list of cities by name and state and a list of the items covered.

Derks, Scott, ed. *Value of a Dollar: Prices and Incomes in the United States, 1860–1989.* Gale, 1994. 559p.   LC 94-163270   0-8103-6841-2 $7

> This book charts the value of a buck for the stated years. A history of each era is given in various areas. There is a miscellany section, and sources are given for the information.

Russel, Cheryl and Margaret Ambry. *Official Guide to American Incomes.* New Strategist, 1993. 350p. index.   0-9628092-2-5 $69.95

How much do Americans have to spend? Readers can find income trends here with historical perspective. There is information on household income, personal income, discretionary income, and poverty trends. There is a glossary of terms and a good index.

Major Companies

★ *Hoover's Guide to Computer Companies: Covers Over One Thousand Key Computer Companies.* Reference Press, 1996. 672p. index. 1-878753-80-0 $34.95 paper with disk

> Hoover's guides are known for their clear, concise, and user-friendly information on companies, and this directory is no exception. Access to information on more than one thousand companies has three main sections: "Industry Leaders" (77 bios), "Selected Industry Players" (173 shorter bios), and "Key Computer Companies" (directory info on the 250 companies profiled and 885 other companies). Company profiles include an overview, history, officers, directory info, list of products, sales, competitors, and financial performance. The disk is in Windows format.

★ *Hoover's Handbook of World Business, 1996–97: Profiles of Major European, Asian, Latin American and Canadian Companies.* 3d ed. Reference Press, 1996. 700p. 1-57311-008-6 $29.95

> Current and accurate information on world companies at a reasonable price is provided by this excellent Hoover guide. The 227 companies headquartered outside the United States are profiled with the usual Hoover information on the background of the company, its place in the industry, and directory information. Almost eighty lists—such as "Thirty-five Wealthiest Individuals," "Europe's Twenty Largest Banks," and "Twenty-five Largest Foreign Investors in the United States"—make this a good acquisition for libraries of all sizes.

★ *Hoover's Masterlist of America's Top Twenty-five Hundred Employers: A Digital Guide to the Largest and Fastest-Growing U.S. Companies That Are Hiring Now.* Reference Press, 1995. 2d ed. 415p. index. 1-57311-013-2 $22.95 paper with disk

> Twenty-five hundred employers are listed by state. There are also indexes by name, industry type, and metropolitan area. Company profiles list addresses, phone numbers, officers, type of business, number of employees, and number of new hires in the past year. Lists such as Hispanic-owned companies, most-admired companies, and companies sympathetic to gay and lesbian workers are especially valuable. Designed as a job-seeking guide, it is also valuable as a directory of companies.

Plunkett, Jack W. *The Almanac of American Employers, 1994.* Rev. ed. Plunkett Research, 1994. index. 0-9638268-0-8 $110

> Because this covers major companies, it would probably not be too useful for job searchers, except for the most qualified prospects. It is, however,

another source for quick facts on major companies. The main criterion for selection is the provision of long-term jobs. It has information on salaries, benefits, hiring practices, and much more.

★ Spain, Patrick J. and James R. Talbot, eds. *Hoover's Handbook of American Business, 1997: Profiles of Major U.S. Companies*. 2d ed. Reference Press, 1996. 1059p.   1-57311-009-4 $34.95

Company profiles in this work give a short overview of the company's market position, history, officers, address, financial information, and competition. The Fortune 500 list and Standard and Poor's 500 and MidCap 400 lists are included in a lists section. Essential for the smallest library.

Standard and Poor's Staff. *Standard & Poor's 500 Guide, 1997*. McGraw-Hill, 1996. 1028p.   0-07-052154-9 $24.95 paper

Standard and Poor's Staff. *Standard & Poor's MidCap 400 Guide*. 1995 ed. McGraw-Hill, 1996. 820p.   0-07-052153-0 $24.95

Standard and Poor's Staff. *Standard & Poor's SmallCap 600 Guide*. McGraw-Hill, 1996.   0-07-052503-X $24.95 paper

The S & P Guides take information from the costly *Standard & Poor's Stock Reports* on the 500 index (large), the MidCap 400 (medium-size), and the SmallCap 600 (smaller). Each company has two-page coverage that gives evaluative comments and a rating. Ten years of financial information is given, and there is a short narrative on company sales and business. The guides are issued annually, as opposed to weekly for the *Stock Reports,* so they will be of use mainly where the *Stock Reports* are not purchased, another addition to sources of information on companies for job seekers or investors.

Business Statistics

Business Rankings Annual, 1998. 94th ed. Gale, 1998. 701p. index.   0-7876-135-76 $183

This book consists of top ten (or less) lists in many areas of business. It is arranged alphabetically by topic. There is a fine outline of the contents and bibliography. The good index will be helpful in locating topics in the main body of the work.

Banking

Hales, Michael Gordon. *The Language of Banking: Terms and Phrases Used in the Financial Industry*. McFarland, 1994. 175p.   LC 94-3646   0-89950-919-3 $24.50

Because it might be alleged that the banking business uses more acronyms, opaque words, and jargon than many others, this book represents the consumer's revenge. More than 850 words define banking phrases, laws, and special terms used in the world of banking—and does so concisely and informatively. It can be used by businesspersons, consumers, or students of finance, economics, and accounting. Such areas as withdrawals, savings, investments, borrowing, trust departments, and foreign exchange services are covered. *Banking* covers commercial banks, savings and loan associations, credit unions, mutual savings banks, and trust companies, making it useful to a wide range of banking workers and customers. Definitions are in alphabetical order, and formulas are given when needed.

Woelfel, Charles J. *The Dictionary of Banking*. Irwin Professional Publishing, 1994. 256p.   1-55738-728-1 $24.95

Four thousand brief definitions, mostly two or three sentences in length, are included in this clear, inexpensive, and user-friendly dictionary. It is suitable for use by bank workers or the average library patron.

Investments

Walker's Manual of Unlisted Stocks. 3d ed. Walker's Manual, 1997. 592p. 0-9652088-8-5 $85

Under-reported companies whose stock has long-term value are what the compilers were looking for, and they have covered five hundred non-NASDAQ stock. All firms are American except six. They range from local phone companies to Rand McNally, and each company has a full page of descriptive and financial information. This is a good tool for small libraries.

Real Estate

Reilly, John W. *The Language of Real Estate*. 4th ed. Dearborn Financial Publishing, 1994. 456p.   LC 93-8367   0-7931-0583-8 $29.95 paper

The emphasis here is on the legalities of real estate, and many revisions and new terms have been entered in keeping with changes in the law. The author is a lawyer and a licensed real estate broker. New environmental legislation that affects real estate is dealt with in extralong entries. Appendixes contain abbreviations, the Code of Ethics, and Standards of Practice; and a sample closing form is provided.

Environment

Allaby, Michael, ed. *The Concise Dictionary of Ecology*. Oxford University Press, 1994. 424p.   0-19-286160-3 $14.95 paper

Five hundred definitions of terms in the fields of ecology and the environment cover many topics such as animal behavior, pollution, climatology, and oceanography. As an added bonus, there are some short biographical entries on ecologists.

Dashefsky, H. Steven. *Environmental Literacy: Everything You Need to Know about Saving Our Planet*. Random, 1993. 298p. index.   LC 92-56808 0-679-74774-5 $13 paper

> Terms from all fields related to the environment are included in this volume, which is designed to help those who have no background in the area. Besides definitions of terms, there are biographies and directory information.

Deal, Carl. *The Greenpeace Guide to Anti-environmental Organizations*. Real Story Series. Odonian Press, 1993. 110p. index.   LC 92-46096   1-878825-05-4 $5 paper

> It goes without saying that this book has a Greenpeace slant, but because groups do not go around categorizing themselves as "anti-environmental," this is a unique tool for finding out about such groups. It is also valuable because many of these organizations masquerade under environmentally friendly names. Fifty-four groups are listed with address, officers, funding source, origin, and focus for each.

★ Eblen, Ruth A. and William R. Eblen, eds. *The Encyclopedia of the Environment*. Houghton Mifflin, 1994. 846p. illus. maps. index.   LC 94-13669   0-395-55041-6 $49.95

> More than three hundred experts on all phases of environmental studies wrote the more than 550 articles in this volume. It is written in a style that is easily used by high school and up and is enhanced by numerous photos, charts, and graphs. "Think globally, act locally" is the guiding principle of this work, and the coverage is broad, including pollution, toxicology, hazardous waste, quality of life, and some biography.

★ Hoyle, Russ. *The Gale Environmental Almanac*. Gale, 1993. 684p. illus. bibliog. maps. index.   LC 93-37699   0-8103-8877-4 $79.95

> The goal of this excellent book is to "encourage environmental literacy by providing a sufficient range of impartial information as the basis for broader understanding." To this end, a series of essays give information on historical, legal, political, business, and personal aspects of environmentalism. At the end of the essays are various resources—directories of resource persons, parks, chronologies, bibliographies, and so forth.

Lean, Geoffrey. *Atlas of the Environment*. ABC-Clio, 1996. 192p. maps. bibliog. 0-87436-849-9 $39.50

> This atlas, by means of tables and graphs, describes the state of the Earth and the impact of man on the environment. The authors emphasize conservation and how destructive conditions can be reversed. Excellent maps and charts make the data in this work easy to use.

Patton-Hulce, Vicki R. *Environment and the Law: A Dictionary*. Contemporary Legal Issues. ABC-Clio, 1995. 361p. bibliog. index.   LC 95-46013   0-87436-749-2 $39.50

> Citizens need to know how environmental law affects us in how we live, what we drive, where we put our garbage, and what fuel we use. This dictionary covers the key concepts of such law in clear and concise language.

All aspects of environmental law are covered with entries for terms, concepts, organizations, persons, and legislation.

Taxes

Crumbley, D. Larry, Jack P. Friedman and Susan B. Anders. *Dictionary of Tax Terms.* Barron's Educational Series, 1994. 358p.   LC 93-23218   0-8120-1780-3 $9.95 paper

> The meanings of tax concepts are often hidden by specialized terms in the definitions. Clear meanings do not help you fill out your tax form, but people who do their own taxes will find their work easier with this book. IRS and taxpayer assistance phone numbers are given, and there is a list of IRS forms by subject. Excise, sales, property, and social security taxes are covered as well.

United Nations

★ *A Guide to Information at the United Nations.* Department of Public Information, United Nations, 1995. 121p. index.   LC 95-152906   92-1-100542-6 $9.95 paper

> This basic guide to the workings of the United Nations is designed for the media, researchers, and other organizations. There are brief descriptions of the United Nations' agencies, departments, and programs. All entries give the administrator's name and country, mandate, programs, publications, and contact information. Not exhaustive but good for quick access to information about the United Nations.

The Constitution

Vile, John R. *Encyclopedia of Constitutional Amendments, Proposed Amendments, and Amending Issues, 1789–1995.* ABC-Clio, 1996. 320p. bibliog. index.
LC 96-19540   0-87436-783-2 $60

> The author, a political science professor, gives a history of the twenty-seven existing amendments and the almost eleven thousand amendments that have been proposed. There are biographical entries and articles on Supreme Court decisions. There is a long bibliography and a list of key proposals by year.

World Constitutions

Maddex, Robert L. *Constitutions of the World.* Congressional Quarterly, 1995. 338p. charts. index.   LC 95-11374   0-87187-992-1 $79.95

> This good ready reference covers "current constitutions as well as the constitutional histories of eighty countries." The reader is able to compare and

contrast the constitutional climate of the various countries because of the format, which treats each topic in a separate section. There is also a "snapshot" chart that lists type of government, type of state, and type of legislature for each country.

Law

Court TV Staff and *American Lawyer* Staff, eds. *Court TV's Cradle-to-Grave Legal Survival Guide: A Complete Resource for Any Question You Might Have About the Law*. Little, Brown, 1995. 520p. index.   LC 94-24900   0-316-03663-3 $19.95 paper

> The Goodfriend family is easily the most legally beset-upon family in years, and all of their troubles, from obtaining a birth certificate to donating their bodies for medical research, are covered in this family law guide. They are sexually harassed, have their taxes audited, and join cults; and, in doing so, they provide us with a window on the American legal system with problems that an average family might encounter (not in such great numbers, with any luck). Helpful lists of organizations and associations are good additions.

A Dictionary of Law. 3d ed. Oxford University Press, 1994. 433p.   0-19-280000-0 $13.95 paper

> Three thousand entries make up this useful work, and asterisks point out the entries with new material added. This is a handy reference tool, written "for the uninformed."

Hauser, Barbara R. and Roberta C. Ramo. *Women's Legal Guide: A Comprehensive Guide to Legal Issues Affecting Every Woman*. Fulcrum, 1996. 528p. bibliog. index. LC 95-46893   1-55592-913-8; 1-55591-303-2 $39.95; $22.95 paper

> Family- and health-related issues and business topics of interest to women are covered in this book. Women attorneys have written advice for women on such problems as estate planning, sexual discrimination, disabilities, and lesbian rights. The writing is clear and objective, and the contents explain procedures and problems well.

★ Hill, Gerald N. and Kathleen Thompson Hill. *Real Life Dictionary of the Law: Taking the Mystery out of Legal Language*. General Publishing Group, 1995. 479p. LC 95-12249   1-881649-74-1 $19.95

> This volume will be a boon to people who love to watch Court TV. Now they have an easy and entertaining way to learn legal lingo. The three thousand entries are accurate and full of quotes to illustrate points of law. A must for all libraries.

★ Knappman, Edward W. *Great American Trials*. Gale/Visible Ink, 1993. illus. index.   0-8103-8875-8; 0-8103-9134-1 $50.00; $17.95 paper

> Two hundred trials "known for their historic or legal significance, political controversy, public attention, legal ingenuity, or literary fame" are summarized in this interesting book that is recommended for public, high school,

and college libraries. No other nonscholarly title covers so many trials; the Salem witch trials, John Peter Zenger, the Rosenbergs, the Scottsboro boys, and Rodney King are discussed in entries of approximately twenty-five hundred words.

★ Leiter, Richard A., ed. *National Survey of State Laws*. 2d ed. Gale, 1997. 605p. 0-8103-9052-3 $60

> Areas of law covered in this state-by-state compilation are those labeled "controversial," but this book will answer many legal questions asked of reference librarians. Eight sections cover business, consumer affairs, criminal law, education, employment, family, real estate, taxes, and general civil law. Charts in each section provide references to statutes or codes as well as solid answers on such topics as marriage age requirements, abortion, child custody, drunk driving, gun purchase waiting periods, and so forth. Because most libraries cannot afford legal codes for states other than their own, this is a great purchase.

★ Mierzwa, Joseph W. *The Twenty-first Century Family Legal Guide*. ProSe Associates, 1994. 452p. index.   LC 93-86934   0-9637285-0-4 $19.95

> Starting with a discussion of Americans' rights, this book goes on to discuss legal problems of interest to the average consumer, such as automobiles, home ownership, insurance, credit, and domestic relations. Such recent phenomena as sperm banks, ATMs, and dread disease insurance are covered. Helpful lists, such as agencies that oversee health services, labor law, and aging, abound. Every chapter gives an overview of its topic as well as ways in which the pertinent law is applied.

Sack, Steven Mitchell. *The Lifetime Legal Guide*. Time-Life, 1996. 295p.   LC 96-22814 0-7835-4859-1 $27.95

> This legal guide, on a par with many other fine contenders, is especially good at answering "what happens if" questions. There are sample forms and letters and checklists that help readers in various legal activities.

★ Sitarz, Daniel. *The Complete Book of Personal Legal Forms*. Nova Publishing, 1997. 253p. index.   LC 93-86773   0-935755-16-0 $16.95

> Self-help legal materials will never go out of style in libraries, and this book provides more than one hundred forms of use in various legal situations. Contracts, powers of attorney, living wills, premarital agreements, leases, property rental agreements, and promissory notes are represented. Users are advised when to seek legal advice.

Strauss, Peter J. and Nancy M. Lederman. *The Elder Law Handbook: A Legal and Financial Survival Guide for Caregivers and Seniors*. Facts on File, 1996. 350p. index.   LC 95-53937   0-8160-3082-0; 0-8160-3410-9 $25.95; $14.95 paper

> The problems of the elderly require special attention, which they are given in this book written by lawyers with experience in the field. Estate planning, housing, health care, insurance, Social Security, and long-term care

are all covered. Agencies, associations, and government offices that help the retired are listed in appendixes.

Public Records

Bentley, Elizabeth Petty. *County Courthouse Book.* 2d ed. Genealogical Publishing, 1995. 405p.   LC 95-79104   0-8063-1485-0 $34.95 paper

> An essential resource for genealogists, this directory features listings for 3,125 county jurisdictions and 1,577 New England towns and independent Virginia cities. Entries are arranged by state and county and give an address and phone number. In addition to genealogists, this book will prove of value to researchers in land title, property rights, and inheritance matters.

Ernst, Carl and Michael Sankey, eds. *The Librarian's Guide to Public Records.* 2d rev. ed. BRB Publications, 1996. 336p.   1-879792-30-3 $39

> A directory of county, state, and federal public record offices in the United States, this lists sources for many types of records. Each entry gives address, time zone, phone, and hours. Each section has tips for researchers, and there is a table of access restrictions. Recommended for any collection.

Copyright and Patent

Elias, Stephen. *Patent, Copyright and Trademark: A Desk Reference to Intellectual Property Law.* Nolo Press, 1995. 430p. illus.   LC 94-352   0-87337-236-0 $24.95

Fishman, Stephen. *The Copyright Handbook: How to Protect and Use Written Works.* 3d ed. Nolo Press, 1996. 320p. illus. index.   LC 96-6923   0-87337-323-5 $24.95 paper

Strong, William S. *The Copyright Book: A Practical Guide.* 4th ed. MIT Press, 1993. 288p.   LC 92-16371   0-262-19330-2 $25

> These guides are for anyone who uses the written word. They feature an overview of copyright law—what copyright does or does not do—and are excellent for librarians and for patrons who work with copyrighted material. Each offers a clear explanation of *fair use.* Any of these titles should prove useful to the people who use copyrighted works or those who create them. The third work, *The Copyright Book,* was written by a copyright lawyer to help the layperson or the librarian in search of advice.

Municipal Government

Griffin, Kenton G. *Managing Your City or Town: A Reference Guide for the New Public Official.* University Press of America, 1994. 292p. index.   LC 93-44355   0-8191-9403-4; 0-8191-9404-2 $57.50; $36.50 paper

Although this book has a somewhat limited focus, dealing only with the issues involving a city manager, it is a good overview. The supporting material includes a glossary and a good index. The body of the work deals with personnel, training, budgeting, purchasing, public relations, public safety departments, and so forth. There are samples of such things as ordinances and employment contracts. Especially valuable in this day and age is the "Bomb Threat Information Form." Good for students of city government and anyone considering public service.

Occupational Licensing

Bianco, David, ed. *Professional and Occupational Licensing Directory*. 2d ed. Gale, 1995. 1400p.   0-8103-9050-7 $89.50

This is the only publication that offers detailed information on state and national licensing in all career areas for the entire United States. The listing is by occupation and by state within the occupation.

Military History

★ Dupuy, Trevor N. and Ernest Dupuy. *The Harper Encyclopedia of Military History: From 3500 B.C. to the Present*. 4th ed. HarperCollins, 1993. 1680p. illus. bibliog. maps. index.   LC 92-17853   0-06-270056-1 $70

Conflicts around the world from 3,500 B.C. to the Gulf War are covered in this newest edition of *The Encyclopedia of Military History*. Revision is found throughout the volume, not just in the addition of newer wars. The book is arranged chronologically, and contains valuable line drawings of weapons and covers battle formations.

Margiotta, Franklin D., ed. *Brassey's Encyclopedia of Military History and Biography*. Brassey's, 1994. 1197p. illus. maps. index.   LC 94-33551   0-02-881096-1 $44.95

Drawn from the pages of its parent set, the six-volume *International Military and Defense Encyclopedia* (Brassey's, 1993), this book has entries on wars from classical times to the Gulf War. Because this is a cut-down version of a larger work, only the major engagements are covered. More than one hundred biographies are included.

Polmar, Norman, Mark Warren and Eric Wertheim. *Dictionary of Military Abbreviations*. Naval Institute Press, 1994. 307p.   LC 93-34566   1-55750-680-9 $23.95

This dictionary was designed to help those in the military who are "forced to deal with the plethora of abbreviations used by the other services." It is also of use to librarians. There are five thousand definitions, each noted with the military branch in which it is used (if appropriate). This is the most up-to-date book of such abbreviations available.

★ Shrader, Charles, R., ed. *Reference Guide to United States Military History, 1919–1945*. Facts on File, 1993. 352p. photogs. maps. bibliog. index.   LC 90-25673 0-8160-1839-1 $50

> Emphasis here is on World War II, but there is good information on the time between the wars and even coverage of land, sea, and air activities. The main portion of the book, the fourth volume of a set of U.S. military history, is given over to a chronology of events, a section of biography, and outlines of specific battles. This is recommended for high school, public, and undergraduate libraries.

Social Work

Barker, Robert L. *The Social Work Dictionary*. 3d ed. NASW Press, 1995. 447p. LC 95-3857   0-87101-253-7 $34.95 paper

> This book is regularly updated and the vocabulary is current. The definitions are well done and cover a range of topics that may surprise non-social workers: family therapy, counseling, moral development, educational equity, criminal justice, health care, and so forth.

Social Action

Walls, David. *Activist's Almanac: The Concerned Citizen's Guide to the Leading Advocacy Organizations in America*. Fireside/Simon & Schuster, 1993. 429p. 0-671-74634-0 $18

> Organizations are listed by broad topic with an introduction to each subject. There is also good material on activism in the main introduction. Key legislation is covered. Group profiles give the address, budget, number of members, number of member groups, staff, tax status, purpose, history, priorities, structure, resources, publications, and services.

Substance Abuse

Gall, Timothy L. and Daniel M. Lucas. *Statistics on Alcohol, Drug and Tobacco Use*. Gale, 1995. 238p. index.   LC 95-32413   0-7876-0526-3 $55

> Even though this compilation of statistics sometimes lacks organization within its sections and the information is free in government reports, this is a good reference work for small libraries that do not receive documents and need an all-in-one combination of substance abuse stats. There is also contact information for relevant organizations.

O'Brien, Robert and Sidney Cohen. *The Encyclopedia of Drug Abuse*. 2d rev. ed. Facts on File, 1990. 496p.   LC 89-71531   0-8160-1956-8 $45

> This standard work is written in simple language that makes it appropriate for the layperson or professional. Many categories of "drugs" are covered—

caffeine and nicotine are here as well as the hard drugs. Terms on all areas of the subject are covered in short entries, including slang. Sidebars feature such topics as the histories of use of certain substances.

Federal Aid

★ Dumouchel, J. Robert. *Government Assistance Almanac 1996–97: The Guide to All Federal Financial and Other Domestic Programs*. 10th ed. Omnigraphics, 1996. 875p. LC 86-658073 0-7808-0051-6 $145

> The main purpose of this work is to present the information needed by persons seeking federal aid. More than one thousand programs are listed, and there is a user-friendly index. The format is much less intimidating than that of *The Catalog of Federal Domestic Assistance* (DIANE Publishing, 1997), from which the material is taken.

Adoption

Paul, Ellen, ed. *The Adoption Directory: A Guide to Agencies, State Laws on Adoption, Exchanges, Support Groups and Professional Services in Domestic and International Adoption Including Foster Parenting and Biological Options*. 2d ed. Gale, 1995. 570p. LC 46-7961 0-8103-74951 $65

> Completely updated from the original 1989 edition, this guide covers most of the information adopting persons would need to know about the many different ways to obtain and care for a child, plus all of the information listed so nicely in the subtitle.

Rappaport, Bruce M. *The Open Adoption Book: A Guide to Adoption without Tears*. Macmillan, 1998. 195p. 0-028621-700 $13.95

> The media have placed focus on the open-adoption cases that have fared badly. Rappaport's book covers the risks of such procedures and deals openly with them, but it is upbeat and reassuring in covering the concerns of prospective adopters. This practical book should be in most libraries.

Police Science

Bailey, William G., ed. *The Encyclopedia of Police Science*. 2d ed. Garland Reference Library of the Humanities, vol. 1,729. Garland, 1995. 888p. index. LC 94-46828 0-8153-1331-4 $95

> Approximately 50 entries have been added to the more than 140 of the previous edition, and many have been updated and revised. More information is given on drug-abuse suppression, new crimes, international crimes, and federal mandates. A must buy for any library that might have crime questions.

Crime

★ Frasier, David K. *Murder Cases of the Twentieth Century: Biographies and Bibliographies of 280 Convicted or Accused Killers.* McFarland, 1996. 496p. bibliog. index.   LC 96-14984   0-7864-0184-2 $65

> A boon to true crime fans everywhere, this was reviewed as a "near-perfect reference source on murder." The 280 serial killers, American and foreign, are presented with dates, aliases, locations, weapons, and number of victims. Movies or plays about the killer are listed along with a critical annotated bibliography. There are author/title indexes and a general index that will lead the reader from a movie title to the true crime story involved. Well written and fascinating, this is for all collections.

Morgan, Kathleen O. and Scott Morgan, eds. *City Crime Rankings: Crime in Metropolitan America.* Morgan Quinto Press. 1995. 284p.   LC 95-131624 1-56692-307-7 $19.95 paper

> Crime statistics for 274 metropolitan areas and the 100 largest U.S. cities are based on 1993 data. There are also data on police officers. The information is taken from the FBI's *Crime in the U.S., Uniform Crime Reports.*

Morgan, Kathleen O., Scott Morgan and Neal Quinto, eds. *Crime State Rankings 1996.* Morgan Quinto Press, 1996. 512p.   1-56692-311-5

> Users of this volume can make easy comparisons among the fifty states on a wide range of crime-related topics. In part 1, there are tables of arrests for various crimes. Part 2 consists of correction statistics, part 3 contains substance-abuse data, part 4 breaks down government expenditures for justice-related activities, and part 5 has statistics on law enforcement agencies. The last section has data on such things as use of guns in particular offenses, changes in numbers of various crimes, and so forth.

Secret Societies

Hicks, Roger, *International Encyclopedia of Secret Societies and Fraternal Orders.* Facts on File, 1997. 320p. bibliog. index.   0-8160-2307-7 $40

> Eight hundred entries contain information on social, service, ethnic, trade, mystical, religious, political, and criminal groups all over the world. Activities, rituals, and symbols are covered, and addresses are given for active groups. There is a detailed bibliography.

Insurance

Green, Thomas E., ed. *Glossary of Insurance Terms: Over Twenty-five Hundred Definitions of the Most Commonly Used Words in the Industry.* 5th ed. Merritt Publishing, 1994. 276p.   0-930868-68-4 $14.95 paper

Each term in this book is categorized by the type of insurance involved. Definitions range from six to one hundred words. Each category chapter begins with a list of acronyms and abbreviations from that field. Explanations are longer than those in general dictionaries but still understandable for laypersons.

Schools and Colleges

★ Barron's Educational Editors. *Barron's Profiles of American Colleges*. 20th ed. Barron's Educational Series, 1994. 1650p. paper with disk   0-8120-1752-8 $25

> This and *Peterson's Guide to Four-Year Colleges* (below) are generally considered two of the best of the college guides. Quick views of accredited colleges give usual directory information such as address, costs, enrollment, admissions, financial aid, and so forth. *Barron's* also has info on handicapped programs, foreign student needs, and computer facilities. *Barron's Compact Guide to Colleges* (Barron's Educational Series, 1998) is an abridged version, offering info on four hundred colleges.

Bear, John and Mariah Bear. *College Degrees by Mail and Modem, 1998*. Ten Speed Press, 1997. 216p. illus. index.   0-89815-934-2 $12.95 paper

> This book is of value for showing nontraditional ways to get college degrees, such as via correspondence, cable television, video, independent study, home computer courses, the Internet, and extension courses. Advice is given, and there is a list of one hundred worldwide schools that offer nontraditional learning.

Borins, Sara, ed. *The Real Guide to Canadian Universities: An Insider's Survey for Undergraduates*. Key Porter Books/Copp Clark Pitman, 1994. 293p. illus. 1-55-013533-3 $24.95 paper

> Contributors to this Canadian guide are recent graduates, who add to the information supplied by the universities. All major universities are covered, each with an entry running to six double-columned pages. Included are figures from 1993 on such topics as tuition, admissions, and housing costs. The graduate contributors provide information on sexual mores, easy courses, and good professors.

Cassidy, Daniel J. *Dan Cassidy's Worldwide College Scholarship Directory*. 4th ed. Career Press, 1995. 288p. index.   LC 95-021618   1-56414-208-6 $19.99 paper

> With information on thousands of aid programs from seventy-five countries, this is an abridged version of the National/International Scholarship Research Services database. Information is given about the amount of aid, deadlines, fields of study, eligibility, and addresses. There is a list of "helpful publications."

College Board Staff. *The College Handbook*. Henry Holt, 1996. 1700p.   LC 41-12971
0-87447-506-6 $21.95 paper

> More than three thousand two- and four-year schools are listed here with information supplied by the institution. Such information as the percentage of applicants accepted, the number of volumes in the library, the number of periodical subscriptions, and types of graduate professional programs offered will be welcomed by more sophisticated applicants.

Fiske, Edward B. *The Fiske Guide to Colleges 1997*. Random, 1996. 741p.
0-8129-2757-5 $19 paper

> More than three hundred colleges are treated in this volume and have been selected with academic quality, geographical location, cost, and general appeal to students in mind. All of the highly selective U.S. colleges have been included. The entries are narrative in form and have sidebars detailing statistical information. Each college is rated according to academics, social life, and quality of life.

Mitchell, Robert. *The Multicultural Student's Guide to Colleges*. Noonday Press, 1996. 839p.   0-614-97730-4 $25 paper

> Designed for African American, Asian, Hispanic, and Native American applicants, this college guide gives basic directory information on the colleges listed with special emphasis on the needs of the minority student. An excellent "how-to-use-this book" section will help in choosing and applying to a college.

★ *Peterson's Guide to Four-Year Colleges, 1997*. 27th ed. Peterson's, 1996. 3176p. illus.   1-5607-9604-9 $24.95 paper with disk

> This college guide gives information on about two thousand colleges around the United States. There is information on admissions, aid, courses of study, and extracurricular activities.

Peterson's Guide to Private Secondary Schools, 1997–98. 18th ed. Peterson's, 1997. 1370p   1-560797-02-9 $29.95

> Fourteen hundred private secondary schools worldwide are listed here. They are divided into college prep and general academic, alternative schools for learning and social needs, and junior boarding schools. Info is given on the faculty, accreditation, facilities, programs, requirements, tuition, athletics, and college placement. There is even a notation as to whether the school provides a promotional video. There are good indexes to identify schools by various types.

Solorzano, Lucia. *Barron's Best Buys in College Education*. 4th ed. Barron's Educational Series, 1996. 706p. index.   LC 96-14330   0-8120-9593-6 $14.95 paper

> Two hundred ninety-nine schools are discussed here to tell prospective students about best buys in colleges based on such things as tuition rates, selectivity, or academic emphasis. The problem with a work like this is, to

have a broad geographic range and offer private as well as public schools, some schools that may be just as much a "best buy" are left out. This work does give a wealth of information on campus life, facilities, and graduate placement, so its information on a particular college could supplement the material from a more traditional directory.

Townsend, Kiliaen V. R. *The College Comparison Guide*. Agee, 1993. 320p. maps. LC 92-73762   0-935265-21-X $20 paper

> A selective guide to schools, this handbook is divided into three sections. Part 1 gives eight key statistics for 250 schools. Part 2 provides tables that rank or group the top 130 schools on the characteristics appearing in part 3. Part 3 is an alphabetical listing of the top 130 schools with a two-page spread for each. Info includes a selectivity rating, location, enrollment figures, class composition, admissions, costs, available aid, housing, sports, and so forth. Institutions were selected on the basis of SAT scores and numbers of out-of-state students.

Yale Daily News Staff. *Insider's Guide to the Colleges 1997*. 23d ed. St. Martin's, 1996. 0-312-14627-2 $14.99 paper

> Although this handbook offers the usual directory information such as admissions, policies, costs, and programs, its main feature is frank students' discussions on various aspects of college life. More than three hundred colleges in the United States and Canada are covered.

Consumer Protection

Klein, David, Marymae E. Klein and Douglas D. Walsh. *Getting Unscrewed and Staying That Way: The Sourcebook of Consumer Protection*. Henry Holt, 1993. 322p. index.   0-8050-2100-0 $14.95 paper

> A handy book to have on your consumer shelf, this outlines deceptive tactics and steps one can take to protect oneself against fraud. There are also lists of agencies to turn to and an overview of high-customer-abuse businesses.

Catalogs

Palder, Edward. *The Catalog of Catalogs V: The Complete Mail-Order Directory*. Woodbine House, 1997. 513p.   LC 96-49762   0-933149-88-3 $24.95

> Fourteen thousand (two thousand new to this edition) catalog companies are listed here under eight hundred categories. They are also indexed by name. There is general information on ordering from catalogs and a request for update information from readers. Need a butter churn, septic tank, gingerbread house, feather, or shed? Send away for it!

Chambers of Commerce

★ *World Wide Chamber of Commerce Directory*. World Chamber of Commerce Directory, 1997. 400p.   0-94358-110-9 $35 paper

> This directory lists state, U.S. Chambers of Commerce, state boards of tourism, convention and visitors' bureaus, economic development organizations, Canadian Chambers of Commerce, American Chambers of Commerce abroad, foreign Chambers of Commerce, foreign embassies in the United States, and U.S. embassies overseas. There is even a directory of the 104th Congress! Aside from the obvious use the book has of looking up addresses for these organizations, the addresses themselves can lead to information for school reports or persons moving or relocating.

Measurement

★ Clark, John and Mike Darton. *The Macmillan Dictionary of Measurement*. Macmillan, 1994. 512p. index.   LC 93-47005   0-02-525750-1 $27.50

> If you are a size twelve in the United States, what size will you wear in England? What is the monetary system of Turkey? This is an exhaustive source of anything and everything that can be measured and contains more than four thousand entries taken from science, electronics, farming, music, sports, architecture, and so forth. Some of the entries include etymology as well as definitions. Each entry also indicates in which field it is used. This book will be useful for all libraries.

The Economist *Desk Companion: How to Measure, Convert, Calculate and Define Practically Anything*. Rev. ed. Henry Holt, 1994. 272p. maps. index.   LC 94-76172   0-8050-3567-2 $40

> An extremely detailed table of contents and topic index make this a user-friendly work on all sorts of formulas and conversions in a variety of fields. Accountancy, weapons, global death, earthquakes, major world measurement systems—all are taken care of here. Historical weights and conversions are given. If, for example, the heroine of the romance you are reading buys a *firkin* of butter, just how much does she have to carry home? Check this book out!

Strauss, Stephen. *The Sizesaurus: From Hectares to Decibels to Calories, A Witty Compendium of Measurements*. Kodansha America, 1995. 272p. illus. index. LC 95-32176   1-56836-110-6 $25

> A humorous approach makes the study of measurement fun for students of all ages. It is a dictionary on the science of measures and weights but many of the samples are chosen for humor or high interest value (fingernails grow four times faster than toenails). This would be a fun resource for teachers of science or for those people looking for bulletin-board ideas.

Broadcasting

Reed, Robert M. and Maxine K. Reed. *The Facts on File Dictionary of Television, Cable and Video.* Facts on File, 1994. 234p.   LC 94-1221   0-8160-2947-4 $24.95

> Broadcasting jargon is well-covered in the three thousand entries in this book. Companies, organizations, awards, and technical, advertising, and accounting terms are covered in language written for broadcasting students as well as professionals.

Transportation

Wilson, Anthony. *Dorling Kindersley Visual Timeline of Transportation.* Dorling Kindersley, 1995. 48p. illus. index.   LC 94-98714   1-56458-880-7 $16.95

> Short, sweet, and to-the-point, this chronology of transportation covers the period from 10,000 B.C.E. to the present. A useful and inexpensive source in the usual stunning Dorling Kindersley style and readable text. All modes of transportation are covered.

Costume

★ Cassin-Scott, Jack. *The Illustrated Encyclopedia of Costume and Fashion: From 1066 to the Present.* Rev. ed. Studio Vista/Cassell and Sterling Publishing, 1994. 192p. illus. index.   0-289-80093-5 $24.95

> Each fashion period is given a page with color illustrations and a description of the clothing of that era. Formal and daily attire are generally covered, as are accessories. Only a brief view of each period is given in the space allotted, but it does contain a good sense of the time. This is a European production, and no American style differences are noted.

Hoffman, Frank W. and William G. Bailey. *Fashion and Merchandising Fads.* Harrington Park, 1994. 317p. index.   LC 92-46-36   1-56023-031-2 $22.95 paper

> Alphabetically arranged entries give brief information about the history of 140 fashion fads with at least one source given for each entry. Because standard reference sources do not often cover fads and information on them is sometimes hard to come by, this work fills a gap in the area.

Events

★ *Chase's Calendar of Events 1997.* NTC/Contemporary Publishing Co., 1996. 704p. index.   LC 57-14540   0-8092-3174-3 $49.95

> The main reason to buy this great reference tool is, of course, the list of events by month and day. Do you want to know the dates of the Wisconsin Dells Flake Out Festival? The International Day of the Seal? The New

York Chocolate Festival? Check out the index and go to the listed date, which gives information on the event. "Firsts" and historic events are also listed for each day, and birthdays are listed for each month. Extras include presidential proclamations, award winners, and abbreviations. The newest edition of this is a must for all libraries.

★ Puckett, Barry and Helene Henderson, eds. *Holidays and Festivals Index: A Descriptive Guide to Information on More Than 3,000 Holidays.* Omnigraphics, 1995. 800p. index.   LC 94-39351   0-7808-0012-5 $75

> In many ways this supersedes *Holidays, Festivals, and Celebrations of the World Dictionary* (below). It is published by the same company and has information on more than three thousand secular and religious holidays around the world. Commercial and trade events are also covered. The entries are alphabetically arranged by name of the event. There is brief information with a reference to the source. Four indexes: ethnic and geographic, name, religious group and denominations, and chronological. *Chase's Calendar of Events* (above) is more inclusive, but *Holidays* has the references, which may provide much more information in many cases.

Thompson, Sue E. and Barbara W. Carlson, comps. *Holidays, Festivals, and Celebrations of the World Dictionary.* 2d ed. Omnigraphics, 1996. 536p. bibliog. index.   1-7808-0074-5 $72

> Fifteen hundred entries cover the history, significance, and observance of each event. Lists of legal holidays for the fifty states and world nations, a glossary of terms dealing with periods of time, and different calendars round out this comprehensive book that complements *Chase's Calendar of Events* (above) and *The Folklore of World Holidays* (Gale Research, 1991).

Weaver, Robert S. *International Holidays: 204 Countries from 1994 through 2015.* McFarland, 1995. 375p. index.   LC 94-19445   0-89950-953-3 $45

> The main part of this book consists of calendars from 1994 to 2015. They are arranged chronologically by year, month, and day and list all events on a particular date. Four appendixes include holidays with fixed dates; holidays with different dates every year; tables for holidays, showing their dates from 1900 to 2100; and each country, with a list of holidays.

Etiquette

Holberg, Andrea, ed. *Forms of Address: A Guide for Business and Social Use.* Rice University Press, 1994. 200p. index.   LC 94-17521   0-89263-333-6; 0-89263-334-4 $27.50; $12.95 paper

> This book has a specific topic—the proper forms of address for titled officials in all levels of U.S. and foreign government, royalty, U.S. military, and others. Proper address is considered for business correspondence, personal correspondence, place cards, introductions, and conversation.

★ Post, Elizabeth L. *Emily Post's Etiquette*. 16th ed. HarperCollins, 1997. 845p.
LC 96-43427   0-06-270175-4 $28

> This easily understood, reasonably current guide to proper behavior (yes,
> there still is such a thing) has a new and useful section on "Your Profes-
> sional Life."

★ Tuckerman, Nancy and Nancy Dunnan. *The Amy Vanderbilt Complete Book of
Etiquette*. Doubleday, 1995. 800p. illus. index.   LC 93-44452   0-385-41342-4 $32

> New technology and new lifestyles bring new problems of etiquette. In-
> cluded in this new edition of a classic are discussions of cellular phone
> use, living together (straight or gay or lesbian), and business travel for
> women.

Folklore

★ Brunvand, Jan H., ed. *American Folklore: An Encyclopedia*. Reference Library
of the Humanities, vol. 1,551. Garland, 1996. 816p. photogs. bibliog. index.
LC 95-53734   0-8153-0751-9 $95

> This may be the first encyclopedia of strictly American folklore. Each arti-
> cle is signed and most include bibliography. Some of the topics covered
> are holidays, festivals, rituals, geographic areas, ethnic groups, types of
> folklore, theories, scholars, characters, music, and dance. Recommended
> for all schools and public libraries.

Cordry, Harold V. *The Multicultural Dictionary of Proverbs*. McFarland, 1997. 344p.
bibliog. index.   LC 96-33264   0-7864-0251-2 $47.50

> The author of this work became fascinated with "the striking similarity of
> proverbs from dissimilar cultures in different times and different places"
> and so produced this delightful thesaurus of proverbs from around the
> world. Most of the citations include the language of origin or the ethnic de-
> rivation of the phrase. This is a good addition to traditional proverb books.

DeLoach, Charles. *Giants: A Reference Guide from History, the Bible, and Recorded
Legend*. Scarecrow, 1995. 326p. illus. index.   LC 94-41625   0-8108-2971-1 $39.50

> Taking the point of view that giants actually existed, DeLoach offers refer-
> ences to giants through history. Bible giants are explained with archaeo-
> logical references, and individual giants since ancient times are discussed
> and documented. Provocative and entertaining, this should be approached
> cautiously for hard-core reference.

Flexner, Stuart and Doris Flexner. *Wise Words and Wives' Tales: The Origins,
Meanings and Time-Honored Wisdom of Proverbs and Folk Sayings Olde and New*.
Avon Books, 1993. 224p. bibliog.   LC 92-97449   0-380-76238-2 $9 paper

> Each saying in this book is listed with examples of usage, starting with the
> earliest date of appearance. The Flexners spent years in collecting mater-

ial, and this is an entertaining book that has a good bibliography. Its reference use is somewhat limited by the fact that there is no index.

Jackson, Guida M. *Encyclopedia of Traditional Epics.* ABC-Clio Literary Companion. ABC-Clio, 1994. 732p. illus. bibliog. index.   LC 94-9303   0-87436-724-7 $65

> Epics from all cultures, familiar and unfamiliar, are covered, with the title of the tale receiving a longer synopsis entry. Cross-references lead the user to related material, and an excellent bibliography sends the user to other titles. This can be used by all ages.

★ Jones, Alison. *Larousse Dictionary of World Folklore.* Larousse Kingfisher Chambers, 1995. 493p. illus.   LC 95-54592   0-7523-0012-1 $27.50

> This dictionary brings together central themes of worldwide folklore. It demonstrates similarities and differences in cultures through folklore, and it explains some ancient beliefs that are precursors to current customs. There are 468 pages of alphabetical entries and 6 pages of biographical notes on folklorists. Twenty-one pages of folklore and ethnic museums and a calendar of appropriate events complete the work. Although it purports to be a world catalog, it favors the myth and lore of Northern Europe. This is a useful title for the general reader.

★ Leach, Maria and Jerome Fried, eds. *Funk & Wagnall's Standard Dictionary of Folklore, Mythology and Legend.* Harper San Francisco, 1984. 1256p. LC 83-48421   0-06250511-4 $40 paper

> This standard work covers various aspects of folklore. Because many anthropologists and sociologists contributed to the work, there is an ethnic rather than a literary emphasis.

Opie, Iona and Peter Opie. *Oxford Dictionary of Nursery Rhymes.* Oxford University Press, 1951. 494p.   0-19-869111-4 $47.50

> This is a scholarly collection of nursery rhymes with notes on the history, literary associations, and portrayal of real people.

Radford, Edwin and Mona A. Radford. *Encyclopedia of Superstitions.* Greenwood, 1969. 269p.   LC 70-88993   0-8371-2115-9 $65

> A wide-ranging list of superstitions from ancient and modern cultures is covered in this useful title.

Rose, Carol. *Spirits, Fairies, Gnomes, and Goblins: An Encyclopedia of the Little People.* ABC-Clio, 1996. 370p. illus. bibliog.   LC 96-8460   0-87436-811-1 $49.50

> The criteria for inclusion in this work are (1) "a spirit must exert active, willful, and supernatural influence on humans or creatures"; (2) "it cannot be divine"; and (3) "it is neither a hero or ghost involved in the human condition." This work is universal and spans all times and all places. There is a full description of each spirit and the places it inhabits. This new standard in the field is well written and a delightful addition to popular literature of folklore.

Simpson, J. A. *The Concise Oxford Dictionary of Proverbs*. Oxford University Press, 1992. 336p.   LC 91-393666   0-19-866177-0 $30

> Illustrations of its use are given for each proverb listed, and the author includes only proverbs current in our time. Arrangement is alphabetical by keyword with cross-references to related keywords.

★ Titelman, Gregory Y. *Random House Dictionary of Popular Proverbs and Sayings*. Random, 1996. 608p. bibliog. index.   LC 95-52189   0-679-44554-4 $30

> Many books of proverbs are more scholarly than this one, but its value lies in the fact that it emphasizes proverbs and their use in the 1980s and 1990s. Examples of old proverbs in current use are taken from popular fiction and other general materials. Definitions are provided for the proverbs, making this useful for non-English speakers or the very young.

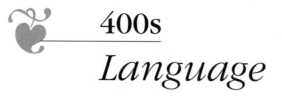

400s
Language

Words, words, words . . . words spoken and unspoken, words in English, words in foreign languages . . . concern with words is what the 400 section is about.

Every library should have at least one title on sign language for the hearing impaired. Most of the sources listed for this topic are inexpensive with clear drawings.

There is a plethora of good dictionaries to chose from, and this list includes only a sampling. Make sure the dictionary you choose has syllable breakdown and part of speech and etymology for each word. It is nice to be able to afford an unabridged dictionary, but a good college dictionary will get the patron and librarian through most word queries.

For writers of all levels and skills, a thesaurus or dictionary of synonyms is a must, as are books that show the richness of our language, such as dictionaries of idioms, metaphors, and slang from all walks of American life. These same writers will also find occasion to check on their grammar and punctuation when they write.

Although the demand may not be high, it is good for small libraries to carry foreign language dictionaries in the "most popular" foreign languages such as Latin, French, Spanish, German, and Italian.

American Sign Language

Butterworth, Rod R. and Mickey Flodin. *The Pocket Dictionary of Signing*. Berkley, 1992. 224p. illus. index. LC 91-30462 0-399-51743-X $6.95 paper

Intended for the beginning signer, this has clear hand-shape illustrations. There are good explanations of usage, such as currency, word endings, and so forth.

★ Costello, Elaine. *Random House Webster's American Sign Language Dictionary*. Illus. by Lois Lenderman. Random, 1994. 1120p. illus. 0-394-58580-1 $50

More than fifty-six hundred words and signs are described for users and learners of the American Sign Language. In the detailed introduction to the language, the point is made that the deaf community sees itself as a "cultural group with a common language." Changes in American Sign Language throughout the years are discussed. This book belongs in all libraries.

Lane, Leonard G. *The Gallaudet Survival Guide to Signing.* Expanded ed. Gallaudet University Press, 1990. 224p. illus. LC 89-25686 0-930323-67-X $6.95 paper

Hand-shape illustrations are good, and each sign is followed by a description of hand movements and positions. Drawings are easy to follow. Both this and Butterworth and Flodin (above) are reference bargains for small libraries.

Sternberg, Martin L. *American Sign Language Dictionary.* Rev. ed. Harper Perennial/HarperCollins, 1994. 576p. illus. 0-06-273275-7 $18

An abridgment (rather than a revision) of the first edition of Sternberg's excellent and well-reviewed *American Sign Language Dictionary: A Comprehensive Dictionary,* this adds more than one thousand new words and illustrations but omits bibliography and numerous useful English and foreign language indexes. If you own the first edition, do not discard it, but use this as a supplement to it. Also available is Sternberg's *American Sign Language Concise Dictionary* (HarperCollins, 1994) for libraries or patrons seeking an inexpensive "carry-around" paperback edition.

The English Language

★ Crystal, David. *The Cambridge Encyclopedia of the English Language.* Cambridge University Press, 1995. 500p. illus. maps. index. LC 94-23918 0-521-40179-8 $49.95

In spite of an emphasis on British English, this highly informative, beautifully illustrated book is recommended for most public, school, and academic libraries. Chapters beginning with "History," going to "Structure," and ending with "Use" consider the history, social, and literary story of the language. Chapters are divided into topics, with a double-paged spread for each.

Abbreviations

★ Barnhart, Robert K., ed. *The Barnhart Abbreviations Dictionary.* Wiley, 1995. 400p. LC 96-115251 0-471-57146-6 $34.95

In a two-way presentation (abbreviations-to-words followed by words-to-abbreviations), editors list abbreviations taken from contemporary English-language sources such as magazines, books, and newspapers. "Most common English-language terms" from all fields are collected here, with technical, scientific, and computing terms getting their due. Many acronyms are included. Affordable and, with more than sixty thousand listings, this is a good replacement for the more expensive *Acronyms, Initialisms and Abbreviations Dictionary* (Gale Research, 1997).

Kerchelich, Karen and Dean Stahl. *Abbreviations Dictionary.* 9th ed. CRC Press, 1995. 1376p.   LC 94-220525   0-8493-8944-5 $79.95

Abbreviations, acronyms, appellations, contractions, eponyms, geographical equivalents, initialisms, nicknames, slang shortcuts, and toponyms—this revised and expanded edition adds more than fifteen thousand of them. The final third of the work is a ready reference in itself, with info on inventors, airlines, vehicle license letters, birthstones, international conversions, superlatives, and more. Recommended for all libraries.

Dictionaries

Bragonier, Reg. *What's What: A Visual Glossary of the Physical World.* Smithmark, 1994. 576p. photogs.   0-831-79469-0 $15.98

More than five hundred pages of objects, mainly in photos, are labeled; and their parts are identified.

★ Brown, Lesley, ed. *The New Shorter Oxford English Dictionary.* 2 vols. Oxford University Press, 1993. 3801p.   0-19-861271-0 $125

The first rewriting of the sixty-year-old *Shorter Oxford English Dictionary* is a useful and affordable historical dictionary of English. Meanings and developments of words used between 1700 and 1990 trace every word back to its first known use. The 500,000 definitions offer the scholarship of the *Oxford English Dictionary* without the twenty-volume bulk or huge price.

★ Neufeldt, Victoria, ed. *Webster's New World Dictionary of American English.* 3d college ed. Prentice-Hall General Reference, 1994. 1574p. illus.   LC 93-2961   0-671-88289-9; 0-671-88243-0 $18; $22 thumb indexed

Two hundred new words and phrases, including *no-brainer, food court, designated driver,* and *factoid,* have been added to this dictionary. The biographical, geographical, and census entries have also been updated. Definitions are presented in historical order. Edged out for user-friendliness only by the American Heritage dictionaries, this is a good choice for public libraries.

Proctor, Paul, ed. *Cambridge International Dictionary of English.* Cambridge University Press, 1995. 1795p. illus.   0-521-48236-4; 0-521-48421-9 $27.95; $21.95 paper

Using Australian, British, and U.S. English, this dictionary offers the foreign-language speaker a guide to usage, pronunciation, spelling, and grammar. The definitions use a controlled vocabulary of less than two thousand words. Sample sentences and definitions are clear and concise. Only one meaning is given per entry. Words with different meanings are listed separate times. Illustrations help with definitions of everyday items.

★ *Random House Unabridged Dictionary.* 2d rev. ed. Random, 1994. 2550p. illus. maps.   LC 93-84591   0-679-42917-4 $100

With a continued tradition of currency, this dictionary owes its life to a computerized Random House database called the "Living Dictionary Project." One thousand new words have been added since 1987, and another fifteen hundred have been revised.

Swanfeldt, Andrew. *Crossword Puzzle Dictionary.* 6th ed. HarperCollins, 1995. 864p. 0-06-272053-8 $14 paper

As crossword "cheaters" know, no definitions of words are provided in crossword puzzle dictionaries. Entries contain lists of words one is trying to locate, such as synonyms for *light* or words for units of light—all in order of the number of letters per word.

Ultimate Visual Dictionary. Dorling Kindersley/Houghton, 1994. 640p. illus. maps. index.   1-56458-648-0 $39.95

This sparkling dictionary is another publishing marvel from Dorling Kindersley. Thirty thousand terms on more than 250 topics are organized into fourteen sections. The text is enhanced by five thousand color photographs and more than one thousand illustrations. An example of the usefulness of this volume is the section on the human body.

Thesauruses

★ American Heritage Dictionaries Editors. *Roget's II: The New Thesaurus.* 3d ed. Houghton Mifflin, 1995. 1216p. index.   0-395-68722-5 $20

All of the synonyms in this title are in one alphabetical list. It is current in words included and usage and is based on the 3d edition of the *American Heritage Dictionary of the English Language.* Main entries are in bold type with the part of speech listed. A brief definition is given, with *see* references to related words. Different meanings of synonyms are listed under different subentries.

★ *Bartlett's Roget's Thesaurus.* Little, Brown, 1996. 1488p. index.   LC 96-18343 0-316-10138-9 $18.95

Grouping more than 350,000 words and meanings under 848 broad topics, this is among the most substantial thesauruses now in print. The vocabulary reflects recent slang and usage, and the book features one hundred word lists on a great variety of subjects.

Hayakawa, S. I. and Eugene Ehrlich, eds. *Choose the Right Word: A Contemporary Guide to Selecting the Precise Word for Every Situation.* HarperCollins, 1994. 608p. index.   LC 93-34206   0-06-273131-9 $17 paper

A revised edition of the still useful *Modern Guide to Synonyms and Related Words,* this adds some words and subtracts others. Although it is less broad in its coverage than some other similar dictionaries, the explanatory essays are longer. Either edition is useful to libraries that need a dictionary of synonyms.

Lutz, William D. *The Cambridge Thesaurus of American English.* Cambridge University Press, 1994. 500p.   LC 93-31878   0-521-41427-X $17.95

> With a double-column format and good, readable type, this handy work offers a "discriminating" list of synonyms for each entry. Its alphabetical arrangement avoids the index approach of some thesauruses. Antonyms are listed for some words and phrases.

Sisson, A. F. and Barbara Ann Kipfer. *Sisson's Word and Expression Locater.* 2d ed. Prentice-Hall/Career and Personal Development, 1994. 404p. index.   LC 94-12091   0-13-814088-X; 0-13-814096-0 $27.95; $14.95 paper

> Unlike your average synonym dictionary, this work gives subheadings of related words under the main-entry word. The example given by one reviewer is that if one is looking for a word on the age of a tree, one can find *dendrochronology* under the subheading *Time* in the main entry *Tree.* More than 3,700 main words lead to more than 100,000 words and expressions.

Rhyming Dictionaries

Young, Sue. *The Scholastic Rhyming Dictionary.* Scholastic, 1994. 224p. illus. index. LC 93-11809   0-590-49460-0 $14.95

> Entries in this rhyming dictionary are divided according to the vowel sounds with which the rhyming sounds begin. There is an alphabetical index of words and rhyming sounds. The book includes instructions on locating a rhyming sound and definitions of the types of rhyme. Advice is also given on dealing with unrhymable words. Although designed for young people, this can be used by poets and songwriters of all ages.

Word and Phrase Origins

Rawson, Hugh. *Devious Derivations: Popular Misconceptions—and More than One Thousand True Origins of Common Words and Phrases.* Crown, 1995. 245p. bibliog. index.   0-517-58066-7 $12

> About one thousand words and phrases are gathered under headings such as "Geographical Ghosts," "Erudite Errors," and "Spurious Acronyms." A good bibliography gives this work value aside from the pleasure word hounds will take in browsing for origins of such words.

Idioms and Expressions

Fergusson, Rosalind, comp. *Shorter Dictionary of Catch Phrases*. Routledge, 1994. 176p.   LC 93-43539   0-415-10051-8 $16.95 paper

> The entries in this work have been taken from *A Dictionary of Catch Phrases,* but they have been rewritten and updated. This alphabetically arranged dictionary explains the meaning of each term and when it was introduced. "Read my lips," "take a rain check," and "TGIF" are all included. This is a nice addition to the collection on word and phrase origins.

Makkai, Adam. *A Dictionary of American Idioms*. 3d ed. Barron's Educational Series, 1995. 455p.   0-8120-1248-8 $12.95 paper

> More than two thousand entries relating to pop culture, slang, and technology have been added to this third edition, which defines more than eight thousand idiomatic expressions. It will perhaps be of most use to non-English speakers, and so an explanation of the book is written in nine languages. No sources of idioms are given, only their meanings.

Spears, Richard A. *NTC's American Idioms Dictionary*. 2d ed. National Textbook, 1994. 539p.   0-8442-0826-4 $12.95

> Eighty-five hundred idioms of American English are defined in the newest edition of this dictionary. More than one thousand have been added since the first edition. More than ten thousand examples are used to define the idioms, and a phrase-finder index gives keyword access to them. Clear definitions and lots of examples make this a great source, especially for those for whom English is a foreign language. No vulgar idioms are included, and no information on sources is given.

Slang

★ Lewin, Esther and Albert E. Lewin. *The Thesaurus of Slang: Over 165,000 Uncensored Contemporary Slang Terms, Common Idioms, and Colloquialisms, Updated for the 1990s and Arranged for Quick and Easy Reference*. Rev. ed. Facts on File, 1994. 456p.   LC 93-42890   0-8160-2898-2 $50

> A revision of the Lewins' 1987 book, this work boasts fifteen thousand additions and deletions, bringing the work up to current language. The only flaw here is that terms under each heading aren't listed in alphabetical order, thus making it difficult for the user to see if a specific term meets her needs. The book is, however, a useful work for writers and the merely curious. Libraries that already own the first edition could benefit from the currency of this one.

Spears, Richard A., ed. *NTC's Dictionary of American Slang and Colloquial Expressions*. 2d ed. National Textbook/NTC Publishing Group, 1995. 568p. index. LC 95-149319   0-8441-0827-2; 0-8442-0828-0 $16.95; $12.95 paper

More than one thousand new expressions have been added to the first edition of this work. Good explanatory material and a keyword index make this an easy work to use. Each entry starts with a code explaining the expression's grammatical function. Origin is sometimes indicated. The definition is followed by sample sentences showing how the expression is used. Aside from the lack of vulgar or obscene expressions, this is a fairly comprehensive and current dictionary.

Black Slang

Smitherman, Geneva. *Black Talk: Words and Phrases from the Hood to the Amen Corner.* Houghton Mifflin, 1994. 384p. illus.   LC 94-591   0-395-67410-7; 0-395-69992-4 $18.95; $10.95 paper

> This listing of words and phrases with "sometimes" examples of use and etymology is definitely aimed at the general reader. Reviewers state that it "lacks the scholarly documentation" that supports many of its claims to origins of terms, but it is "an excellent glossary of the current vocabulary of young, urban African Americans."

Western Slang

Adams, Ramon F. *Cowboy Dictionary: The Chin Jaw Words and Whing-Ding Ways of the American West.* Perigee Books/Berkely, 1994. Rev. ed. 384p. LC 93-30210   0-399-51866-5 $10.95 paper

> First appearing in 1936 as *Cowboy Lingo,* this work has gone through several editions until it was "revised and enlarged" in 1968. As it was revised, more "western" occupations were added so that the dictionary now covers loggers, boatmen, miners, packers, and so forth, as well as cowboys. Many words are included that we would not consider precisely western slang, but this is an inexpensive book for libraries that need or want information on this topic.

Clark, Thomas L. *Western Lore and Literature: A Dictionary for Enthusiasts of the American West.* University of Utah, 1996. 320p. photogs. bibliog.   0-87480-510-4 $24.95

> Words in this volume cover western life and folklore. Definitions are short, and the entries include pronunciation, parts of speech, sources, etymology, and dates of first occurrence.

Hendrickson, Robert. *Happy Trails: A Dictionary of Western Expressions.* Facts on File Dictionary of American Regionalisms, vol. 2. Facts on File, 1994. 288p. index. LC 93-42888   0-8160-2112-0 $24.95

> Because the author frequently uses quotations to underscore a meaning, this is an entertaining as well as informative dictionary. The subject index is excellent, and the work complements Adams (above). Hendrickson's defi-

nitions are a bit longer on the average, but Adams includes pronunciation, important where so many Spanish and Native American words are involved. Highly readable and useful where needed.

Military Slang

Dickson, Paul. *War Slang: Fighting Words and Phrases of Americans from the Civil War to the Gulf War.* Pocket Books, 1994. 416p. index. LC 93-16264 0-671-75024-0 $18 paper

> "War slang" in this instance is a broad term, referring to the slang of soldiers in the Civil War, the two world wars, Korean War, Vietnam War, Gulf War, and cold war. One chapter is devoted to each war, with the chapter on World War II accounting for more than three thousand terms alone. Etymologies are given, and sidebars give the history of some more-popular expressions. This will become a standard reference work on soldier slang.

Metaphors

Sommer, Elyse and Dorrie Weiss, eds. *Metaphors Dictionary.* Gale, 1995. 833p. index. LC 94-36728 0-8103-9149-X $65

> Libraries serving customers who do public speaking, creative writing, or criticism will want this book. More than six thousand metaphors are arranged by themes, which are listed in alphabetical order. Cross-references are given to help readers find other pertinent information. There is also a valuable list of sources.

Grammar and Punctuation

Gordon, Karen Elizabeth. *The New Well-Tempered Sentence: A Punctuation Handbook for the Innocent, the Eager and the Doomed.* Rev. ed. Ticknor & Fields, 1993. 148p. LC 93-18454 0-395-62883-0 $14.95

> Witty and irreverent, Gordon points out the rules of punctuation in full chapters. Our friend, the comma, rates thirty-seven pages of "mirthful discussion" of its proper use. Word lovers will enjoy reading it; students in need will enjoy scanning for the information. Alas, no index. Gordon treats grammar issues with equal élan in *The Deluxe Transitive Vampire* (Pantheon Books, 1993).

Shaw, Harry. *Errors in English and Ways to Correct Them.* 4th ed. HarperPaperbacks/ HarperCollins, 1993. 306p. index. LC 92-5313 0-06-461044-6 $11

> According to one reviewer, the main audience for this book is "self-conscious people who do not write often," a group that probably includes the larger portion of the U.S. population. Part 1 offers advice on how to avoid major writing errors. The main portion of the text relates to grammar, usage, sen-

tence structure, punctuation, and mechanics. Clear examples are given as well as practice exercises and answers. Another book bargain.

★ Shaw, Harry. *Punctuate It Right!* 2d ed. HarperPaperbacks/HarperCollins, 1993. 208p. index. 0-06-100813-3 $4.99

> Easier to use than more-detailed works such as *The Chicago Manual of Style* (see 800s), this book is based on the idea that punctuation is necessary for clear communication. The main portion of the work is an alphabetical listing of individual punctuation marks with specific rules and their exceptions. There are many examples of correct and incorrect usage. This is an excellent pocket guide for writers, professionals, and amateurs and an excellent bargain.

Weiner, Edmund and Sylvia Chalker. *The Oxford Dictionary of English Grammar.* Oxford University Press, 1994. 460p. LC 94-19818 0-19-861314-8 $11.95 paper

> Not a book of grammar, this dictionary gives brief definitions for terms used in grammar and linguistics. Cross-references between related meanings help explain differences in similar terms. This work is unique and will provide help for students of English and writing.

Usage

★ Burchfield, R. W., ed. *The New Fowler's Modern English Usage.* 3d ed. Oxford University Press, 1996. 640p. 0-19-869126-2 $25

> This, the first update of the classic work since 1965, brings the charm of *Fowler's* into the nineties. There are pronunciation guides, British versus American usage, and the politicizing of speech. Even though some of the charm has gone with the new revision, this is a book for those who love words and language.

Williams, Deborah K. *NTC's Dictionary of Tricky Words: With Complete Examples of Correct Usage.* National Textbook/NTC Publishing Group, 1996. 193p. LC 96-21920 0-8442-5472-X; 0-8442-5764-8 $16.95; $12.95 paper

> English words that are alike in sound or often mixed up in usage are listed and carefully defined. An inexpensive book that should be a part of every library's reference collection, this is a good place to find the difference between *infer* and *imply, hanged* and *hung,* and *shall* and *will.*

German Language

Sykes, J. B. and W. Scholze-Stubenrecht, eds. *The Oxford-Duden German Dictionary: German-English, English-German.* Clarendon Press, 1990. 1696p. LC 90-30292 0-19-864171-0 $39.95

> Some 260,000 entries and 450,000 translations are given, designed with both German and English speakers in mind. British and American English and Swiss, German, and Austrian German are covered. There is a section on grammar and a section on letter writing.

Terrell, Peter, ed. *Collins German-English, English-German Dictionary: Unabridged Edition*. 2d ed. HarperCollins, 1993. 902p.   LC 93-157577   0-06-275511-0 $50

> This excellent dictionary is up-to-date on such recent terms as *grunge, wimp,* and *pantyhose!* Many computer terms are listed as well as Americanisms and vulgarities (the latter with offensiveness ratings). Its only flaw, for us, is that pronunciation is given in British English. The one German dictionary that should be in every library.

French Language

Correard, Marie-Helen and Valerie Grundy. *The Oxford-Hachette French Dictionary*. Hachette and Oxford University Press, 1994. 2016p.   0-19-864519-8 $39.95

> These 350,000 entries and 530,000 translations draw examples from sources such as newspapers, magazines, and advertisements. Special attention is made of "false friends" (e.g., *figure* means *face* in English).

French-English/English-French Dictionary. Dictionnaire Francais-Anglais/Anglais-Francais. Unabridged ed. Larousse Kingfisher Chambers, 1993. maps.   2-03-420100-0 $40

Larousse Concise French-English/English-French Dictionary. Larousse Kingfisher Chambers, 1993.   LC 93-86203   2-03-420300-4; 2-03-420500-6 $16.95; $10.95 paper

> If you need an unabridged French dictionary containing more than 300,000 terms, the Larousse has been judged by some reviewers to be "remarkably superior to most other French-English dictionaries on the market." Vocabulary is advanced, and there is emphasis on historical contexts of words. Usage notes and sample sentences are liberally provided, and there is equal coverage of British and American usage. The abridged edition covers 90,000 terms and is designed for students beyond the beginning levels.

Rowlinson, William, Michael Janes and Dora Latiri-Carpenter. *The Oxford Paperback French Dictionary and Grammar*. Oxford University Press, 1995. 832p. 0-19-864529-5 $12.95

> This wonderfully organized dictionary has an excellent French grammar section and treats more than fifty thousand words and phrases. It seems largely based on the 1992 *Oxford Guide to the French Language,* so if you have that title, you can pass on this one.

Italian Language

The Oxford-Duden Pictorial Italian and English Dictionary. Oxford University Press, 1995. 872p.   0-19-864517-1 $19.95 paper

> This book has listings for more than twenty-eight thousand objects in its illustrations. It is divided into major headings, including transport, communications, and information technology; office, bank, and stock exchange;

and recreation, games, and sport. Excellent illustrations will help the user find the word he or she seeks. This is recommended as a supplement to standard Italian-English dictionaries.

Ragazzini, Guideppe and Adele Biagi. *Zanichelli New College Italian and English Dictionary*. National Textbook, 1990. 1200p. 0-8442-8449-1 $29.95

There are many business and technical terms in the almost seventy-five thousand words defined here. Usage examples are given, as are abbreviations, monetary systems, weights and measures, and irregular verbs.

Spanish Language

Spanish-English/English-Spanish Dictionary. Gran Diccionario Espanol-Ingles/Ingles-Espanol. Unabridged ed. Larousse Kingfisher Chambers, 1993. LC 93-086201 2-03-420200-7 $40

Larousse Concise Spanish-English/English-Spanish Dictionary. Larousse Diccionario Manual Espanol-Ingles/Ingles-Espanol. Larousse Kingfisher Chambers, 1993. 1248p. LC 93-086204 2-03-420400-X; 2-03-420402-6 $16.95; $10.95 paper

As with their French counterparts, the Spanish unabridged dictionary provides many more usage examples in its more than 220,000 entries. The concise version contains more than 120,000. The unabridged provides a Spanish grammar section, and the concise gives a conjugation chart. Both include slang and vulgarisms. They are easy-to-use and belong in all collections.

Latin Language

★ Ehrlich, Eugene. *Amo, Amas, Amat and More: How to Use Latin to Your Advantage and to the Astonishment of Others*. HarperCollins, 1993. 328p. 0-06-272017-1 $13 paper

Thanks to Hollywood, we all know what *carpe diem* means, but when someone says they have had a *lapsus linguae* (slip of the tongue) or someone is *oleo tranquillior* (smooth as oil), do you stand with your mouth open? No more. In this book, twelve hundred Latin phrases and proverbs are made stunningly clear to the reader. This is a must and a pleasure for lovers of words and history.

★ Ehrlich, Eugene. *Veni, Vidi, Vici: Conquer Your Enemies, Impress Your Friends with Everyday Latin*. HarperPerennial/HarperCollins, 1995. LC 94-42354 0-06-273365-6 $13 paper

A useful addition to all libraries, this "sequel" to *Amo, Amas, Amat and More* (above) starts with notes and short biographies on thirty-three quotable Romans. The more than one thousand phrase entries each gives the phrase, pronunciation, a translation, and the meaning of the words in context. Fun for word lovers to browse and good for reference.

Stone, Jon R. *Latin for the Illiterati: Exorcising the Ghosts of a Dead Language.*
Routledge, 1996. 240p. index. LC 95-47985 0-415-91775-1 $14.95 paper

> Similar to the works of Ehrlich (above) but much wider in range, this work is also a delight to read and a fine reference tool. Translations are given for more than five thousand phrases, and a section on abbreviations that come from Latin—such as "A.M."—also lists the months of the years, days of the week, Seven Hills of Rome, and Roman numerals to two thousand. Highly recommended.

Woodhouse, S. E. and James Morwood. *The Pocket Oxford Latin Dictionary.* Rev. ed. Oxford University Press, 1994. 368p. LC 94-11749 0-19-864227-X $15.95

> Although the term *pocket* conjures up a small, flimsy *vade mecum* (look *that* up in your Latin dictionary), this is not a pocket-size book either by size or by contents. The word count totals about thirty thousand and includes botanical terms, mythological names, and geographical names. A summary of Latin grammar rounds out the work.

500s
Natural Sciences and Mathematics

Although historical facts are important to the scientist, even the smallest library should check its science collection to make sure it contains current, basic science information.

Dictionaries of science are a great help to patrons and to librarians trying to help patrons in a field that may be unfamiliar to both! Books of scientific discovery and biography are in demand for students writing reports and need to cover a wide range of the sciences.

A small library does not have to keep a section of extremely technical mathematics materials, but a good dictionary of math terms and some books that will help the math impaired do their banking, wallpapering, and mortgage paying are a must.

Biology, the earth sciences, the physical sciences, and astronomy see new discoveries and theories every year. Many publishers are working with exciting and attractive new formats to help encourage reading and browsing in the sciences.

Many fine field guides to the natural world, such as Peterson's, Audubon Society, and Golden Guides, are not discussed here (with a few exceptions—Madame Audrey is noted for exceptions) because it is felt that most small libraries know of their existence and have a good selection in their circulating collections. These can be great additions to reference collections if individual libraries so choose. The important thing is to have a good collection of nature materials and information about the other living creatures, plant and animal, with whom we share the earth.

Dictionaries of Science

★ Barnes-Svarney, Patricia. *The New York Public Library Science Desk Reference.* Macmillan, 1995. 758p. illus. maps. index.   LC 94-40445   0-02-860403-2 $39.95

A clearly written reference book for high school and public libraries, this work includes among its many topics formulas, endangered species lists, and computer technology. The major divisions of science are each covered in a chapter giving basic facts, terms, and processes. There is also a chapter of "useful resources."

Lafferty, Peter and Julian Rowe, eds. *The Dictionary of Science.* Simon & Schuster, 1994. 678p. illus. index.   0-13-304718-0 $45

> This fine dictionary, with five thousand entries, does not aim to be exhaustive but is oozing with quality. The entries place terms in historical context and are full of interesting tidbits of information. Good illustrations, lots of cross-references, occasional quotations, chronologies, and a thematic index add to the value found here. This is an excellent supplement to more comprehensive works.

Moran, Andrea and Cynthia O'Neill, eds. *Visual Encyclopedia of Science.* Larousse Kingfisher Chambers, 1994. 320p. illus. maps. index.   LC 93-43118   1-85697-998-9 $22.95

> An alphabetical index makes it easy for students and interested adults to access the plethora of information in this highly condensed science reference. Scientific knowledge is divided into four sections: Earth, the living world, stars and planets, and science and technology. Using photographs, charts, tables, good illustrations, maps, and "fact boxes," the authors impart a world of information that will prove especially valuable for students looking for science project ideas.

★ Parker, Sybil P., ed. *McGraw-Hill Dictionary of Scientific and Technical Terms.* 5th ed. McGraw-Hill, 1994. 2194p. illus.   LC 93-34772   0-07-042333-4 $125 with disk

> Clear, concise definitions for the general public, 105,000 of them, are the stock-in-trade of this dictionary, last published in 1989. Unlike some dictionaries, the *McGraw-Hill* offers pronunciation. The disk includes a subset of the entries for basic technical terms. Both are excellent for school and public libraries.

Walker, Peter M. B., ed. *Larousse Dictionary of Science and Technology.* Larousse Kingfisher Chambers, 1995. 1236p. illus.   LC 94-73123   0-7523-0010-5 $45

> This work is an update of *Chambers Science and Technology Dictionary.* Forty thousand terms are defined, and five hundred black-and-white illustrations complement the text. All scientific topics are covered, and new term coverage is excellent. This is a relatively inexpensive way to cover the sciences in a good one-volume dictionary.

Natural History

Burnie, David. *Dictionary of Nature.* Dorling Kindersley, 1994. 192p. illus. index. LC 93-30696   1-56458-473-9 $19.95

More than two thousand nature concepts are discussed in this thematically arranged dictionary. Main headings include general information, terms, and explanation. Illustrations include three-dimensional models, diagrams, and photos. This book would be good for school children as well as adults looking for answers to questions on nature.

Scientific Discovery

Bruno, Leonard C. *Science and Technology Firsts*. Gale, 1996. 636p. photogs. bibliog. index.   LC 96-43595   0-7876-0256-6 $65

> Because there are many books out that stress inventions, Bruno places his stress on science firsts. More than four thousand entries are divided among twelve subject chapters, with entries arranged in chronological order within the chapters. The topics covered include biology, chemistry, computers, and transportation. More than 150 photos enhance the text.

★ Schmittroth, Linda, Mary Reilly McCall and Bridget Travers, eds. *Eureka! Scientific Discoveries and Inventions That Shaped the World*. Gale, 1995. 6 vols. illus. maps. index.   0-8103-9802-8 $99.95

> An excellent addition to any science collection, this set of books covers familiar and less-familiar scientific breakthroughs in an alphabetical arrangement. Lots of photos, drawings, charts, and sidebars make the work interesting for browsing as well as for reference. Male and female scientists of various racial backgrounds are included.

Travers, Bridget and Jeffrey Muhr, eds. *World of Scientific Discovery*. Gale, 1993. 776p. illus. index.   0-8103-8492-2 $69.95

> This work has wide coverage of topics and covers those topics in depth. Included in the 1,083 discoveries discussed here are DNA, Earth's mantle, penicillin, bubonic plague bacteria, and krypton. There is especially good material here on the lives of the scientists involved. It would provide a good starting place for school science reports.

Scientific Biography

Bailey, Martha J. *American Women in Science: A Biographical Dictionary*. ABC-Clio, 1994. 463p. illus. bibliog. index.   LC 94-10096   0-87436-740-9 $60

> Four hundred women scientists who worked before 1950 are covered as to specialty, education, employment, biography, awards, and a bibliography of sources. Recommended for any type of library.

Isely, Duane. *One Hundred and One Botanists*. Iowa State University Press, 1994. 352p. illus. index.   LC 94-28380   0-8138-2498-2 $32.95

> Three- to five-page essays on botanists from the time of Aristotle to 1991 include personal facts, major contribution, and a short bibliography.

Ninety-eight male and three female botanists are covered. Two indexes help this work, which features the usual "suspects" plus some lesser-known names in the field.

★ Millar, Ian, Margaret Millar, David Millar and John Millar. *The Cambridge Dictionary of Scientists*. Cambridge University Press, 1996. 387p. illus. index. LC 95-38471   0-521-56185-X; 0-521-56718-1 $39.95; $16.95 paper

An expansion of the *Concise Dictionary of Scientists,* out-of-print, this has been revised and updated. It covers thirteen hundred scientists, including more than seventy women. Articles are well written and include the fields of physics, chemistry, biology, geology, astronomy, mathematics, medicine, meteorology, and technology. Good for academic and public libraries.

★ Muir, Hazel, ed. *Larousse Dictionary of Scientists*. Larousse Kingfisher Chambers, 1994. 608p. index.   LC 94-75739   0-7523-0002-4 $35

Twenty-two hundred two-hundred-word essays give information on persons noted in the areas of natural sciences, mathematics, and medicine. There is some information on ancient natural philosophers and modern technologists as well. The emphasis here is on scientific accomplishment rather than personal biography.

Porter, Roy, ed. *The Biographical Dictionary of Scientists*. 2d ed. Oxford University Press, 1994. 960p. illus. index.   LC 94-10982   0-19-521083-2 $95

For each of seven fields (astronomy, biology, chemistry, engineering, geology, mathematics, and physics), essays tell about major developments and events in the lives of the scientifically inclined. Twelve hundred men and women are discussed with their contributions and biographical information. A glossary and appendix of Nobel Prize–winners are useful. Not as many women are included as one would like.

Yount, Lisa. *Contemporary Women Scientists*. American Profiles. Facts on File, 1994. 144p. illus. index.   LC 93-26821   0-8160-2895-8 $17.95

Arranged by year of birth, this dictionary covers women born from 1899 to 1946. A picture, a biographical chronology, and a bibliography about the subject's work are included in each entry. Although the intended audience is junior high and high school girls who might consider a career in science, all ages and levels can benefit from the identifying material and bibliographies here.

Mathematics

★ Downing, Douglas. *Dictionary of Mathematics Terms*. 2d ed. Barron's Educational Series, 1995. 393p. illus.   LC 95-12039   0-8120-3097-4 $10.95 paper

Downing covers the level of math that is studied in high school and early college. Aside from subjects and terms, there is some biographical infor-

mation. There is also a list of symbols, a common logarithm table, a trigo-
nometric function table, standard normal distribution tales, a chi square,
and a brief table of integrals.

Hopkins, Nigel and John W. Mayne. *The Numbers You Need.* Gale, 1993. 349p.
index. LC 92-4305   0-8103-8373-X $45

> Here are all the numbers you "meet" in everyday life—credit card num-
> bers, tips, car-buying figures, the CPI—explained for you! This user-
> friendly title has information and explanations on numbers in banking,
> health, weather, sports, gambling, hobbies, tools, and popular science.

★ Sutcliffe, Andrea. ed. *Numbers: How Many, How Far, How Long, How Much.*
HarperPerennial/HarperCollins, 1996. 656p. index.   LC 95-52658
0-06-273362-1 $20

> Meant as a home reference, this will nonetheless be useful for small li-
> braries. Tables and charts show loan amortization tables, a perpetual cal-
> endar, weights and measures conversions, zip codes, and food values.
> There is demographic data and consumer info on money, travel, the uni-
> verse, transportation, and so forth.

Averages

Droste, Kathleen and Jennifer Dye, eds. *Gale Book of Averages.* Gale, 1993. 600p.
index.   LC 93-29316   0-8103-9138-4 $49.95

> Information for the 1,147 charts, tables, graphs, and narratives in this work
> was collected from periodicals, newspapers, books, government documents,
> reports, company studies, research centers, and organizations. Data are
> arranged in fifteen subject chapters, and a source is listed with each table. A
> thirty-page subject index and thirty-page table of contents will lead the user
> to the correct information. This book would be useful in any library.

Astronomy

★ Audouze, Jean and Guy Israel, eds. *The Cambridge Atlas of Astronomy.* 3d ed.
Cambridge University Press, 1994. 472p. illus. maps. bibliog. index.   LC 95-112181
0-521-43438-6 $90

> This greatly enjoyable text combines with an impressive array of illustra-
> tions to make one of the nicest astronomy books for reference and general
> reading. It is divided into subject areas and subdivided into more specific
> topics. Lots of tables of information are included.

★ Bakich, Michael E. *The Cambridge Guide to the Constellations.* Cambridge
University Press, 1995. 320p. illus. maps.   LC 94-4678   0-521-46520-6; 0-521-44921-9
$49.95; $19.95

The first section of this book is devoted to lists on fact and myth related to the constellations, and the second section gives detailed information about each constellation. This is a delightful book for discovering or rediscovering the stars. Recommended for all types and sizes of libraries.

Clark, Stuart. *Stars and Atoms: From the Big Bang to the Solar System*. The New Encyclopedia of Science. Oxford University Press, 1995. 160p. illus. maps. index. LC 94-30783   0-19-521087-5 $39.95

The physics of modern astronomy is the emphasis in this book that is, nevertheless, readable and does not assume much prior knowledge. The first section consists of a glossary of terms. The balance of the volume is made up of essays grouped by topics, and the emphasis is on stellar astrophysics and not the constellations or appearance of the sky. Attractive as a coffee-table book, this will be a useful addition to the astronomy collection.

Gribbin, John. *Companion to the Cosmos*. Little, Brown, 1996. 504p. illus. bibliog. LC 96-26772   0-316-32835-9 $29.95

Beginning with an essay on current knowledge of the universe, this book is an encyclopedia with long articles, short entries, and biographies. A time line shows astronomical discoveries with general science discoveries and historical events.

Illingworth, Valerie, ed. *The Facts on File Dictionary of Astronomy*. 3d ed. Facts on File, 1994. 528p. illus.   LC 94-26275   0-8160-3184-3; 0-8160-3185-1 $27.95; $14.95 paper

Entries in this work are concise and well cross-referenced. As well as the standard terms one might expect, there is information on abbreviations, equipment, organizations, and observations.

Lankford, John, ed. *History of Astronomy: An Encyclopedia*. Encyclopedias in the History of Science, vol. 1. Garland, 1996. 733p. illus. bibliog. index.   LC 96-28558 0-8153-0322-X $95

This is the first one-volume encyclopedia on the history of astronomy. It focuses on the period after the scientific revolution and is written by a group of astronomy and space scholars. Some areas covered are general astronomical history, astronomy in national contexts, social history of astronomy, and some biographies. A good bibliography complements this fine work.

★ Lippincott, Kristen. *Astronomy*. Eyewitness Science. Dorling Kindersley, 1994. 64p. illus. index.   LC 94-18479   1-56458-680-4 $15.95

In a work produced in association with the Old Royal Observatory in Greenwich, England, the history of astronomy is emphasized. Information is chronological, finishing with facts about each planet in the solar system. Excellent cutaways and fact charts will sell this book to the most determined nonscientist.

Paschoff, Jay and Donald H. Menzel. *A Field Guide to the Stars and Planets.* Rev. ed. Houghton Mifflin, 1992. 528p. illus. maps.   LC 92-17556   0-395-53764-9; 0-395-53759-2 $24.95; $16.95 paper

> Numbers can best be used to describe this useful work—approximately 250 photographs, about 75 sky maps of northern and southern hemispheres, and more than 50 charts of the entire sky.

Peltier, Leslie C. *The Binocular Stargazer: A Beginner's Guide to Exploring the Sky.* Kalmbach Publishing, 1995. 160p. illus. maps. index.   0-913135-25-9 $19.95

> Recommended for public, secondary school, and college collections, this is a book written by an advocate of amateur astronomy. The intended audience is the beginning amateur, who would use binoculars instead of a telescope—hence the title. It serves its purpose well and provides a good introduction to the topic.

Chemistry

Eagleson, Mary, trans. *Concise Encyclopedia Chemistry.* Walter de Gruyter, 1994. 1203p. illus.   LC 93-36813   3-11-011451-8 $89.95

> An English-language version of *ABC Chemie,* this mainly covers physical properties and associated structures of substances. There are some short entries, but processes and concepts are covered in detail. Useful and reasonably priced, this book is recommended for all libraries as a handy reference.

Stwertka, Albert. *A Guide to the Elements.* Oxford University Press, 1996. 238p. illus. bibliog. index.   LC 96-24992   0-19-508083-1 $35

> History, theory, and arrangement of the periodic tables precedes the one-to seven-page articles on each of the 112 elements. Modern applications are given as well as properties and history for each element. Most of this can be found in a good encyclopedia, but this is a handy collection for science reference.

Earth Science

★ Farndon, John and Neil Ardley. *Dictionary of the Earth.* Dorling Kindersley, 1994. 192p. illus. maps. index.   LC 94-35497   0-7894-0049-9 $19.95

> Divided into such major themes as the Earth in space, the Earth's structure, rocks and minerals, soil, seas and oceans, and the impact of human beings, this dictionary provides definitions, photographs, and appropriate charts and tables. The text is clear and concise without being condescending. There are some biographies and a world map with major physical features. This is a good introductory reference source.

Ritchie, David. *The Encyclopedia of Earthquakes and Volcanos*. Facts on File, 1994. 240p. illus. bibliog. index.   LC 93-7670   0-8160-2659-9 $40

> A science writer has written a book for the lay reader with 632 alphabetically arranged entries and eighty-five black-and-white photos. Significant eruptions, quakes, and faults are covered, as are terms related to their study. Appendixes include a chronology of quakes and eruptions, eyewitness accounts to historic occurrences, and a bibliography.

Simkin, Tom and Lee Siebert. *Volcanoes of the World*. 2d ed. Geoscience Press, 1995. 349p. illus. maps.   LC 93-77813   0-945005-12-1 $25

> About one-third of this book is a directory of volcanoes arranged by geographic regions and country. Maps of particular volcanoes give location, elevation, times of eruption, type, and eruptive characteristics. Another section gives a chronology of eruptions over a ten thousand–year period. There is a list of references by geographic area.

van Rose, Susanna. *The Earth Atlas*. Dorling Kindersley, 1994. 64p. illus. maps. index.   LC 94-8765   1-56458-626-X $19.95

> Thirty topics in geology are each given a two-page spread in this gorgeously illustrated book. Most of the examples are drawn from actual facts or cases (e.g., Mount St. Helen's typifies volcanoes). Everyone from children to adults will be attracted to this book and find it useful.

Water

Ganeri, Anita. *The Oceans Atlas*. Dorling Kindersley, 1994. 63p. illus. maps. index. LC 93-28724   1-56458-475-5 $19.95

> This is not a traditional atlas as those familiar with Dorling Kindersley publications can probably guess, but it still gives important information on ocean features. Two-page layouts each focus on a different topic, such as coral reefs, waves, winds, and so forth. Color drawings and photographs show animals and oceanographic features. For junior high and public libraries.

Weather

★ Wagner, Ronald L. and Bill Adler Jr. *The Weather Sourcebook: Your One-Stop Resource for Everything You Need to Feed Your Weather Habit*. Globe Pequot Press, 1994. 320p. illus. maps. index.   LC 93-46757   1-56440-384-X $18.95 paper

> Almost every aspect of weather is mentioned and discussed in this book, but many of the discussions are very brief and will only whet the appetite for further reading. The book includes historical information and discusses all types of severe weather. Weather organizations and weather resources are covered thoroughly. A great addition to your collection for weather buffs and young science students.

Watts, Alan. *The Weather Handbook*. Sheridan House, 1994. 187p. illus. maps. index. 0-924486-76-7 $19.95

> If you own previous books by Watts, this might be a repetitious purchase. If this is your first, it is a good one. Among the topics covered are observational meteorology, forecasting techniques, local effects, a glossary of terms, and safety tips. A good, readable weather book for the general public.

Williams, Jack. *The* USA Today *Weather Almanac, 1995*. Random, 1994. 0-679755-47-0 $14 paper

> Although not a comprehensive book, this inexpensive title contains much information that will be helpful to librarians in answering weather questions: weather guides for vacation and travel, weather radio and extreme weather information, a city-by-city guide (including fifty foreign cities), and six-month forecasting.

Gems and Minerals

Hall, Cally. *Gemstones*. Eyewitness Handbooks. Dorling Kindersley, 1994. 160p. illus. index.   LC 93-28348   1-56458-499-2; 1-56458-498-4 $29.95; $17.95 paper

> We have become so jaded with the plethora of color material that makes up any Dorling Kindersley book that we forget how wonderful the pictures can be when used to illuminate a topic such as gemstones. "Spectacular" photos show 130 varieties of stones, and the text tells where they are found, how they can be located, and their properties. A good portion of the book is given over to cut stones, and photographs display the various cuts and characteristics. A beautiful book with lots of information, this will be picked up if you just leave it out where it can be seen!

Hochleitner, Rupert. *Minerals*. Barron, 1994. 240p. illus. index.   LC 93-40790 0-8120-1777-3 $14.95 paper

> After an opening that defines what a mineral is and discusses the properties of minerals, three hundred minerals are identified. Each entry has a color photo, and identifying features are given for each mineral. Easy-to-use and attractive, this has a place in most libraries.

Paleontology

Lambert, David and the Diagram Group. *The Field Guide to Prehistoric Life*. Facts on File, 1994. 256p. illus. maps. index.   0-8160-1389-6 $14.95 paper

> Instead of an actual field guide, it is better to think of this book as a brief summary of the major groups of ancient life classified by paleontologists. What are fossils? How are they distributed? These questions are answered by the good introductory material. An especially valuable chapter is devoted to the geological time periods and epochs.

Lessem, Don and Donald F. Glut. *The Dinosaur Society Dinosaur Encyclopedia*. Random, 1993. 576p. illus. index.   LC 94-117716   0-679-41770-2 $25

> *Jurassic Park* aside, just what is a dinosaur? The group in general is defined in nontechnical language. The majority of the text is a listing of 450 genera and 600 species of these fascinating critters. Each genus entry gives name of species, classification, name history, size, period, range, and diet. This is not a technical book or a children's book but a good, authoritative name glossary for the average adult whose interest in dinosaurs has been piqued by recent media attention.

Dictionaries of Biology

Concise Dictionary of Biology: New Edition. Oxford University Press, 1990. 288p. illus.   0-19-286109-3 $10.95 paper

> This work is taken from the larger *Concise Science Dictionary* put out by Oxford University Press and includes all the entries from that work on the biological sciences and related terms in other fields.

Dictionaries of Botany

Pankhurst, R. and R. Hyam. *Plants and Their Names: A Concise Dictionary*. Oxford University Press, 1995. 512p.   0-19-866189-4 $29.95

> Brief information is given on sixteen thousand scientific and vernacular plant names. The common names included are those that were encountered in literature and reflect everyday usage.

Forests

Kricher, John. *Peterson First Guide to Forests*. Peterson First Guide Series. Houghton Mifflin, 1994. 128p. illus. index.   LC 94-23719   0-395-71760-4 $4.95 paper

> Well put together and well written, this reasonably priced book is a good introduction to the ecology of North American forests. Most of the book consists of two-page descriptions of forty-eight North American forest types listing common trees, birds, animals, reptiles, amphibians, and plants for each. One page has a picture of the type, and the second page has a brief description.

Plants and Flowers

Heywood, Vernon, ed. *Flowering Plants of the World*. Updated ed. Oxford University Press, 1993. 336p. illus. maps. index.   LC 93-14014   0-19-521037-6 $55

An updated reissue of an old classic in the field, this includes common names of flowers, habitat, distribution, classification, and economic uses. Of the 306 families described, 205 have half-page or full-page illustrations. Recommended for all levels of study.

Edible and Medicinal Plants

The Encyclopedia of Medicinal Plants. Dorling Kindersley, 1996. 336p. photogs. bibliog. index.   LC 96-15192   0-7894-1067-2 $39.95 paper

Information on habitat and growth is given for herbs from all over the world. A history of herbal medicine and traditions has a visual guide to one hundred herbs, with current usage, research, and cautions.

Livingston, A. D. and Helen Livingston. *Edible Plants and Animals: A Compendium of Unusual Foods from Aardvark to Zamia.* Facts on File, 1993. 304p. illus. index. LC 92-42501   0-8160-2744-7 $25.95

Not really a book to take on your next camping trip, this is actually an "off-beat" collection of information about what has been eaten, how, and why. Medical, nutritive, and cultural significances are noted, as are poisonous parts of plants or animals. As for showing the diversity of the human palate, it can probably be said with no fear of contradiction that this is the only book in your collection where you will find a recipe for Scythian boiled horse.

Poisonous Plants and Venomous Animals

★ Foster, Steven and Roger A. Caras. *A Field Guide to Venomous Animals and Poisonous Plants: North American, North of Mexico.* Peterson Field Guide Series, no. 46. Houghton Mifflin, 1994. 244p. illus. index.   LC 94-1641   0-395-51594-7; 0-395-35292-4 $22.95; $15.95 paper

The hills are alive . . . with the sting of venom, apparently! This field guide to disaster shows us more than 250 poisonous plants and ninety venomous animals. Each animal included is given a short entry telling where it can be found and remarks on its venom and hazards. Black-and-white drawings illustrate the text. The plant section is arranged by color and comments on poisons and symptoms. Recommended.

Shells

Abbott, R. Tucker and Percy A. Morris. *A Field Guide to Shells of the Atlantic and Gulf Coasts and the West Indies.* 4th ed. Peterson Field Guide Series, no. 3. Houghton Mifflin, 1995. 350p. illus. bibliog. index.   LC 94-14421   0-395-69780-8; 0-395-69779-4 $26.95; $16.95 paper

Seven hundred eighty species are described in readable text that gives names, range, type of habitat, physical description, and life cycle. The book is aimed at the average shell collector and helps him or her with color plates showing each shell. There is more of an emphasis on the living animal rather than the collectible dead shell. Lists of clubs, a bibliography, and a glossary make this a valuable work for younger students and adults.

Insects

★ Evans, Arthur V. and Charles L. Bellamy. *An Inordinate Fondness for Beetles.* Holt, 1996. 208p. photogs. illus. bibliog. index.   0-8050-3751-9 $40

Beetles are marvelous creatures who have been on Earth since before the time of the dinosaurs. They are portrayed here in highly readable text and beautiful color photos that show more than 220 species. Body functions, history, habits, defenses, evolution, and conservation are just a few of the topics covered on these amazing insects.

Miller, Millie and Cyndi Nelson. *Painted Ladies: Butterflies of North America.* Johnson Books, 1993. 64p. illus.   1-55566-103-3 $5.95 paper

Designed as a personal vade mecum rather than a library book, this will still be of use to small libraries who need identification books. Few reference books can be said to have "charm," but watercolor illustrations and author comments give this a character of its own. Only about one hundred species are covered, but those are the most common. A good intro to butterfly watching.

Opler, Paul A. *Peterson First Guide to Butterflies and Moths.* Peterson First Guide Series. Houghton Mifflin, 1994. 128p. illus. index.   LC 93-5751   0-395-67072-1 $4.95 paper

One hundred eighty-three of the most common butterflies and moths in North America are shown in color, with descriptions of and features for each family and creature. There is a good beginning section on butterfly anatomy and how it differs from that of the moth.

Fishes

Nelson, Joseph S. *Fishes of the World.* 3d ed. Wiley, 1994. 600p. illus. bibliog. index. LC 93-37462   0-471-54713-1 $79.95

This new edition of a classic fish book has increased its bibliography by half and has information on almost forty more families of fish than its predecessors. The book is an asset to persons working with fishes and is suitable for public library reference. A standard work in the field.

Reptiles

Ernst, Carl H., Roger Barbour and Jeffrey E. Lovich. *Turtles of the United States and Canada.* Smithsonian, 1994. 682p. illus. maps. index.   LC 93-34939 1-56098-346-9 $60

> This is the best and most detailed book on turtles of Canada and the United States published. It is authoritative but not too technical, and it is well written. Accounts of each of the fifty-six species include habitat, behavior, reproduction, and distribution maps. Many species have color photographs.

★ Mattison, Chris. *The Encyclopedia of Snakes.* Facts on File, 1995. 288p. illus. maps. index.   LC 95-2501   0-8160-3072-3 $35

> An excellent, relatively inexpensive book, this is highly recommended for all types of libraries. It is well written and detailed and full of color photos. Snaky things in general are covered in the first of ten chapters. Habits and distribution, feeding, reproduction, human-snake relationships, myths, and taxonomy are just a few of the topics covered in this fine book.

Smith, Hobart M. *Handbook of Lizards: Lizards of the United States and of Canada.* Comstock Classic Handbooks. 1946. Reprint, Comstock Publishing/Cornell University Press, 1995. 580p. illus. maps. index.   LC 94-40090   0-8014-8236-4 $39.95 paper

> Even though this is a reprint of a 1946 work, reviewers report that it is useful and relevant for the study of lizards today. Because some of the taxonomy has changed, the publisher provides a chart that compares current nomenclature with that used in the book. Part 1 of this classic work discusses lizards in general, and part 2 has information on families. A more technical work than some, it is still the best scientific resource on lizards of the area covered. Useful where high school and college students use the public library.

Wareham, David C. *The Reptile and Amphibian Keeper's Dictionary: An A-Z of Herpetology.* Blandford/Sterling Publishing, 1993. 248p. illus.   0-7173-2318-1 $24.95

> This is an inexpensive source that most college, school, and public libraries will want and be able to afford. Not a "snake" book, it is a dictionary of more than two thousand terms for hobbyists, students, teachers, and zoologists, with information on reptiles and amphibians in clear, concise prose. Small black-and-white drawings add to the value of the work.

Wright, Albert Hazen and Anna Allen Wright. *Handbook of Frogs and Toads of the United States and Canada.* 3d ed. Comstock Classic Handbooks. 1949. Reprint, Comstock Publishing/Cornell University Press, 1994. 584p. illus. maps. index. 0-8014-8232-1 $39.95

As with Smith's lizard handbook (above), the publisher of this Comstock Classic updates the taxonomy in an introduction. Full information on frog and toad families, anatomy, habitat, appearance, development, and range are given.

Birds

Baerg, Harry J. *Common American Birds.* Naturegraph, 1994. 64p. illus. index. 0-87961-235-5 $8.95 paper

> This is a very inexpensive introduction to familiar birds of North America. More than three hundred species are covered in beautiful full-color paintings, generally of the males. The text has brief coverage of calls, songs, behavior, diet, nests, and so forth. For children or adults who want the basics.

Harrison, Colin and Alan Greensmith. *Birds of the World.* Eyewitness Handbooks. Dorling Kindersley, 1993. 416p. illus. maps. index.   LC 93-7065   1-56458-296-5; 1-56458-295-7 $29.95; $19.95 paper

> Each species account includes color photographs of each bird and information on behavior and ecology. Range maps and pictorial keys to basic information complete the entries. Simple, clear, and concise, this is current and informative for students or birdwatchers.

Kaufman, Kenn. *Lives of North American Birds.* Peterson Natural History. Houghton Mifflin, 1997. 640p. photogs. index.   LC 96-20285   0-395-77017-3 $35

> A companion to field guides, this work gives us six hundred species of birds and groups them by family. It includes color photos and range maps with concise information on life and conservation status. This is a quick reference rather than an exhaustive resource.

★ Rosair, David and David Cottridge. *Photographic Guide to the Shorebirds of the World.* Facts on File, 1995. 175p. illus. index.   LC 95-2502   0-8160-3309-9 $29.95

> Seven hundred fantastic photographs show plovers, sandpipers, oystercatchers, coursers, jacanas, and other shorebirds with variations in plumage. The text is organized by species. This is the best title available for identifying these birds.

Mammals

Carwardine, Mark. *Whales, Porpoises, and Dolphins.* Dorling Kindersley, 1995. 256p. illus. maps. index.   LC 94-33301   1-56458-621-9; 1-56458-620-0 $29.95; $17.95 flexibinding

> This pocket-size field guide consists of species accounts filled with illustrations, sidebars, and bits of information. Each species is illustrated in color, and there are detailed drawings of the parts of an animal. This is an excellent guide for whale watchers or for students.

Nowak, Ronald M. *Walker's Mammals of the World*. Rev. Johns Hopkins University Press, 1991. 1732p. photogs.   LC 91-027011   0-80183-970-X $95

> Animals in this authoritative work are arranged by family. There are black-and-white photos identifying species of creatures from all over the world. Such information as range, habitat, color, and measurements are given with each entry, and there are several pages of distribution charts. Not a pretty or exciting animal book, this is nonetheless useful in identifying and giving brief information on hundreds of wild animals.

O'Brien, Tim. *Where the Animals Are*. Globe Pequot Press, 1992. 320p. LC 92-20081   1-564400-77-8 $12.95 paper

> Zoos, aquaria, and wildlife attractions in the United States and Canada are covered in this guidebook with full directory information and travel tips. It is arranged by state or province.

Stuart, Chris and Tilde Stuart. *Africa's Vanishing Wildlife*. Smithsonian, 1996. 198p. photogs. index.   1-56098-678-6 $39.95

> Encyclopedia-style entries provide information on the status of African animals and show a photo, distribution map, behavior, and conservation efforts. Good information for school reports.

★ Whitaker, John O., Jr. *Audubon Society Field Guide to North American Mammals*. Alfred A. Knopf, 1996. 780p. photogs.   0-67944-631-1 $19.99

> Mammals from north of Mexico are covered in three hundred pages of color plates, arranged by type of animal. Captions under the photos list the animals measurements as explained in a chart. The second half of the book is given over to descriptions of the pictured animals. Entries include a description of the animal, a list of similar species, habitat, range, and habits.

600s
Technology and Applied Sciences

While the 500s represent pure science or the natural sciences, this category represents man's attempts to use science and its various applications. Although, once again, history is important in any field, this is an area where up-to-date information is often required.

Medicine is one section where "five years old is too old." Combining this fact with the difficulty of finding good, clear consumer medical information makes the 610s an essential area to check when weeding or selecting new titles. Information on health care, illnesses, sex, drugs, pediatrics, and preventive medicine are important elements in a good consumer-health collection.

Technical fields such as mechanics and transportation also need attention from library staff. Information on history and current happenings in the space program are of interest to library users, and every librarian knows the importance of having plenty of auto and motorcycle repair manuals on hand.

The agricultural arts, such as gardening, are popular with patrons seeking advice on adding to or changing a vegetable or flower garden. Books on care and training of horses, dogs, and cats are a necessary part of any collection; and information on breeds will be in demand. Cookbooks will be a part of any library's circulating collection, but books on food terms and definitions should be in reference, as should books on nutrition.

Child-care and home-maintenance titles are an important part of the 600s, as are business books, which provide information for secretaries needing help, for students and businesspeople seeking explanations of terms, and for those looking for material on marketing and advertising.

Technology and Trademarks

Freiman, Fran Locher and Neil Schlager. *Failed Technology: True Stories of Technological Disasters*. 2 vols. Gale, 1995. illus. index.   0-8103-9794-3 $34.95

A unique reference, this work gives details on failed technology in the areas of ships and submarines; airships, aircraft, and spacecraft; automobiles; dams and bridges; structures; nuclear plants; chemicals and the environment; and medical practice. Background and particulars are given for each disaster, as is the impact of the catastrophe. There are seventy photographs and a list of sources for further reading.

★ James, Peter and Nick Thorpe. *Ancient Inventions*. Ballantine, 1994. 544p. illus. bibliog. index. 0-345-40102-6 $17.50 paper

> To quote a reviewer and give one an idea of the importance of this book, "You leave your seventh-floor apartment, curse the congested traffic . . . stop at a fast food restaurant on your way to have cataract surgery. You live in Rome A.D. 25." Well researched and well illustrated, this amusing book can be used for its accounts of daily life as well as for information on technology of the past.

Levy, Richard C. *Inventing and Patenting Sourcebook*. 2d ed. Gale, 1992. 1024p. index. 0-8103-7616-4 $90

> Mainly a compendium of information on how to protect and license your patent, this book is a directory of inventing information with many useful forms and tables. There is an index, a glossary, and appendixes, including patent classifications, the patent office phone directory, the copyright office phone directory, a fee schedule, and the top two hundred corporations receiving patents in 1990.

Morgan, Hal. *Symbols of America*. Viking/Penguin, 1987. 240p. illus. bibliog. index. 0-14-008077-5 $22.50

> Not only a delightful presentation of well-known symbols and logos of American-made products, this is also a good reference book. Background is given, and any changes in the logo over the years are illustrated.

Rose, Sharon and Neil Schlager, eds. *CDs, Super Glue, and Salsa: How Everyday Products Are Made*. 2 vols. Gale, 1994. illus. index. LC 94-35243 vol. 1, 0-8103-9792-7; vol. 2, 0-8103-9793-5 $44.95

> The stories of popular products used at home, work, and school make fascinating reading. Chocolate (yes!), salsa, and cheese are covered, and running shoes, zippers, and bulletproof vests are examined. How do CDs work? What about optical fiber or bar-code scanners or the combination lock? Essays are about eight pages each and give a background of the product and design and a description of the manufacturing process.

Travers, Bridget, ed. *World of Invention*. Gale, 1993. 750p. illus. bibliog. index. 0-8103-8375-6 $75

> This one-volume book covers much work from women and minorities, two groups likely to have been left out of previous compilations. More than eleven hundred entries describe inventions from the Industrial Revolution to the present, presenting information in layperson's terms. There is a good bibliography.

Health Care

★ Freudenheim, Ellen, *Healthspeak: A Complete Dictionary of America's Health Care System*. Facts on File, 1996. 288p. bibliog. index   LC 95-10965   0-8160-3210-6 $30

> It is difficult for the consumer to follow the changes in federal and state policies that address the American health-care system. The two thousand health-care terms and their definitions found here at least give the average citizen a fighting chance. The author has a master's degree in public health and has put together a highly useful and recommended work for all reference collections.

Miller, Marc S., ed. *Health Care Choices for Today's Consumer: The Families USA Guide to Quality and Cost*. Living Planet Press, 1995. 352p. index.   1-879326-23-X $14.95 paper

> Families USA is a nonprofit consumer group offering advice on how to be an informed health-care consumer. Issues covered are consumer rights; selecting health plans, providers, and hospitals; services for women, children, and the elderly; alternative care; long-term care; and home care. Lists of organizations are especially helpful.

★ Wright, John W. and Linda Sunshine. *The Best Hospitals in America*. 2d ed. Gale, 1995. 630p. index.   0-614219-91-4 $18.95 paper

> Hospitals in this guide were chosen after consultation with physicians representing various parts of the United States and Canada. The book is arranged by state or province, and a four- to five-page section on each hospital tells about specialty areas, patient satisfaction, research programs, and admission policies. There is also information on number of beds, number of staff, charges, and directory data. Lists include hospitals recommended by the Joint Commission on Accreditation of Healthcare Organizations, the *U.S. News and World Report* list of the top forty hospitals, and cancer centers designated by the National Cancer Institute.

Medicine

Bynum, W. F. and Roy Porter, eds. *Companion Encyclopedia of the History of Medicine*. 2 vols. Routledge, 1993. 1792p. index.   LC 92-26013   0-415-04771-4 $199.95

> As an outstanding survey of medical history, these volumes have astonishing coverage. Seventy-two essays range from ten to more than forty pages and are international in scope. Each chapter has a bibliography. Some of the best medical scholarship available is evident in these books, which cover such topics as geriatrics, alternative health practices, theories, body systems, Chinese medicine, and clinical medicine.

Smith, Trevor. *An Encyclopedia of Homeopathy*. 2d ed. Insight Editions/Atrium Publishers Group, 1994. 317p.   0-946670-22-6 $19.95 paper

The author is a doctor with thirty years of practice in the field of homeopathy. There are brief biographies and an outline of common illnesses with a list of remedies. The essential areas of homeopathic medicine are compared with conventional medicine. The writing is clear and the print is large. This is a good source of information on the history and practice of homeopathy, with information not easily found elsewhere.

★ Walton, John, Jeremiah A. Barondess and Stephen Lock. *The Oxford Medical Companion*. Oxford University Press, 1994. 800p. illus. 0-19-262355-9 $60

Articles about medicine in various geographical areas, psychiatry, and art make this a welcome addition to any library. It has appeal as a reference book and a tome that is fun to browse through. It is a cross between a dictionary and a one-volume encyclopedia of medical topics.

Medical Dictionaries

★ *Merriam-Webster's Medical Desk Dictionary*. Merriam-Webster, 1995. 816p.
LC 96-15564 0-87779-125-2 $24.95

A list of signs and symbols, a handbook of style, biographical notes on individuals whose names are part of medical terminology—all of these and more are included in this excellent medical dictionary. The editors maintain a program of scanning medical publications to keep up with the latest in terminology. *Merriam-Webster's Medical Dictionary* published in 1995 is an abridged version of this volume.

Stedman's Medical Dictionary. 26th ed. Williams & Wilkins, 1995. illus.
0-683-07922-0 $44.95

A classical medical dictionary, this work is comprehensive and scholarly. More than one hundred thousand entries cover terms in all fields of medicine. Color plates are included.

★ Thomas, Clayton, ed. *Taber's Cyclopedic Medical Dictionary*. 18th ed. Davis, 1997. 2700p. illus. 0-8036-0195-6; 0-8036-0194-8 $62.00; $27.50 paper

More than two thousand color illustrations and charts help define the more than forty thousand main definitions in basic medical terminology, nursing, and allied health fields.

Anatomy

★ *Atlas of the Human Body*. HarperPerennial/HarperCollins, 1994. 140p. illus. index. LC 94-4162 0-06-273297-8 $20 paper

Each chapter in this text has a single topic—for example, female reproductive organs—and explains the purpose and shows the parts of this system. Diagrams show individual processes. Color drawings, sketches, and stylized studies of relationships of parts and systems give students and patients a clear look at the body's workings.

Walker, Richard. *The Visual Dictionary of the Skeleton*. Eyewitness Visual Dictionaries. Dorling Kindersley, 1995. 64p. illus. index.   0-7894-0135-5 $16.95

> A detailed index contains anatomical and popular terms that refer to the appropriate illustration in the text, more an atlas than a dictionary. Functions of the bones and joints are illustrated. Skeletons other than human are used for comparisons.

Health

★ American Medical Association Staff. *American Medical Association Complete Guide to Women's Health*. Random, 1996. 759p. illus. index.   LC 96-33738 0-679-43122-5 $39.95

> Although this was compiled by a woman gynecologist and a team of physicians, it has a somewhat more conservative slant than the classic *Our Bodies, Ourselves* (Peter Smith Publisher, 1998). It is patterned after the *American Medical Association Family Medical Guide* (Random House, 1994), and is illustrated with flow charts and diagrams in the manner of that title. There is a FAQ section on women's health issues and preventive medical advice. The book gives authoritative and reliable medical advice.

Ammer, Christine. *The New A to Z of Women's Health: A Concise Encyclopedia*. 3d ed. Facts on File, 1995. 576p. illus. index.   0-8160-3121-5 $40

> Although general diseases and conditions are treated, the emphasis here is on gynecology and obstetric issues. Updates include information on alternative medicine and HIV. The language is clear and terms are explained. A good addition to the consumer-health collection.

Carlson, Karen J., Stephanie A. Eisenstadt and Terra Ziporyn. *The Harvard Guide to Women's Health*. Harvard University Press Reference Library. Harvard University, 1996. 704p. illus. bibliog. index.   0-674-36768-5; 0-674-36769-3 $39.95; $24.95 paper

> An up-to-date guide on women's health, this is written by women physicians. More comprehensive than *Our Bodies, Ourselves* (Peter Smith Publisher, 1998), this covers a wide range of topics. Women's heart disease and reproductive issues are well handled. Internet resources are listed as well as a print bibliography. The alphabetical arrangement makes for easy use.

Gottlieb, Bill, ed. *New Choices in Natural Healing: Over One Thousand of the Best Self-Help Remedies from the World of Alternative Medicine*. Rodale, 1995. 440p. illus. index.   LC 95-15907   0-87596-257-2 $27.95

> If libraries have hesitated to purchase materials on alternative medicine, this significant work is a good place to start. The editors of *Prevention* magazine have devoted twenty chapters to different natural therapies. There is also a list of 163 health problems and possible natural treatments.

★ Inlander, Charles. *The People's Medical Society's Men's Health and Wellness Encyclopedia: Everything a Man Needs to Know for Good Health and Well-being*.

Macmillan/People's Medical Society, 1998. 518p. illus. bibliog. index.
0-028-62153-0 $29.95

> Cosmetic surgery, men's role in pregnancy and childbirth, circumcision, vitamins, male menopause, gay health, and prostate cancer are among a few of the topics covered in this useful and comprehensive aid to consumer health education. Patient participation in health care is strongly touted. The author, a physician, lists web sites on men's health and includes a good bibliography.

★ Inlander, Charles B. and People's Medical Society Staff. *The Consumer's Medical Desk Reference: Information Your Doctor Can't or Won't Tell You; Everything You Need to Know for the Best in Health Care*. Hyperion/Little, Brown, 1995. 672p. index.
0-7868-6056-1 $24.95

> Designed to assist the layperson in making medical decisions, this helps with choices concerning procedures, tests, medication, hospitals, nursing homes, providers, and insurance. The chapter on providers gives a comparison between MDs and osteopaths. Agencies and societies are listed. Complication and morbidity rates for the top eighteen high-risk surgeries may or may not be good to know! Not a typical health guide, this book is about weighing options.

Kastner, Mark and Hugh Burroughs. *Alternative Healing: The Complete A-Z Guide to Over 160 Different Alternative Therapies*. Halcyon Publishing, 1993. 368p. index.
LC 93-77385   0-9635997-1-2 $15 paper

> The 169 alphabetically arranged articles deal with alternative therapy systems designed to help the body heal itself. The coverage is broad and the articles well written. A glossary and a directory of alternative therapy organizations are included. A well-balanced book, this does not claim that the therapies should be used without resorting to conventional medicine.

★ Merck Staff. *The Merck Manual of Medical Information: Home Edition*. Merck, 1997. 1536p. illus. index.   LC 96-080494   0-911910-87-5 $29.95

> *The Merck Manual* is one of the most widely used medical books in the world, but until now it was still a book for the medical professional. This version has almost all of the same information but is accessible to the average consumer. Divided into sections by organ system or specialty, this is illuminated by helpful drawings and lots of cross-references. Comparable to other family home medical guides, this also has special information on men's, women's, and children's health.

Napoli, Maryann, ed. *The Center for Medical Consumers Ultimate Medical Answerbook*. Hearst Books, 1995. 416p. illus. index.   LC 95-60   0-688-12753-3 $23

> The *Answerbook* describes seventy-five common conditions with an average of five pages for each entry. The editor is a regular contributor to *Family Circle* magazine and founded the Center for Medical Consumers. Not as comprehensive as some books of its type, it is noteworthy for its balanced treatment of medical opinion. Recommended for consumer-health collections.

Null, Gary. *The Woman's Encyclopedia of Natural Healing: The New Healing Techniques of Over One Hundred Leading Alternative Practitioners.* Seven Stories, 1997. 480p. index.   LC 96-28291   1-888363-35-5 $19.95 paper

> Twenty-eight ailment categories are arranged alphabetically with prevention, symptoms, diagnosis, and conventional and alternative treatments. Each chapter has a good bibliography. Contributing specialists are listed in the back of the book with addresses and credentials. There is an emphasis on nutrition.

Rees, Alan M. *Consumer Health USA: Essential Information from the Federal Health Network.* Oryx, 1995. 552p. illus. index.   LC 94-37594   0-89774-880-1 $55

> This is essentially a reprint of 151 federal publications giving answers to questions on AIDS, allergies, women's health, and other areas of concern. The publications are arranged by body system and give the source of the original document. There is also a reprint of the National Library of Medicine's Health Hotlines.

Stoppard, Miriam, ed. *Woman's Body.* Dorling Kindersley, 1994. 224p. illus. index. LC 94-6290   1-56458-617-0 $29.95

> Not just another women's health book, this well-illustrated volume gives information about diet, exercise, health care, contraception, pregnancy, infertility, and sexually transmitted diseases. An excellent companion for other studies of women's health, this book's fine color photographs and graphic materials make the study of women's health more understandable.

★ Time-Life Books Editors. *The Medical Advisor: The Complete Guide to Alternative and Conventional Treatments.* Time-Life, 1996. 1152p. illus. bibliog. index. LC 95-45803   0-8094-6737-2 $39.95

> The major portion of this book is given over to an eight-hundred-page section on two hundred ailments with symptoms, causes, prevention, and treatments, both conventional and alternative. There are descriptions of the therapies, first aid information, health guidelines, an index of medicines, a directory of health organizations, and a very good index. The book includes an illustrated diagnostic guide, an anatomical atlas, a map of acupressure points, a foot reflexology chart, and yoga positions. Highly recommended for small libraries.

Wertheimer, Neil. *Total Health for Men: How to Prevent and Treat the Health Problems That Trouble Men Most.* Rodale, 1995. 600p.   LC 95-15909   0-87596-309-9; 0-87596-459-1 $31.95; $17.95 paper

> Because in previous years much medical research was done strictly on groups of men, many general health books can be said to be books on men's health. However, men have shown a growing awareness of health problems, from alcoholism to prostate cancer, and this book is a good popular treatment of their concerns. Information is included on nutrition, fitness, and lifestyle, as well as diseases and conditions. This is a good choice for popular health collections.

Sex

Bechtel, Steven and the Editors of Prevention Magazine. *The Practical Encyclopedia of Sex and Health: From Aphrodisiacs and Hormones to Potency, Stress and Vasectomy.* Rodale, 1993. 352p. index.   LC 92-35043   0-87596-163-0 $26.95

> Alphabetically arranged short articles deal with sexual health in layperson's terms. Human sexual "equipment," function, behaviors, diseases, and therapies are covered. Sources for further information are included in the text. This would be a good addition to consumer-health collections.

Bullough, Vern L. and Bonnie Bullough, eds. *Human Sexuality: An Encyclopedia.* 2 vols. Garland, 1994. 688p. index.   LC 93-32686   0-8240-7972-8 $95

> One hundred medical specialists have written two hundred articles on all aspects of sexuality, including moral development. There are biographical entries for pioneers in the sometimes controversial field, and a good index helps readers follow through with a topic. The articles are well written, and this is one of the few works of its kind.

Francoeur, Robert T., Timothy Perper and Norman Scherz, eds. *The Complete Dictionary of Sexology.* New expanded ed. Continuum Publishing, 1995. 784p. illus. 0-8264-0672-6 $29.95 paper

> One hundred thirty more entries have been added to this dictionary, the aim of which is to provide a "common basis for communications by bringing together terms and definitions from all the disciplines." Sexual terms from a variety of contexts are brought together so there can be a consistent vocabulary across fields.

Westheimer, Ruth K., ed. *Dr. Ruth's Encyclopedia of Sex.* Continuum Publishing, 1994. 324p. illus. bibliog. index.   LC 94-5009   0-8264-0625-4 $29.50

> A good source for high school and college students or other members of the general public, this book covers a wide range of topics and has, to quote the title of a book from another era, *Everything You Always Wanted to Know about Sex But Were Afraid to Ask.* Its emphasis is not on analysis, but rather on description. Entries range from a paragraph to several pages. There is a glossary that includes slang and a bibliography of general works in this field.

Drugs and Medicines

Fried, John J. and Sharon Petska. American Druggist *Complete Family Guide to Prescriptions, Pills and Drugs.* Hearst Books, 1995. 352p. illus. index.   LC 94-39831 0-688-12385-6 $17.95 paper

> The first thirteen chapters in this book talk about general drug-related issues. The rest of the chapters cover various therapeutic categories. Prescription and over-the-counter drugs are covered. There is a useful suggestion section with ideas for stocking a home medicine cabinet. This is an up-to-date source for the general reader.

★ Griffith, H. Winter. *Complete Guide to Prescription and Non-Prescription Drugs, 1997.* Berkley, 1996. 1104p.   0-614-17511-9 $16.95 paper

> Four thousand brand name and 490 generic drugs are listed in this work that provides information about the drugs in a chart form: brand names, side effects, dosage, interaction, and so forth.

Leber, Max, Robert Jaeger and Anthony Scalzo. *The Handbook of Over-the-Counter Drugs.* Celestial Arts, 1995. 464p. bibliog. index.   0-89087-734-3 $14.95 paper

> This guide to nonprescription drugs explains what the products are designed to do and their potential hazards. Cost and effectiveness are compared for different drugs recommended for the same condition. The substances are arranged by care categories. Besides drugs, such products as bottled water, shampoos, and cosmetics are covered. The emphasis is on ingredients with an index to brand names.

★ Long, James W. *The Essential Guide to Prescription Drugs, 1997.* HarperCollins, 1996. 1184p. index.   0-06-273429-6 $20 paper

> Full information on prescription drugs is provided for the consumer. Written by a physician, this is one of the best guides to medicines. It will supplement the direction received from a physician. Three hundred profiles of common drugs are given. The index lists both generic and brand names. Patrons accustomed to trying to use the *Physician's Desk Reference* (below) will be pleased at the layperson's language in this title.

Oppenheim, Mike. *One Hundred Drugs that Work: A Guide to the Best Prescription and Nonprescription Drugs.* Lowell House, 1994. 348p. index.   LC 93-223654 1-56565-115-4 $22.95

> This book is a listing of more than one hundred drugs, including antibiotics, hormones, and cardiovascular, digestive, neurological and psychological, pain, respiratory, skin, and nutrient agents. A "how-to" section tells the user how the book is set up and gives advice on how to use the text. An appendix has a list of ten underused drugs and ten overused drugs and ten drugs that don't work.

★ *The PDR Family Guide to Prescription Drugs.* 3d ed. Medical Economics Data, 1995. 1024p. illus. index.   1-56363-134-2 $25.95 paper with CD-ROM

> The information contained in this book is based on the product labeling published in the *Physician's Desk Reference* (below) and is supplemented with other sources. Part 1 consists of drug profiles in plain English. Part 2 has overviews of disease, and part 3 has "glamour shots" of the pills themselves as seen in the *Physician's Desk Reference*. There is a general index, a disease index, and a list of sugar-free products, alcohol-free products, photosensitive drugs, and poison-control centers.

★ *Physicians Desk Reference, 1996.* American Medical Association, 1996. illus. 0-614-1972-8-7 $69.95

This standard source of information on prescription drugs gives full information for more than twenty-eight hundred drugs. Arrangement is by drug name. The information given comes from the drug companies and includes a product description, why the drug is prescribed, dosage, and contraindications.

Winter, Ruth. *A Consumer's Dictionary of Medicines: Prescription, Over-the-Counter, and Herbal*. Crown, 1993. 507p.   LC 92-45595   0-517-88046-6 $20 paper

This book is unique in that it covers prescription, over-the-counter, and herbal medicine in one volume. Numerous *see* references are helpful in locating related materials. A long introduction defines the three types of medications covered and discusses the elderly, women, pregnancy, safety issues, sexual dysfunction, drug-food interaction, and generic drugs.

Poisons

Turkington, Carol. *The Home Health Guide to Poisons and Antidotes*. Facts on File, 1994. 372p. index.   0-8160-3316-1 $12.95

This book covers natural and man-made poisons and shows the reader how to recognize the symptoms of poisoning. It does not give first-aid instructions but tells how to contact poison-control centers when poisoning is suspected. There is a listing of toxic substances and a discussion of drug interactions and inhalation of noxious substances.

Vitamins

Navarra, Tova and Myron A. Lipkowitz, M.D. *Encyclopedia of Vitamins, Minerals and Supplements*. Facts on File, 1996. 288p. bibliog. index.   0-8160-3183-5 $35

The authors of this worthwhile resource certainly have the proper credentials—Navarra is a registered nurse and Lipkowitz is an M.D. and former pharmacologist with training in nutrition. Each substance is described, and information is given on where it is found and its uses. Health conditions that may be helped by vitamins are covered, as are terms on nutrition. There are five hundred entries in all. Good appendixes include a food pyramid and a glossary of terms.

Sultenfuss, Sherry Wilson and Thomas J. Sultenfuss. *A Women's Guide to Vitamins and Minerals*. Contemporary Books, 1995. 270p. index.   0-8092-3509-9 $16.95

Confused by magazine, newspaper, and TV information on vitamins? Are they necessary? What about supplements? Should herbs be used "over-the-counter"? This book is a review of medical and nutritional journal articles on vitamins, minerals, and herbs designed to give the average woman information on healthy use of these substances. Suggestions for buying and recommended dietary allowances are listed, but no dosages are given and professional advice is highly recommended. The main portion of the book is devoted to nutritional supplements.

Illness

American Diabetes Association Staff. *American Diabetes Association Complete Guide to Diabetes*. American Diabetes Association, 1996. 446p. index.   0-945448-64-3 $29.95

> Actually a "beginner's guide" to diabetes, this book discusses the condition, the effects, and the importance of management. A good section on diabetes tools explains the use and cost of each one. Prevention of complications is addressed as well as issues of discrimination. Essential for health collections.

Kohn, George C., ed. *Encyclopedia of Plague and Pestilence*. Facts on File, 1995. 408p. bibliog. index.   LC 94-23135   0-8160-2758-7 $40

> The basic facts of history's "great" epidemics are given in entries of approximately one page each. There is a time line and a geographic list of epidemics. The index has to be used, as most outbreaks are listed by location. A unique reference source for general readers.

★ Stoffman, Phyllis. *The Family Guide to Preventing and Treating One Hundred Infectious Illnesses*. Wiley, 1995. 320p. bibliog. index.   LC 94-23832   0-471-00014-0 $18.95 paper

> This easily understood guide was written by a public health nurse. Parts 1 and 2 are an overview of infectious disease and its prevention. A list of recommended vaccinations and a guide for travelers are included. Part 3 covers one hundred diseases, with information on how the disease is contracted and what its symptoms are, care of a patient, and medication. Highly recommended.

First Aid

American Medical Association Handbook of First Aid and Emergency Care. American Medical Association, 1990. 332p. index.   LC 89-43545   0-679-72959-3 $9.95

> One copy for the home, one copy for the car, and at least one copy for the library! That's the formula for purchasing this handy aid to all types of injuries and emergency situations. There is information on preparing for an emergency, supplies to keep on hand in home and car, what to expect in the emergency room, sports injuries, and lifesaving techniques. All of this is in alphabetical order for easy access.

First Aid for Children Fast. Dorling Kindersley, 1995. 128p. illus.   LC 94-26716
1-56458-702-9 $11.95 paper

> Whatever you need to know about children's emergency care is included
> in this handy 128-page volume. Step-by-step procedures are given for each
> emergency, and there are sections on what to put in a first-aid kit, how to
> apply dressings, and how to keep a safe home environment.

Isaac, Jeff and Peter Goth. *The Outward Bound Wilderness First-Aid Handbook*.
Lyons Press, 1998. illus.   LC 97-43329   1-55821-682-0 $14.95 paper

> Medical information about situations that arise in wilderness activities can
> be easily transferred to less-rural injuries. This is a good source of infor-
> mation on emergency procedures for any library. A glossary is included.

Kusick, James. *A Treasury of Natural First Aid Remedies from A to Z*. Prentice-Hall
Career and Personal Development, 1995. 313p. index.   LC 94-30472   0-13-063181-7
$11.95 paper

> If you don't have a well-stocked medicine cabinet, this book will tell you
> about first aid with substances most people have on hand or can acquire
> from a grocery or health food store. Included are kitchen remedies, herbs,
> splints, and homeopathic remedies. Articles describe health conditions and
> recommend treatment. This will be a good supplement to traditional first-
> aid books.

Mental Health

Kahn, Ada P. and Jan Fawcett. *Encyclopedia of Mental Health*. Facts on File, 1993.
480p. bibliog. index.   LC 92-35148   0-8160-2694-7 $45

> This overview of the mental health field was written by a medical admin-
> istrator and a psychiatrist. The alphabetically arranged entries cover all as-
> pects of mental health with some biographical entries. There is a list of
> organizations and a long bibliography.

Sports Medicine

Micheli, Lyle J. with Mark Jenkins. *The Sports Medicine Bible: Prevent, Detect, and
Treat Your Sports Injuries Through the Latest Medical Techniques*. HarperPerennial/
HarperCollins, 1995. 352p. illus. index.   0-06-273143-2 $20 paper

> Prevention of sports injuries, proper clothing, exercise tips, strength, and
> flexibility are covered in this text that provides the reader with a lot of eas-
> ily read and digested material. The majority of the book deals with specific
> injuries and addresses various treatments. A good addition to the reference
> shelf or the health collection.

Pediatrics and Childbirth

★ Evans, Nancy. *The A-to-Z of Pregnancy and Childbirth: A Concise Encyclopedia.*
Hunter House/Publishers Group West, 1994. 336p. illus.   LC 93-2247   0-89793-136-X;
0-89793-129-7 $29.95; $16.95 paper

> Evans is a medical writer, and she offers clarification of some of the con-
> fusing words and phrases dealing with pregnancy and childbirth. More
> than 850 terms are defined and contemporary issues are discussed. The
> ease of use and intelligent discussions make this a recommended work for
> libraries.

Markel, Howard and Frank A. Oski. *The Practical Pediatrician: The A to Z Guide to
Your Child's Health, Behavior, and Safety.* Freeman, 1996. 364p. illus. index.
LC 96-17604   0-7167-2896-6 $16.95 paper

> The authors are practicing pediatricians, and they have written a child-care
> dictionary that gives information on child health, behavior, and safety of
> the child from birth to eight years of age. The topics are readable and
> helped by good illustrations. Titles for further reading are suggested.

Mayo Foundation for Medical Education and Research. *Mayo Clinic Complete Book
of Pregnancy and Baby's First Year.* Morrow, 1994. 750p. illus. index.   LC 94-7264
0-688-11761-9 $30

> This thorough guide deals with conception to birth, delivery, and the first
> year of a baby's life. There is, thank goodness, a section dealing with the
> impact a baby has on a family's or a couple's life. Medical information is
> presented in a clear and readable manner with loads of tips and numerous
> illustrations. A useful work for all libraries.

Nathanson, Laura Walthier. *The Portable Pediatrician for Parents.* HarperCollins, 1994.
544p. illus. index.   LC 93-24395   0-06-271562-3; 0-06-273176-9 $40; $20 paper

> Part 1 of this book zeroes in on the well child and discusses normal de-
> velopment and stages of life. Part 2 deals with illness and injury and what
> to do in case of either. The third part covers problems that are sources of
> miscommunication between parents and doctors. The fourth section, titled
> "Handouts," is full of pages to copy for neighbors, friends, and relatives.
> Part 5 is a medical glossary.

★ Zand, Janet, Rachel Watson and Bob Rountree. *Smart Medicine for a Healthier
Child: A Practical A-to-Z Reference to Natural and Conventional Treatments for
Infants and Children.* Avery Publishing Group, 1994. 464p. bibliog. index.
LC 94-16594   0-89529-545-8 $19.95 paper

> An overview of conventional medicine and homeopathy and their basic
> techniques; an alphabetical listing of childhood health problems; and illus-
> trated instructions for specific treatment approaches make up the three ba-
> sic parts of this volume written by a nurse, a physician, and a naturopath.
> A handy glossary, a bibliography, and a resource list make up the rest of
> this fine book, recommended for all collections.

Electronics

Gibilisco, Stan. *Amateur Radio Encyclopedia*. McGraw-Hill, 1994. 593p. illus. index. 0-07-023561-9 $29.95 paper

> Material in this work on a technical topic is easy to understand and well presented. Line drawings and appendixes add to the book's value. The appendixes include continuous wave abbreviations, ham radio talk, physical conversions, and schematic symbols. Highly recommended.

★ Gibilisco, Stan. *The Illustrated Dictionary of Electronics*. 7th ed. McGraw-Hill, 1996. 640p. illus.   0-07-024186-4 $34.95

> The illustrations—graphs, tables, drawings, and schematics—are what set this dictionary apart. Terms on electricity, robots, lasers, and medical imaging are here, as well as more jargon than most electronics dictionaries. This edition has several hundred more entries than the previous one.

Markus, John and Neil Sclater. *McGraw-Hill Electronics Dictionary*. 5th ed. McGraw-Hill, 1994. 596p. illus.   LC 93-39121   0-07-040434-8 $49.50

> This book can be compared with *The Illustrated Dictionary of Electronics* (above). Gibilisco seems to define more words, but a study by one reviewer shows that there are enough differences to warrant purchasing both if you have questions in this field. This work has fourteen thousand entries and fifteen hundred illustrations. There is new emphasis on integrated circuitry and consumer electronics. About twelve hundred new words have been added.

Mechanical Engineering

★ Oberg, Erik, ed. *Machinery's Handbook*. 25th ed. Industrial Press, 1996. 2511p. illus. index.   0-8311-2575-6 $65

> This standard reference tool gives information on shop practice and practical mechanical engineering and has done so for more than seventy-five years. There are new sections on numerical control and machinery noise.

Weingartner, Clarence, comp. *Machinist's Ready Reference*. 8th ed. Prakken, 1994. 294p. index.   0-911168-90-7 $14.50 spiral-bound

> This book consists of tables, charts, and tabular data likely to be required by the apprentice machinist. The information applies mostly to metalworking tools and techniques.

Weapons

★ Diagram Group. *Weapons: An International Encyclopedia from 5,000 B.C. to 2,000 A.D.* St. Martin's Press, 1991. 336p. illus.   0-312-03951-4; 0-312-03950-6 $29.95; $18.95 paper

Twenty-five hundred illustrations on the development and use of weapons for hunting, self-defense, and warfare, from the hand ax to the neutron bomb. Not an in-depth work but valuable for its illustrations and short answers on many weapons.

Evangelista, Nick. *The Encyclopedia of the Sword*. Greenwood Press, 1995. 720p. illus. index.   LC 94-7426   0-313-27896-2 $79.50

According to reviews, this is the "first comprehensive treatment of the weapon that has played a key role in human history." Every artistic, cultural, historical, literary, popular, and symbolic aspect of the sword is covered in this valuable book. There is heavy emphasis on European fencing, but Japanese sword culture and legendary and literary swords are covered as well. Appendixes list types of swords, fencing masters, swashbuckler films, actors who fenced, and fencing organizations.

Quertermous, Russell C. and Steven C. Quertermous. *Modern Guns: Identification and Values*. 11th ed. Collector Books, 1996. 496p. illus.   0-89145-731-3 $12.95 paper

This essential guide is a must for checking the value of new and used firearms and family heirlooms. Each firearm is described and pictured and a value given.

Schwing, Ned and Herbert Houze. *Standard Catalog of Firearms*. 5th ed. Krause, 1995. 912p. illus.   0-87341-351-2 $27.95

New firearms and updated prices are given in this book, which deals with ten thousand models of guns and more than one thousand manufacturers. There is often a brief note on the history of the company and the gun. One of the best sources for those who need basic information on pricing and identifying firearms.

Maritime Matters

Jeans, Peter D. *Ship to Shore: A Dictionary of Everyday Words and Phrases Derived from the Sea*. ABC-Clio, 1993. 425p. bibliog. illus.   LC 93-28533   0-87436-717-4 $55

This Australian teacher brings us fifteen hundred words and phrases from our language that have a nautical origin. Entries include the etymology of the phrase and examples of its use. Most of the phrases here are not included in the *Dictionary of Nautical Terms* (below), which is technical in nature. The bibliography includes nautical fiction as well as research titles. This would make an excellent gift for a sea buff and a great addition to many reference collections.

Lenfestey, Thompson with Tom Lenfestey Jr. *The Facts on File Dictionary of Nautical Terms*. Facts on File, 1993. 560p. illus.   LC 92-31490   0-8160-2087-6 $40

Not a dictionary for historical maritime terms, this is a valuable update containing materials on new shipbuilding products and techniques, new cordage, and new advances in navigational technology. Nine thousand entries illuminate words used by the navy, the merchant marine, fishers, yachtspersons, and so forth. Slang is included, and there are numerous diagrams, illustrations, and tables.

Railroad Trains

Drury, George H., comp. *Guide to North American Steam Locomotives*. Railroad References Series, no. 8. Kalmbach Publishing, 1993. 448p. illus. index.
LC 93-41472   0-89024-206-2 $24.95

> Libraries who have railroad buffs should consider purchasing other titles in the Kalmbach Railroad Reference Series. These guides are noted for accuracy and conciseness of information and are a good first resource for railroad questions. The book at hand covers the history and development of railroad steam power and specific companies. Many chapters deal with types of equipment and major locomotive builders. Four hundred photos enhance the text.

Aviation

★ Aviation Week Group Staff. *The Aviation and Aerospace Almanac, 1997*.
McGraw-Hill, 1996. 816p. index.   0-07-006062-2 $75 paper

> The *American Reference Books Annual* reviewer of this book calls it "an absolutely essential purchase for any library or individual with an aviation/aerospace collection." It provides historical and current statistics dealing with civil aviation, which covers international and domestic carriers. Directories of U.S. government boards and departments relating to aviation and statistics on the aerospace industry will prove valuable. There is an excellent index.

Baker, David. *Flight and Flying: A Chronology*. Facts on File, 1993. 559p. illus. index.   LC 92-31491   0-8160-1854-5 $65

> More comprehensive than many similar chronologies, this book covers the topic from 850 B.C.E. to 1991. Entries include the significance of the event in the history of flight as well as facts, statistics, and other events, far beyond the usual chronology entry. Almost seven thousand entries cover the two world wars in depth. Aircraft name and subject indexes will be a great help in locating particular bits of information. There are many photos to illuminate the events covered.

Automobiles

Berliant, Adam. *The Used Car Reliability and Safety Guide*. Betterway Books/F & W Publications, 1994. 320p. index.   1-55870-371-3 $12.99

> Wanna buy a used car? Wanna buy a *good* used car? Check this book out first. It will tell you if a particular car has a reputation for problems as based on complaints to the National Highway Traffic Safety Administration. Models covered are from 1983 to 1993. To receive a bad rating, a car has

to have accumulated at least fifty complaints, four on the same problem. Theft likelihood is also noted. This book is a must for the public library consumer-information collection.

★ Chilton Staff. *Chilton's Auto Repair Manual, 1988–92*. Chilton, 1992. 1548p. illus. index.   0-8019-7906-4 $30.95

★ Chilton Staff. *Chilton's Auto Repair Manual, 1993–1997*. Chilton, 1996. illus. index.   0-8019-7919-6 $28.95

> These volumes, covering seven years, have repair help for cars grouped under their manufacturers, which are arranged in alphabetical order. Handy subject and cross-reference indexes help the would-be repairperson find the needed section easily. No library can be caught without enough auto repair manuals, and these are great for small libraries.

Consumer Reports Books Editors and Bill Hartford. *New Car Buying Guide 1996*. Consumer Reports, 1995. 208p. photogs.   0-89043-716-5 $8.99 paper

> A feast for the eyes of the car lover as well as a reference tool, this work has more than two thousand good quality photographs. The first part of the book is devoted to histories and styling changes of each make, and the second part deals with specifications—year-by-year weight, price, and production figures as well as engine specs.

IntelliChoice, Inc., Staff. *The Complete Car Cost Guide, 1996*. IntelliChoice, 1996. 0-941443-21-3 $59.50 paper

> Although some people swear by the annual car issue of *Consumer Reports, The Complete Car Cost Guide* makes it possible for prospective car owners to compare the costs of owning various models of cars. Information on gas mileage and repair frequencies will help purchasers make informed decisions.

★ Kimes, Beverly Rae. *Standard Catalog of American Cars, 1805–1943*. 2d ed. Krause Publications, 1996. 1598p. illus. index.   LC 85-50390   0-87341-428-4 $55 paper

> Although the black-and-white illustrations are sometimes not the best quality, this is the first place to go for information on makes and years of cars. There are brief histories, descriptions, specs, factory prices, and estimates of current value for more than five thousand cars. If this is useful in your library, you should also have these two.
>
> > ★ Gunnell, John, ed. *Standard Catalog of American Cars, 1946–1975*. 3d ed. Krause Publications, 1992. 864p. illus. LC 82-84065   0-87341-204-0 $27.95 paper
> >
> > ★ Flammang, James, ed. *Standard Catalog of American Cars, 1976–1986*. 2d ed. Krause Publications, 1990. illus.   LC 82-84065 0-87341-133-1 $19.95 paper

Willson, Quentin. *The Ultimate Classic Car Book*. Dorling Kindersley, 1995. 224p. illus. index.   LC 95-11903   0-7894-0159-2 $29.95

> If you have patrons who enjoy material on historic and classic cars, this is a good coffee-table book or reference. The collection here is subjective

and personal, covering a wide range of the term *classic*. U.S. automobiles from the fifties and sixties are included as well as popular and unpopular models that comprise "the interesting and the diverting."

Motorcycles

Bennett, Jim. *The Complete Motorcycle Book: A Consumer's Guide.* Facts on File, 1995. 228p. illus. index. LC 94-20012 0-8160-2899-0; 0-8160-3181-9 $24.95; $14.95 paper

> Want to purchase, maintain, and ride a motorcycle? This is one of the most complete and readable books on all of the above! The first chapter asks readers to decide if they really want to ride a motorcycle. Types, mechanics, selection, used bikes, maintenance, safe riding, road rules, and products are all covered. This is recommended for high school, public, and college libraries.

Wilson, Hugo. *The Encyclopedia of the Motorcycle.* Dorling Kindersley, 1995. 320p. illus. bibliog. maps. index. 0-7894-0150-9 $39.95

> Three thousand marques are covered in this book—at the same time a coffee-table book and a useful reference work. Major motorcycles are featured in a two-page color photo with specs, history, and early advertising. The second part of the book is a catalog of manufacturers, a glossary of terms, a bibliography, and a good index. This attractive volume will have audience appeal as a reference or circulating work.

Wilson, Hugo. *The Ultimate Motorcycle Book.* Dorling Kindersley, 1993. 192p. illus. index. LC 93-21884 1-56458-303-1 $29.95

> An oversize picture book, *The Ultimate Motorcycle Book* shows full-color pictures of international motorcycles, both famous and obscure. There is a history of motorcycles, a section on manufacturers, and a section on motorcycle sports and the major systems of a motorcycle featuring cutaway pictures.

Space Flight

Curtis, Anthony. *Space Almanac.* 2d ed. Gulf Pub., 1992. 955p. illus. maps. index. 0-88415-039-9; 0-88415-030-5 $36.95; $24.95 paper

> All aspects of space and technology—from the planets to the astronauts—are covered in this handy compilation of international scope.

Neal, Valerie, Cathleen S. Lewis and Frank H. Winter. *Spaceflight: A Smithsonian Guide.* Macmillan/Simon & Schuster, 1995. 256p. illus. 0-02-860007-X; 0-02-860040-1 $24.95; $18.00 paper

> At a reasonable price, this title covers space vehicles, space exploration, and space flights in an easy-to-read manner. The 350 photographs and drawings, mostly in color, enhance the excellent text. For further information, there is a forty-page glossary, a fifteen-page chronology, and a foldout on the history of spaceflight.

Agriculture

Lipton, Kathryn L. *Dictionary of Agriculture: From Abaca to Zoonosis.* Lynne Rienner, 1995. 375p.   LC 94-25260   1-55587-523-8 $75

> Thirty-four hundred agricultural terms are defined in this book, with the entries varying from a sentence to a paragraph. The defined terms are grouped by topic in an appendix. There is also a list of acronyms, discussions of agricultural legislation, agricultural aspects of the North American Free Trade Agreement, and state rankings in nine different crops.

Gardening

★ Bush-Brown, James and Louise Bush-Brown. *America's Garden Book.* 4th ed. Macmillan, 1997. 1042p. photogs.   LC 96-18752   0-02-517971-3 $50 paper

> The emphasis here is on home gardens, which it has been since 1939, the year of the first edition. There is information on plant types, special gardens, indoor gardens, and edible plants. New varieties have been added, and there is new information on seaside gardening, tools, and mulches. Black-and-white line drawings have given way to beautiful color photographs, a must in today's garden books.

Halpin, Anne. *Horticulture Gardener's Desk Reference.* Macmillan, 1996. 608p. illus. index.   0-02-860397-4 $35

> The main feature of this work is lists on such topics as herbs for bathing, shade flowers, most popular annuals, and so forth. Aside from the lists, there is a lot of information on hardiness zones and gardening techniques. The index is not detailed, but the excellent table of contents makes that unnecessary.

Lancaster, Roy. *What Plant Where.* Dorling Kindersley, 1995. 256p. illus. index. LC 95-8172   0-7894-0151-7 $24.95

> This is a marvelous book for the beginning gardener and will be of use to the experienced horticulturist as well. Five chapters list perennials, annuals, biennials, trees, climbers, and shrubs and give information on how and where they should be used. Soil, sunlight, size, position, seasonal features, and color are some of the features taken into consideration. It goes without saying that the illustrations are wonderful.

★ Tenenbaum, Frances, ed. *Taylor's Master Guide to Gardening.* Houghton Mifflin, 1994. 612p. illus. maps. index.   LC 93-48865   0-396-64995-1 $60

> Another "one-stop shopping" guide to gardening, this book is a large and colorful addition to any library or home collection. "Taylor" is a well-known name in this field, and thirty consultants added to the knowledge contained herein.

Houseplants

Brookes, John. *The Indoor Garden Book: The Complete Guide to the Creative Use of Plants and Flowers in the Home.* Dorling Kindersley, 1994. 288p. illus. index. LC 93-34262   1-56458-527-1 $14.95 paper

> Most of the coverage here is on the houseplants themselves, with a shorter portion on how they can be used in a home. There are many pages on display of live plants, cut flowers, and dried flowers. Clear pictures show the techniques of plant care. This is a good book for the beginner.

★ Stuckey, Maggie. *The Houseplant Encyclopedia.* Berkley, 1995. 400p. illus. 0-425-14617-0 $12 paper

> A great bargain, *The Houseplant Encyclopedia* should probably be purchased for both the circulating and reference collections if one can afford two copies. One- or two-page descriptions of popular plants are arranged alphabetically, and there is information on history and care in each entry. The instructions and information are clear and easy-to-read. Recommended for the beginner.

Herbs

★ Bown, Deni. *The Encyclopedia of Herbs and Their Uses.* Dorling Kindersley, 1995. 424p. illus. index.   LC 95-8171   0-7894-0184-3 $39.95

> This book is an educational tool of the Herb Society of America and provides comprehensive information in a catalog of more than one thousand herbs. A dictionary makes up the largest part of this work. Color photos show every variety, and the range, hardiness, and part of the plant used is indicated. The dictionary has information on uses and associations with legend and lore. There are handy warnings on medical use and legality of herbs. The herb garden design section of the book is lovely, and there is a list of herb gardens to visit in North America. This is probably the definitive work for the herb gardener.

Bremness, Lesley. *Herbs.* Eyewitness Handbooks. Dorling Kindersley, 1994. 304p. illus. index.   LC 93-26815   1-56458-497-6; 1-56458-496-8 $29.95; $17.95 paper

> Each entry in this internationally flavored work gives a description, natural habitat, uses, illustration, and common and scientific names. Leaves, roots, flowers, fruits, and seeds are colorfully displayed against a white background. *Herbs* here means *useful plants,* and 470 entries cover 700 species of trees, shrubs, perennials, annuals, biennials, and vines.

Hoffman, David. *The Complete Illustrated Holistic Herbal: A Sage and Practical Guide to Making and Using Herbal Remedies.* Element/Penguin, 1996. 256p. photogs. index.   1-85230-758-7 $18.95 paper

This list of more than two hundred herbs gives detailed information on their use in the treatment of ailments for each body system. There are instructions for making preparations, and there is a glossary. The book covers North American herbs.

Tyler, Varro E. *Herbs of Choice: The Therapeutic Use of Phytomedicinals.* Haworth Press, 1994. 209p. index.   LC 93-41977   1-56024-894-7; 1-56024-895-5 $24.95; $17.95 paper

This is one of the few books that proposes a scientific approach to the study of herbs for medicine. Information is provided for health professionals and those who medicate themselves using herbs. Factual information about herb efficacy and safety is given, and the author presents a plan for reform that would encourage the study and regulation of therapeutic herbs.

Veterinary Medicine

★ Fraser, Clarence. *Merck Veterinary Manual.* Merck, 1991. 7th ed. illus. 0-911910-55-7 $24

A technical manual of use to veterinary personnel and informed laypeople. It includes authoritative information on all phases of veterinary medicine.

West, Geoffrey P., ed. *Black's Veterinary Dictionary.* 18th ed. Barnes and Noble, 1994. 624p. illus.   0-7136-3946-6 $99

Nontechnical language is a plus in this guide for the veterinarian and the animal owner. Many entries have been expanded. It is a British work but is still excellent for any library that needs info on anatomy, physiology, diseases, and treatment of animals.

Horses

★ Edwards, Elwyn Hartley. *The Encyclopedia of the Horse.* Dorling Kindersley, 1994. 400p. illus. maps. index.   LC 94-644   1-56458-614-6 $39.95

Each breed of horse covered in this illustrated reference work is given a two-page spread with origins, background, size, conformation, and characteristics. As well as chapters that deal with breeds, there are chapters that tell of the history of the horse, its use, and its physical development from earliest times. The chapters on horses in war and sports are up-to-date and excellent. The only flaw in this horse-lover's dream is that the fine breed pictures cover two pages, and the horses, like Playboy Bunnies, have a crease down their middles.

★ Hendricks, Bonnie L. *International Encyclopedia of Horse Breeds.* University of Oklahoma Press, 1995. 479p. photogs. bibliog. index.   0-8061-2753-8 $65

In alphabetical order, Hendricks lists nearly four hundred breeds of horses. Entries include info about origins, background, size, and appearance and use of each breed. Most entries include a photograph. A list of breed associations is included in the appendix. Highly recommended.

UC Davis Book of Horses: A Complete Medical Reference Guide for Horses and Foals. HarperCollins, 1996. 512p. illus. index.   LC 96-10907   0-06-270139-8 $30

There are plenty of family medical guides—this is one for horses. There are thirty-seven contributors, mostly veterinarians from the School of Veterinary Medicine at the University of California, Davis. Horse owners will be able to find basic information about their horses' health and performance. There is material on breeds, how to purchase a horse, and health issues. This is useful for professionals and horse owners.

Visual Dictionary of the Horse. Eyewitness Visual Dictionaries. Dorling Kindersley, 1993. 64p. illus. index.   LC 93-20819   1-56458-504-1 $15.95

Two-page spreads cover a number of "horsey" topics such as anatomy, history, gaits, and equipment. The text gives basic facts on the pictures. This will have a limited use as an adult reference tool but is recommended for school libraries at all levels and will be a welcome addition to the adult browsing collection for all the horse lovers a library serves.

Dogs

★ Fogle, Bruce. *The Encyclopedia of the Dog.* Dorling Kindersley/Houghton, 1995. 312p. photogs. index.   LC 95-6745   0-7894-0149-5 $39.95

Fogle, an animal behavior expert and veterinarian, has practical and informative advice to give on development of the dog, behavior and care, and travel. Many excellent photographs illuminate each of four hundred entries.

Yamazaki, Tetsu. *Legacy of the Dog: The Ultimate Illustrated Guide to Over Two Hundred Breeds.* Chronicle Books, 1995. 344p. photogs. index.   LC 95-2059 0-8118-1123-9; 0-8118-1069-0 $45.00; $24.95 paper

Well-organized into seven standard categories (herding, working, sporting, hound, terrier, toy, nonsporting), this includes a brief history of domestic dogs and a group chart displaying each dog in a category. Yamazaki is a photographer, and the focus here is on the beautiful illustrations.

Cats

Altman, Roberta. *The Quintessential Cat.* Macmillan, 1994. 289p. illus. index. LC 94-14095   0-671-85008-3 $27.50

Although there are some access problems (sidebars appear with no relation to the text and literary "bits" are indexed only by author), this is a purrr-fectly charming book of facts and fancies that will delight all cat lovers and those seeking information about cats. Cats in history, myth, and literature; celebrity cats; and cat expressions are only a few of the treated topics, and there are loads of full-color photographs. Listings of clubs, breeder's associations, advocacy groups, boutiques and catalogs, and medical societies round out this work.

★ Morris, Desmond. *Cat World: A Feline Encyclopedia*. Viking/Penguin Reference, 1997. 496p. illus. index.   LC 96-28314   0-670-10006-4 $29.95

The focus of this encyclopedia, by a trained zoologist, is on the domestic cat. Information is given on eighty breeds, thirty-six types of wild cats, and famous cats or famous cat owners. All aspects of cat behavior are covered. Those interested in the arts will enjoy the lists of "100 Best Cat Books," cat movies, and the numerous illustrations. Great as a gift for cat lovers, as a circulating title, or as part of the reference collection.

Aquarium Fishes

Mills, Dick. *Aquarium Fish*. Eyewitness Handbooks. Dorling Kindersley, 1993. 304p. illus. maps. index.   LC 93-3155   1-56458-294-9; 1-56458-293-0 $29.95; $17.95 paper

This colorful guide is excellent and easy-to-use for the beginning hobbyist. There is useful information on more than five hundred freshwater and marine fish, and each type is shown in a photograph. The description includes habitat and any information needed to keep finny friends happy in your aquarium.

Sakurai, Atsushi, Yohei Sakamoto and Fumitoshi Mori. *Aquarium Fish of the World: The Comprehensive Guide to Eight Hundred Species*. Chronicle Books, 1992. 296p. illus. index.   LC 92-16784   0-8118-0269-8 $29.95

Mainly a pictorial book, this provides some of the best color photos of aquarium fish available. More than eleven hundred color photos describe 650 species of freshwater and brackish water fish. There are brief descriptions of behavior and care of fish. Excellent for identification purposes.

Food

Albyn, Carole Lisa and Lois Sinaiko Webb. *Multicultural Cookbook for Students*. Oryx, 1993. 312p. maps. index.   0-89774-735-6 $25.95

What do you do when your child comes home from school and says he or she has to bring a Sudanese dessert to the World Banquet? Look in this book! It might not have everything, but there are at least two recipes for every country listed. There are locator maps to tell students where the country is and where the recipe came from. A glossary and index and a "Getting Started" section for young cooks are valuable.

Anderson, Kenneth N. and Lois E. Anderson. *The International Dictionary of Food and Nutrition*. Wiley, 1993. 336p. illus.   LC 92-38971   0-471-55957-1 $34.95

> Words from menus, cookbooks, and periodicals are included in this dictionary, with more than seventy-five hundred entries on food processing, production, and preparation. With increased interest in foreign cooking, this will prove helpful in identifying terms.

Bartlett, Jonathon. *The Cook's Dictionary and Culinary Reference: A Comprehensive, Definitive Guide to Cooking and Food*. Contemporary Books, 1996. 488p.
LC 96-3055   0-8092-3120-4 $24.95

> Comparable to *The Dictionary of American Food and Drink* (below), this is an excellent tool for beginners and gourmet cooks. In alphabetical order, foods, methods, tools, and phrases are defined in entries ranging from a sentence to three pages. The writer has an excellent sense of humor and has created a work that is easy to consult quickly and entertains during the consultation.

★ Bissell, Frances. *The Book of Food: A Cook's Guide to Over One Thousand Exotic and Everyday Ingredients*. Henry Holt, 1994. 275p. illus. index.   LC 93-80835
0-8050-3006-9 $40

> An aid to cookbooks though not a cookbook itself, this volume gives advice on buying potatoes, skinning a rabbit, cracking a coconut, and so forth. There is information on more than one thousand foods, including descriptions, origins, purchasing advice, storage, and preparation. This is an authoritative resource on foods, where they are popular, and how to use them.

★ *Foods That Harm, Foods That Heal: An A-Z Guide to Safe and Healthy Eating*.
Reader's Digest, 1997. 400p. illus. index.   LC 96-24477   0-89577-912-9 $30

> Three hundred experts have made sure that this book is up-to-date and scientifically sound. Aside from the usual information on the relationship between diet and health, there is information on such current problems as genetically altered foods and diet-related stress. Many charts, tables, and illustrations illuminate an easy-to-read text. This is an essential purchase for public libraries.

Horn, Jane, ed. *Cooking A to Z: The Complete Culinary Reference*. 2d rev. ed. Cole Group, 1992. 672p. illus. index.   1-56426-577-3 $29.95 paper

> This beautifully illustrated book of cooking techniques is suitable for adults and children alike. Six hundred recipes show how to use the procedures in easy-to-follow steps.

★ Mariani, John. *The Dictionary of American Food and Drink*. Rev. ed. Hearst Books, 1994. 379p. index.   LC 92-44649   0-688-10139-9 $19.95

> A standard ready-reference tool, this is recommended for anyone interested in food—in short, anyone! Each entry gives variant terms, derivations, and the time when the food was introduced. The coverage of beverages

includes Coca-Cola and Gatorade. This new edition adds four hundred entries and many revisions. There is a greater emphasis on ethnic and authentic native dishes. Read about all this plus lunch counters, candy bars, and airline food!

Orstad, Dianne. *The Whole Foods Companion: A Guide for Adventurous Cooks, Curious Shoppers and Lovers of Natural Food*. Chelsea Green, 1996. 400p. illus. bibliog. index.   0-930031-83-0 $25 paper

> This book's mandate is to educate and entertain, and it fulfills that nicely. The book is first organized into broad categories such as "Fruits," "Vegetables," and "Grains"; then, individual items are discussed in detail. Properties, buying tips, uses, and nutritional information are covered in each entry. Sidebar highlights add to the visual interest of this book.

Trager, James. *The Food Chronology: A Food Lover's Compendium of Events and Anecdotes, from Prehistory to the Present*. Henry Holt, 1995. 783p. illus.   LC 95-6710   0-8050-3389-0 $40

> Beginning at one million B.C., more than thirteen thousand entries detail happenings and history relating to food, glorious food. Divided into politics, economics, arts, and humanities, this work records the trivia and milestones in the history of food.

Additives

Winter, Ruth. *A Consumer's Dictionary of Food Additives*. 4th ed. Crown, 1994. 425p. 0-517-88195-0 $15 paper

> "Good," "bad," and "inadvertent" additives to processed food are all covered in this consumer classic. New research is covered, and the sources cited have been updated. Sometimes a bit too subjective for a scientific topic, this is still an excellent work for people who care about what they eat.

Nutrition

★ Duyff, Roberta Larson. *The American Dietetic Association's Complete Food and Nutrition Guide*. Chronimed, 1996. 520p. illus.   1-56561-098-9 $29.95

> This timely nutrition book discusses the food pyramid, foods not to eat with medicine, making your own baby food, the iron content of food cooked in iron pots, and the calories found in the glue on a postage stamp (a postage stamp?). There is a good list of organizations involved in nutrition. This is recommended for public libraries.

Pennington, Jean A. T., rev. by. *Bowes and Church's Food Values of Portions Commonly Used*. 17th ed. Lippincott-Raven Publishers, 1997. 512p. index. LC 97-02466   0-395-55435-4 $34

This is a standard work in the health and nutrition fields, and it distinguishes between brand names, fast foods, and frozen-food brands. Serving portions of more than eighty-five hundred foods (more than four thousand new in this book) are detailed as to calories, water, protein, carbohydrates, dietary fiber, fat, cholesterol, vitamins, and minerals. There are also tables of caffeine content, pectin, amino acids, and salicylates. Recommended for all sizes of libraries.

★ Tamborlane, William V., M.D., ed. *The Yale Guide to Children's Nutrition.* Yale University Press, 1997. 412p. illus. index.   LC 96-44774   0-300-06965-0; 0-300-07169-8 $40; $18 paper

One hundred physicians and other health-care providers have prepared this excellent work, which dispels many myths on children's eating and discusses nutritional management of many childhood ailments and conditions. All of the nutritional "building blocks," such as vitamins, fats, and proteins, are discussed at length; and the authors give good suggestions for selecting meals and snacks for children. The last part of the book is given over to a section of handy recipes. This will be an excellent addition to the health-care selection in small and large libraries alike.

Consumer Information

Lesko, Matthew and Andre Naprawa. *The Great American Gripe Book.* 2d ed. Information USA, 1994. 367p.   0-878346-18-0 $12.92

This book was designed to give the reader a quick and easy reference to hundreds of state and federal complaint-handling agencies and the laws they enforce. There is information on the complaint, the contacts, available help, and "what happens next."

Cleaning and Household Problems

Consumer Reports Books Editors. *How to Clean Practically Anything.* 4th ed. Consumer Reports, 1996. 256p. illus.   LC 95-37498   0-89043-843-9 $11.95 paper

This is mainly an analysis of household cleaning equipment and supplies with material on the cost-effectiveness of various cleaning products. Homemade substitutes for most types of products are suggested. There is a chapter on stain removal.

Palma, Robert J., Sr. with Mark Espenscheid. *The Complete Guide to Household Chemicals.* Prometheus Books, 1995. 325p.   0-87975-983-6 $24.95

Because most of us know little about the household products we use daily, the authors provide the necessary background on safe use and storage of commonly used household chemicals. They take us on a walk through a typical house, looking at the laundry room, medicine cabinet, living room, bar, kitchen, car, garage, and backyard. There is a glossary, metric equivalents, chemical symbols, and contact information for manufacturers.

Hotels

Dane, Suzanne G. *The National Trust Guide to Historic Bed and Breakfasts, Inns and Small Hotels.* 3d ed. Wiley, 1994. 510p. illus. maps.   LC 93-32374
0-471-74370-7 $15.95 paper

> More than six hundred historic lodgings are entered in this book, which is designed to show the diversity of U.S. architecture as much as it gives information about accommodations. Selection criteria demand that the structures listed herein be at least fifty years old and retain architectural integrity. Listings are in order by state, and the location of each inn is marked on a state map. Directory information is given as well as rates, methods of payment, handicapped accessibility, and local activities.

Lanier, Pamela. *The Complete Guide to Bed and Breakfasts, Inns and Guesthouses.* 14th ed. Ten Speed Press, 1996. 571p. illus.   0-89815-885-0 $16.95

> Arranged alphabetically by state and province, this book provides a list of featured establishments in each area. The entries for these include directory info, type of accommodations, number of private baths, type of meals served, liquor license, payment options, rating, and so forth. A list of further establishments with only directory information follows. Altogether, about thirty thousand inns are listed. Supporting material includes a list of special features (gourmet food, shopping, antiques) offered by various inns. There is also a list of reservation service organizations that handle many of the establishments.

Parenting and Child Care

Carpenter, Kathryn Hammell. *Sourcebook on Parenting and Child Care.* Oryx, 1995. 288p. index.   LC 94-39012   0-89774-780-1 $35 paper

> Infants, children, and adolescents are "taken care of" in nine hundred annotated entries from popular and professional books and journals. Recommended titles are starred, and the titles are arranged in subject chapters. There are directories of agencies and lists of videotapes and statistical data.

★ DeFrancis, Beth. *The Parent's Resource Almanac: Where to Write, Who to Call, What to Buy and How to Find Out Everything You Need to Know.* Adams Publishing, 1994. 770p. index.   LC 94-15476   1-55850-396-X; 1-55850-394-3 $39.95; $15.00 paper

> The reviewer agrees with *Parent's Choice* magazine on the quality of this title and claims that it should be a mandatory purchase for all libraries. Chapters on such topics as parenting, grandparenting, family travel, health, education, children's lit, and child development are full of book lists, peri-

odical citations, associations, software, videos, and businesses. Appendixes list youth orchestras, government publication, national parks, and mail-order catalogs. A valuable resource.

Stoppard, Miriam. *Complete Baby and Child Care.* Dorling Kindersley, 1995. 351p. illus. index.   LC 94-26720   1-56458-850-5 $29.95

> The author starts with the period directly after birth and explains hospital procedures and terms a new parent is likely to encounter. Also for the new parent are sections on types of birthmarks and the sounds that might issue forth from a new baby. The work then discusses child development and medical conditions that might be encountered at various age levels. Case histories and wonderful photos make this an appealing book for parents. A great baby-shower gift and great for libraries!

Business Dictionaries

Friedman, Jack P. *Dictionary of Business Terms.* Barron's Business Guides. 2d ed. Barron's Educational Series, 1994. 700p.   0-8120-1833-8 $11.95

> One thousand new terms have been added to this edition. There are many useful cross-references. Sixteen specialists had a hand in the compilation of this work, and it is a good complement to dictionaries such as Rosenberg (below).

★ Rosenberg, Jerry M. *Dictionary of Business and Management.* Business Dictionary Series. 3d ed. Wiley, 1993.   LC 92-7977   0-471-57812-6; 0-471-54536-8 $45.00; $14.95 paper

> According to one reviewer, this has no equal in comprehensiveness, clarity, and price. More than ten thousand business terms are defined in concise language that is understandable to the average reader. Major fields of business and major topics are covered.

Terry, John V. *Dictionary for Business and Finance.* 3d ed. University of Arkansas Press, 1995. 432p.   1-55728-344-3 $18 paper

> Because businesspeople need to be familiar with terms in the financial world, they either need to memorize them all or have a dictionary such as this one handy. Accounting, banking, economics, estate planning, finance, insurance, investments, management, real estate, securities, and statistics all have terms represented here. Two hundred more terms have been added to this third edition, and it is highly recommended for the businessperson or student.

Secretarial Handbooks

★ *Merriam-Webster's Secretarial Handbook.* 3d ed. Merriam-Webster, 1993. 608p. illus. index.   LC 93-10632   0-87779-236-4 $15.95

This is one of the most thorough and easy-to-follow of all the secretarial guides offered. The low price and easy access to material, plus the basics necessary for the novice or experienced secretary, make this a highly recommended purchase for all libraries. There is information on letters, etiquette, office management, records, and basic accounting and bookkeeping. Guidelines for English grammar and a desktop publishing glossary add to the value.

Prentice-Hall Editors. *Professional Secretary's Encyclopedic Dictionary.* 5th ed. Prentice-Hall, 1994. index.   LC 94-28490   0-13-030-453-0 $29.95

In dictionary format, this work not only gives definitions of terms, but explains the form or special technique involved. There are many charts, as well as examples, and sections on procedures, communication, business law, finance, real estate, and insurance.

Marketing and Advertising

Carter, David E., ed. *Living Logos: How Corporations Renew Their Image.* Art Direction Book/Reference Press, 1993. 160p. illus.   LC 92-074314   0-88108-108-6 $17.50 paper

A reasonably priced book, this will be of interest to many patrons. The editor takes seventy companies and shows the changes in their logos throughout the years. My, Betty Crocker, how you've changed! There is not much text, often only a sentence or two about the company, but the logos speak for themselves.

Wiechmann, Jack G. *NTC's Dictionary of Advertising.* 2d ed. National Textbook, 1993. 222p.   0-8442-3486-9 $29.95

One thousand new terms have been added to this dictionary of research, production, media, marketing, publicity, finance, and service. Good for use by professionals and nonprofessionals, this is a book of brief definitions with many useful cross-references.

Franchises

Bond, Robert E. *The Source Book of Franchise Opportunities.* Irwin Professional Publishing, 1994.   0-7863-0338-7 $10

This book includes specific information on the financial aspects of franchises. There is some analysis of the place of each company within its field.

Wine and Beer

Foulkes, Christopher, ed. *Larousse Encyclopedia of Wine.* Larousse Kingfisher Chambers, 1994. 608p. illus. maps. index.   2-03-507022-8 $40

More than one hundred experts assisted editor Foulkes in compiling the various portions of this delightful book. The wine topics covered include history, selection, laws, storage, serving, tasting, wine with food, and wine making. Vineyards are the main topic of the second section of the book, and a third section includes information on labels, vintages, quality, zones, statistics, and terms.

Johnson, Hugh. *Hugh Johnson's Modern Encyclopedia of Wine.* Simon & Schuster, 1991. 544p. illus. index.   0-671-73638-8 $35

> Seven thousand wine producers from thirty countries are covered as to type of wine, address, amount of land, worth, name of wine maker, and so forth. There is also general material on wine. Johnson's *The World Atlas of Wine: A Complete Guide to the Wines and Spirits of the World* (Simon & Schuster, 1994) has some of the same information but also includes more maps and information on the wine-growing regions of the world.

Koplan, Steven, Brian H. Smith and Michael A. Weiss. *Exploring Wine: The Culinary Institute of America's Complete Guide to Wines.* Van Nostrand Reinhold, 1996. 720p. photogs. maps. bibliog. index.   LC 95-35579   0-442-01831-2 $59.95

> How to select a wine from the flood of types and brands available, how to match food and wine, how to make wine, how to have a wine-tasting experience—all are covered here and all are illustrated by beautiful photographs. There is a section on wine collecting and a glossary. "Highly recommended."

Rhodes, Christine P., ed. *Encyclopedia of Beer: The Beer Lover's Bible.* 512p. Henry Holt, 1995.   LC 95-24963   0-8050-3799-3 $35

> Thirsting for knowledge about beer? This is the book that can quench that thirst. All aspects of the brew are covered, such as history, judging, and brewing of beer; types of beer; ingredients and flavoring; methods and equipment; and cultural practices. Even beer signs and bottle caps are discussed.

★ Robinson, Jancis, ed. *The Oxford Companion to Wine.* Oxford University Press, 1994. 1040p. illus. maps. index.   0-19-866159-2 $60

> Considered by some reviewers to be the most complete wine book, this boasts three thousand entries by seventy wine authorities. U.S. and foreign wine regions are covered, and the text is enhanced by color and black-and-white illustrations, charts, and maps.

Wood

Constantine, Albert, Jr. *Know Your Woods.* Rev. ed. Scribners Reference, 1987. 360p. illus. maps. bibliog. index.   0-684-18778-7 $14 paper

> The first half of this book is made up of fourteen chapters on such subjects as identification of woods, a listing of state trees, woods of the Bible, and little-known facts about trees. The second half is a dictionary with entries for more than three hundred trees giving description and properties of the wood and how it is traditionally used. There is index access by country of origin, products, and properties of the woods.

Arts and Recreation

What was our friend Melvil thinking when he crammed most of the world's "goodies" into one small category? It was not enough for him to put all of the graphic, plastic, and performing arts into one section—he had to add sports and recreation as well!

Starting with the graphic and plastic arts, we have tried to identify those books that would give a patron quick answers to art questions. This includes dictionaries of art and artists, histories of art, and handbooks on art techniques. This is also the area for materials on architecture and antiques. Even the smallest library needs some antique price guides for patrons with full attics and basements.

Many musical questions involve songs, recordings, or biographical information, so this category has an emphasis in those areas. It is necessary for the smallest library to have basic information on popular music, rock and roll, country, jazz, and classical works.

The 700s are the home of the performing arts, an extremely popular topic. Many fine tools have been developed to deal with questions on movies, theater, radio, and television and the people who made them possible. The nice thing about many of these titles is, although they go out of date, the information they contain is still useful for the period covered.

Sports, games, and recreation finish this section off with statistics and information on favorite pastimes.

Art

Apostolos-Cappadonna, Diane. *Dictionary of Christian Art*. Continuum Publishing, 1994. 380p. illus. bibliog. index.   0-8264-0779-X $39.50

> Designs, symbols, figures, and topics that play a large part in Christian art are covered in entries that range from fifty to several hundred words. One hundred sixty pictures show the use of various symbols. There is a bibli-

ography, list of illustrations, and an index. This will be a good addition to public or private art-lovers' libraries.

★ Chilvers, Ian and Harold Osborne, eds. *The Oxford Dictionary of Art.* Oxford University Press, 1988. 560p.   0-19-866133-9; 0-19-280022-1 $49.95; $17.95 paper

> This successor to the Oxford Companions to art has tightened up a bit and no longer includes the sections on national art movements. The majority of entries relate to the significance of the works of individual artists. Art terms are defined.

Dictionary of the Arts: Movements, Terms, People—from Ancient Arts to World Music. Facts on File, 1994. 564p.   LC 94-16276   0-8160-3205-X $29.95

> The title says it all! More than six thousand entries cover the graphic, visual, and performing arts with movements, terms, and people included. Entries are arranged alphabetically, and ancient to present time is covered. There are chronologies and quotations, and the entries are brief but informative.

Dunlap, Carol. *The Culture Vulture's Guide to Style, Period, and Ism.* Wiley, 1994. 320p. illus. bibliog. index.   LC 93-1394   0-471-14423-1 $19.95 paper

> This handy reference book will be of use to students, browsers, or those generally interested in the arts. It consists of more than 250 articles on periods, styles, and movements. The focus here is on American culture. There is a large bibliography in which the author has indicated her favorite titles.

Earls, Irene. *Baroque Art: A Topical Dictionary.* Greenwood, 1996. 352p. LC 95-51397   0-313-29406-2 $95

> Nicely written entries, listed in alphabetical order, have a good system of cross-references. The seventeenth-century baroque style is well treated here, and the reader is helped to an understanding of many works of art and the meaning of symbols. There are no pictures in this Topical Dictionary series, but there are citations to pictures in other works.

Earls, Irene. *Renaissance Art: A Topical Dictionary.* Greenwood, 1987. 345p. bibliog. index.   LC 87-250   0-313-24658-0 $89.50

> Because the Renaissance period is what many people think of when they think of *art,* this work will be useful for schools and public and academic libraries. The complicated legends and symbolism of myth and religion that fill paintings of this period are fully explained. Techniques and materials are also covered.

★ Janson, Anthony F., ed. *History of Art.* Abrams, 1995.   0-8109-3421-3 $60

> This is one of the best one-volume narrative histories of art available. Maps of sites in the text are included as well as chronological tables to correlate art history with other history.

★ Mayer, Ralph. *Artist's Handbook of Materials and Techniques.* 5th rev. and updated ed. VikingPenguin, 1991. 800p.   0-670-83701-6 $40

This is an excellent guide for the amateur artist or for the experimenting professional. Its information on the basics and tools of art belongs in every collection.

★ Osborne, Harold. *The Oxford Companion to Twentieth-Century Art*. Oxford University Press, 1988. 800p. illus.   0-19-282076-1 $22.50 paper

International in coverage, this work gives concise information on twentieth-century artists. There are longer articles on movements and the state of art.

Ross, Leslie. *Medieval Art: A Topical Dictionary*. Greenwood, 1996. 312p. LC 96-160   0-313-20329-5 $75

Early Christian and Byzantine art is well covered in this guide to art of the Middle Ages. Good explanations of the artworks are given. There are lists of artists and excellent bibliographies.

Steer, John and Antony White. *Atlas of Western Art History: Artists, Sites and Movements from Ancient Greece to the Modern Age*. Facts on File, 1994. 335p. illus. maps. index.   LC 92-11226   0-8160-2457-X $59.95

Beautiful photographs and good maps illuminate the world of art in terms of social and political circumstances. There are 142 map spreads with a five-hundred-word summary on the century each represents. A good index will help the novice user. The attractive format makes it a good book for browsers as well as for reference.

★ Stokstad, Marilyn, Stephen Addiss and Marion S. Grayson. *Art History*. Abrams, 1996. 1224p. illus. maps. bibliog. index.   LC 95-13402   0-8109-1960-5 $60

One reviewer describes this as "a new eight-pound entry in the one-volume history-of-art battle of the titans." It couldn't happen to a nicer field. The illustrations in this book are almost all in color, a definite plus for an art book. The book claims to be user-friendly to today's students, who "lack a deep knowledge of cultural history." There are lots of explanatory text boxes and explanatory drawings. This is the most inclusive of the "titans."

The Business of Art

★ Cox, Mary and Alice P. Buening. *Artist's and Graphic Designer's Market, 1998: Twenty-Five Hundred Places to Sell Your Art and Design*. F & W Publications, 1997. 0-898797-94-2 $24.99

Basic information on marketing, promotion, organizing an art business, and an overview of the industry lead off in this useful reference for the artist or designer who wants to sell his or her work. There are lists of markets for works with directory information for each market. Tips for each market may include how to approach a particular company. There are indications of whether a market is a good one for a beginner to try.

DuBoff, Leonard. *The Art Business Encyclopedia.* Allworth Press, 1994. 320p. index.
LC 93-71921   1-880559-14-5; 1-880559-13-7 $29.95; $18.95

> This is a useful compilation of terms for those wanting to sell their own works, establish a gallery, or collect art. Three hundred fifty terms used in business and law are defined for the intended audience. Appendixes include law, organizations, dealer consignment statutes, art sellers, and a brief bibliography.

Grant, Daniel. *The Artist's Resource Handbook.* 2d rev. ed. Allworth Press, 1994.
224p. index.   1-880559-58-7 $18.95 paper

> More than a book about where to sell art, this gives answers to many questions artists might ask. Students graduating from art-school programs will find this information invaluable to gain a foothold in the art world. There is career assistance, info on arts organizations, funding sources, legal services, networks, studio space, and ethical conduct.

Symbols

Bruce-Mitford, Miranda. *The Illustrated Book of Signs and Symbols.* Dorling
Kindersley/Houghton, 1996. 128p. photogs. bibliog. index.   LC 96-14202
0-7894-1000-1 $24.95

> A great variety of symbols are covered in this title, with emphasis on cultural perspective and coverage of ancient and modern symbols. The entries are divided into categories. There is cross-referencing on many pages and a great index.

Carr-Gomm, Sarah. *The Dictionary of Symbols in Western Art.* Facts on File, 1995.
240p. illus. index.   LC 95-17577   0-8160-3301-3 $22.95

> The stated goal of this dictionary is to explain the meanings of artworks by providing meanings of symbols and their use in art. Entries are alphabetical and describe their subjects and give examples of its use. "Feature panels" discuss important themes, such as flowers, religious orders, and so forth. Recommended for basic art history collections.

Hall, James. *Illustrated Dictionary of Symbols in Eastern and Western Art.*
IconEditions/HarperCollins, 1996. 256p. illus. index.   0-06-433314-0; 0-06-430982-7
$30; $15 paper

> Incorporating the symbols of ancient Egypt and the East, this work adds to the information found in its predecessor, *Dictionary of Subjects and Symbols in Art* (HarperCollins, 1979). Six parts divide the symbols into themes: abstract signs, animals, artifacts, earth and sky, human body and dress, and plants. Entries each have a black-and-white drawing that shows one aspect of the symbol. Groups of symbols, such as the four seasons or the cardinal virtues, are also discussed. An index gives access to specific objects.

Sill, Gertrude. *A Handbook of Symbols in Christian Art*. Macmillan, 1975. 256p. illus. 0-02-000850-3 $13.95 paper

> Arranged by categories (flowers, the body, and so forth), the symbols are listed and traced to a scriptural source. Illustrated with black-and-white drawings.

Artists

Cummings, Paul. *Dictionary of Contemporary American Artists*. 6th ed. St. Martin's Press, 1994. 800p. illus. index.   LC 93-46372   0-312-08440-4 $85

> In this latest edition, twenty-seven artists are deleted and forty-one have been added. The resulting nine hundred entries give information on where and with whom the artist studied, teaching positions, commissions, awards, address and dealers who have handled his or her works, important exhibitions, and a bibliography. Much information is abbreviated, and users will have to resort to a key.

Ergas, Aimee G. *Artists: From Michelangelo to Maya Lin*. Gale, 1995. 2 vols. 504p. illus. bibliog. index.   0-8103-9862-1 $43

> Information on personal experiences, motivations and social climates gives new life to the sixty-two biographies of North American and European artists. The biographies are designed for students but are informative and highlighted by sidebars of information that will make them useful for adults seeking basic information about these artists. There is a glossary and a good bibliography.

Fielding, Mantle. *Dictionary of American Painters, Sculptors, and Engravers*. Edited by Genevieve Doran. Associated Books, 1974. 480p.   0-913274-03-8 $17.50

> Brief biographies of eight thousand American artists are given. A supplemental list of twenty-five hundred has dates and art-form specialty. This includes artists who are not easy to locate elsewhere.

Gowing, Lawrence, ed. *A Biographical Dictionary of Artists*. Rev. ed. Facts on File, 1995. 784p. illus. index.   0-8160-3252-1 $50

> The 1,340 alphabetical entries in this work give a good balance of information on each artist's life and work. Most of the entries include a bibliography, and the book also has a chronology, glossary, and index. An English work, English artists are emphasized, but coverage of other Western countries is excellent. Fine illustrations round out a useful work.

Heller, Jules and Nancy G. Heller. *North American Women Artists of the Twentieth Century: A Biographical Dictionary*. Rev. ed. Garland, 1997. 736p. illus. bibliog. index.   LC 94-49710   0-8240-6049-0; 0-8153-2584-3 $125.00; $29.95

> More than fifteen hundred female artists born between 1850 and 1960 are listed in alphabetical order. Artists are treated in a few paragraphs that conclude with a bibliography. More than one hundred illustrations display the far-ranging talents of the women listed here.

Henkes, Robert. *Native American Painters of the Twentieth Century: The Works of Sixty-one Artists.* McFarland, 1995. 200p. illus.   LC 95-16637   0-7864-0092-7 $38.50

> Although it only includes sixty-one artists, many tribes and many styles are covered. The introduction focuses on the need of Native American artists to incorporate Native American attitudes and culture into their work and yet speak to as broad an audience as possible. Each entry focuses on the artist's work, with brief biographical information. Most photographs of works are unfortunately in black-and-white, although eleven are in color.

Architecture

★ Carley, Rachel. *The Visual Dictionary of American Domestic Architecture.* Henry Holt, 1995. 272p. illus. index.   LC 94-20071   0-8050-2646-0; 0-8050-4563-5 $40.00; $19.95 paper

> This discussion of the American house starts with Native American dwellings and runs through the 1990s. Styles are presented in chronological order. Elements that identify a particular style are detailed, and the renderings give several exterior views; in fact, five hundred drawings of floor plans, interior features, exteriors, details, and "anatomy" give this volume great value for libraries. Highly recommended.

Packard, Robert T. and Balthazar Korab. *Encyclopedia of American Architecture.* 2d ed. McGraw-Hill, 1995. 724p. illus. index.   0-07-048010-9 $89.50

> The combination of descriptive data for the general reader, biography, and bibliography makes this a unique title and a classic in the field of American architecture. New biographical articles have been added and contemporary issues such as accessibility are included. Great color illustrations are excellent for displaying the buildings under discussion.

★ Rifkind, Carole. *Field Guide to American Architecture.* NAL, 1980. illus. 0-452-26269-0 $24.95

> This work covers three centuries of American building and all types of architecture.

Design

★ Byars, Mel. *The Design Encyclopedia.* Wiley, 1994. 612p. illus. 0-471-02455-4 $60

> If you need information on designers, firms, movements, manufacturers, groups, and materials of the past 125 years, this book is for you. Furniture, textiles, glass, metalware, wallpaper, interiors, ceramics, and industrial design are only a few of the topics discussed, with international coverage. Entries are arranged alphabetically and include some biographical material on designers. This excellent reference tool has more than one hundred black-and-white illustrations.

Julier, Guy. *The Thames and Hudson Encyclopedia of Twentieth Century Design and Designers*. Thames & Hudson/Norton, 1993. 216p. illus. index.
LC 93-60123   0-500-20269-9 $12.95 paper

> This useful compilation covers a wide range of design topics and people. Entries range from fifty to one hundred words in length. Illustrations point out references in the text. This is a good beginning to further study of design topics.

Sculpture

Opie, Mary-Jane. *Sculpture*. Eyewitness Art. Dorling Kindersley, 1994. 64p. illus. maps. index.   LC 94-2593   1-56458-495-X $16.95

> As beautiful and enjoyable to browse as other Dorling Kindersley titles, this work also gives an overview of the history of Western and non-Western sculpture and provides a good survey of the subject. Tools, models, sketches, and techniques are all covered in this well-laid-out book. There are individual sections on African, Mesoamerican, and Eastern art. Western sculpture is treated chronologically. Not an in-depth study, but an excellent look at the basics of the history and techniques of sculpture.

Coins

Breen, Walter. *Walter Breen's Complete Encyclopedia of U.S. and Colonial Coins*. Doubleday, 1988. 768p. illus. index.   LC 79-6855   0-385-14207-2 $100

> One reviewer flatly states that this is "without any question the definitive book on colonial and U.S. coins of all kinds, a landmark publication." More than eight thousand coins are lovingly described, and there are more than four thousand good black-and-white photos. The historical material is excellent and provides a background for the main part of the book. Unfortunately expensive but good.

★ Yeoman, R. S., ed. *Guide Book of U.S. Coins, Red, 1997*. Western Press, 1996. 0-307-19905-3 $8.95 paper

> Famous as "The Red Book," this is a standard in the field of coin collecting. There are definitions of terms, background on American coins, and a listing of colonial and U.S. coins and related materials. Prices reflect conservative market values. The photos are clear and sharp, sometimes a rarity in identification books.

Craft Marks

Cushion, J. P. *Handbook of Pottery and Porcelain Marks: Definitive 5th Edition*. Faber and Faber, 1996. 304p.   0-571-17923-1 $55

This work, arranged by country, includes mostly nineteenth- and twentieth-century marks but does contain some older ones. Europe, Japan, and China are covered.

★ Kovel, Ralph and Terry Kovel. *Kovel's New Dictionary of Marks: Pottery and Porcelain 1850 to the Present*. Crown, 1986. 290p. illus. bibliog. index. 0-571-55914-5 $19

> Thirty-six hundred marks—American, European, and Oriental—are arranged by pictorial symbol or name of mark. Special features, such as dating information on marks, are excellent.

Antiques

Atterbury, Paul and Lars Tharp, eds. *The Bulfinch Illustrated Encyclopedia of Antiques*. Little, Brown, 1994. 332p. illus. index. LC 94-75734 0-8212-2077-2 $50

> Because the beautiful color illustrations in this work come mainly from Christie's and each represents an unusual and rare object, this is truly a work in the history of design and style and not a compendium of items persons might identify from their attics. It is an excellent introduction to the field of antiques. Sidebars, timelines, lists, and glossaries enhance the good text and great color plates.

★ Kovel, Ralph and Terry Kovel. *Kovel's Antiques/Collectibles*. Crown Publishing, 1997. illus. index. 0-609-80142-2 $14.95 paper

> One of the classic price guides, this lists all kinds of antiques by type and gives a current price or price range for each one. Approximately fifty thousand antiques are listed in the price guide section, and there are also tips on buying, collecting, and restoring.

Maloney, David J., Jr. *Maloney's Antiques and Collectibles Resource Directory*. 3d ed. Antique Trader Books, 1995. 560p. index. 0-930625-40-4 $24.95

> More than ten thousand resources for antique collectors are listed in this directory. Under twenty-six hundred categories, listings for auction services, clubs and associations, collectors, dealers, experts, museums, libraries, periodicals, repair, matching services, and reproduction sources include names, addresses, and phone numbers.

★ Rinker, Harry L., ed. *Warman's Antiques and Collectibles Price Guide*. 30th ed. Chilton's, 1996. index. 0-87069-746-3 $15.95 paper

> For the middle-range prices found in this classic work, the editor consults with dealers and collectors, reads trade literature, and scans price lists. Entries are alphabetical by the name or type of object. Many entries have a brief history of the "brand" or type of article discussed, with references to other sources. There is an index to pull together all references to a particular type of item. Reproduction alerts are helpful to collectors. This is a library standard.

Needlework

Reader's Digest Editors. *Complete Guide to Needlework*. Reader's Digest, 1981. 504p. illus.   0-89577-059-8 $28

> Ten different needlecrafts in all their aspects are covered in this fine reference tool put out by the editors of *Reader's Digest*. *ABC*s of each type, as well as various stitches and techniques, are covered.

Fashion

Martin, Richard, ed. *Contemporary Fashion*. St. James Press, 1995. 575p. photogs. illus. index.   LC 95-233329   1-55862-173-3 $135

> This encyclopedia of the past fifty years in the fashion business covers designers and retailers that have made an impact on the fashion world. The biographical essays are well researched and cover mostly American and European designers. Black-and-white illustrations and photos provide portraits of the designers and samples of their collections. The impact of various designers is also discussed. Expensive, but useful where there is demand.

Furniture

★ Aronson, Joseph. *Encyclopedia of Furniture*. Rev. ed. Crown, 1961. 496p. illus. 0-517-03735-1 $27.50

> This classic work covers many periods and eras, both Eastern and Western, ancient and modern. There are lots of black-and-white photos to help the novice identify furniture styles and periods.

★ Boyce, Charles. *Dictionary of Furniture*. Henry Holt, 1988.   0-8050-0752-0 $19.95 paper

> The entries in this book are short but well written. It is international in scope, and both ancient and modern furniture are covered. This is not a definitive work, but handy for quick answers and covers a bit more of the modern era than Aronson (above).

Butler, Joseph T. *Field Guide to American Antique Furniture: A Unique Visual System for Identifying the Style of Virtually Any Piece of American Antique Furniture*. Henry Holt, 1986. 400p. illus. bibliog. index.   0-8050-0124-7 $19.95 paper

> The main section of this work is a narrative on the history of American furniture. The second portion consists of drawings of pieces of furniture arranged by purpose and period.

Painting

★ Beckett, Wendy. *The Story of Painting*. Dorling Kindersley, 1994. 400p. illus. index.   LC 94-6322   1-56458-615-4 $39.95

In every reference section, there is room for the general overview of art history that is so magnificently represented by this title. As with most Dorling Kindersley books, this one is a feast of color, but the text is also highly readable and informative. The fascinating little "sidebars" for which Dorling Kindersley is famous abound, as do discussions of various paintings. Time lines and chronologies help not only to place activities and events in the art world, but to place art in its historical context.

Gottsegen, Mark D. *The Painter's Handbook*. Watson-Guptill, 1993. 320p. illus. index. LC 93-14996 0-8230-3003-2 $29.95 paper

For the budding painter or the experienced artist, this book covers everything from studio safety to building a crate to ship one's work. Painting terms cover and describe accessories, papers, boards, and other painting materials. Care for tools, techniques of painting, making one's own paints, and protecting the finished work are covered. This would be a good reference book or an instructional book for a classroom.

Music

Baker, Richard. *Richard Baker's Companion to Music: A Personal A-Z Guide to Classical Music*. BBC/Parkwest, 1995. 208p. illus. 0-563-36414-9 $27.95

Often, a reference book put together by one author will strongly reflect that individual's personality. This delightful book is such a title. The host of a BBC radio program, "Melodies for You," Baker emphasizes classical, jazz, and musicals. He spews forth a plethora of facts about composers, works, genres, terms, halls, instruments, and voice types. There are entries covering choral, film, and folk music. Many photographs, lots of them in color, enhance the text. Make sure a copy of this book is in your browsing collection. It would make a great gift for music lovers.

Baker, Theodore, ed. *Schirmer Pronouncing Pocket Manual of Musical Terms*. 5th ed. Schirmer Books/Simon & Schuster, 1995. 350p. 0-02-874567-1 $5.95 paper

A small book, this is meant mainly for beginning musicians looking up terms they encounter in printed music. There is also information on music basics such as notation, chord structure, scales, keys, and tempo. Pronunciation is given, and there is a list of "noteworthy" musicians.

Davis, Elizabeth A. *A Basic Music Library: Essential Scores and Sound Recordings*. 3d ed. Music Library Association Staff/American Library Association, 1997. 650p. LC 96-47351 0-8389-3461-7 $85

Although costly, the third edition of this work includes sound recordings for the first time and is an excellent source for libraries trying to build an audio collection. More than seven thousand recordings and three thousand scores are listed. The listings are coded for various levels of collections—again, useful for smaller libraries. There are many listings for world music, and the music of black composers and women is indexed.

Hall, Charles J. *A Chronicle of American Music, 1700–1995*. Schirmer/Macmillan, 1996. 768p. bibliog. index.   LC 96-16458   0-02-860296-X $65

> In this chronological treatment of the American music scene, highlights are listed for each year. After the highlights, commercial and art music are treated in separate sections. Births and deaths, debuts, publications, and compositions are covered. There is a detailed index and a good bibliography.

★ Kennedy, Michael and Joyce Bourne, eds. *The Oxford Dictionary of Music*. 2d ed. Oxford University Press, 1995. 985p.   0-19-869162-9 $39.95

> Much of this classic book's appeal can be described by the numbers. Out of twelve thousand total entries, more than nine hundred have been newly added. Two thousand composers are covered, twenty-two hundred terms and forms are defined, and there are more than 550 descriptions of musical instruments. Bibliographies have also been brought up-to-date. Some jazz performers are present, although the work is still short on popular music and musicians. This new edition has a stronger representation of American artists than did the previous edition. This is a highly readable and indispensable standard on many phases of music.

Sadie, Stanley, ed. *The Norton/Grove Concise Encyclopedia of Music*. Rev. and enlarged. Norton, 1994. 850p. illus.   0-393-03753-3 $42.50

> This "child" of the *New Grove Dictionary of Music and Musicians* presents the music lover with ten thousand short entries on composers, instruments, artists, works, and genres. There is also a considerable amount of information on non-Western music. This will complement similar works.

The Music Business

★ Laufenberg, Cindy. *Songwriter's Market 1998: Twenty-five Hundred Places to Sell Your Songs*. F & W Publications, 1997.   0-8987979-5-0 $22.99

> After an introduction on the business of songwriting, this work has up-to-date American and international listings for record companies and commercial firms that publish songs. There is helpful information on writer's organizations, workshops, contests, and useful publications.

Composers and Musicians

Di Martino, Dave. *Singer-Songwriters: Pop Music's Performer-Composers, from A to Zevon*. Billboard Books/Watson-Guptill, 1994. 320p. illus. index.   LC 93-44845 0-8320-7629-6 $21.95

> Only pop singers are included here—no R & B or country. The artists must be regarded as soloists and write the majority of the music they sing and have enjoyed some measure of commercial success. The 208 singers have an average of a page and a half, double columns. Almost all of the entries have a black-and-white photo, and there is a song index.

Ewen, David. *American Songwriters: One Hundred Forty-Six Biographies of America's Greatest Popular Composers and Lyricists*. Wilson, 1987. 489p. illus. 0-8242-0744-0 $68

> One hundred forty-six biographies on the lyricists and composers of all types of American music, from ragtime to soul, give excellent information about their lives and careers.

Sadie, Julie A. and Rhian Samuel, eds. *The Norton/Grove Dictionary of Women Composers*. Norton, 1994. 450p. illus. bibliog. index. 0-393-03487-9 $45

> This work consists of nine hundred articles written especially for it. Each entry gives the expected works lists and bibliographies but also offers a thoughtful essay on the composers' lives and works through achievements and illustrations of their scores. An excellent addition to material on music and composers.

★ Slonimsky, Nicolas. *The Concise Baker's Biographical Dictionary of Musicians*. 8th ed. Schirmer Books, 1993. 1155p. LC 93-30229 0-02-872416-X $50

> *Baker's Biographical Dictionary of Musicians* (Macmillan Library Reference, 1984) has short information on almost twelve thousand musicians, critics, and teachers. The *Concise* version listed here contains less than half of the classic parent volume at a bargain cost for small libraries.

Discography

Country Music Foundation Staff. *Country on Compact Disc: The Essential Guide to the Music*. Edited by Paul Kingsbury. Grove Attic Press, 1993. 286p. illus. LC 93-11887 0-8021-3379-7 $16 paper

> As with all books of this type, by the time the reader reads this annotation, the book is mainly of use as a retrospective collection builder rather than a guide to the best in current country. Albums are rated one to five stars. Zydeco, Cajun, Tex-Mex, bluegrass, and rockabilly are included. Lists of four- and five-star CDs are given, as well as Billboard's number-one country songs from 1944 to 1992. Reviews are somewhat uneven, but one reviewer of this book suggests that the reader can depend on writers from the *Journal of Country Music* and its related publications. Recommended.

★ Erlewine, Michael, ed. *All Music Guide: The Best CDs, Albums and Tapes*. 3d ed. Miller Freeman, 1996. 1417p. index. 0-87930-423-5 $27.95 paper

> This is a solid guide to the best recordings and the best of artists in various fields of music. Twenty-two categories cover rock/pop/soul, blues, gospel, children's, jazz, classical, gay, women's, world, and New Age, among others. Each entry includes birth and death dates and places, instruments, biographical profiles, and a list of major albums. More than one hundred editors have added to the listings, recommending titles as "essential, first purchase, and landmark." Each category is headed up by an essay on that type of music and time lines that show its progression. The only serious

omission is the lack of coverage of classical vocalists. A must for music collections. If you are mainly interested in rock, Erlewine's *All Music Guide to Rock: The Best CDs, Albums and Tapes* (Miller Freeman/Group West, 1995) has reviews of more than fifteen thousand rock recordings.

Gruber, Paul, ed. *The Metropolitan Opera Guide to Recorded Opera.* Norton, 1993. 550p. index.   LC 92-32618   0-393-03444-5 $35

> This companion volume to *The Metropolitan Opera Stories of the Great Operas* (see under "Opera") includes all of the operas in that book with two exceptions (because of recording availability). It is aimed at the new or casual opera lover, and the reviews are by well-known opera critics. Highly recommended for the audience it intends to serve.

Levi, Erik and Calum MacDonald, eds. BBC Music Magazine *Top One Thousand CDs Guide: A Critical Guide to the Best Classical Music CDs.* Amadeus/Timber, 1996. 352p. index.   1-57467-018-2 $12.95

> CDs are arranged in five categories: chamber music, choral and song, instrumental, opera, and orchestral. Entries cover composer, title, performers, label, number-recording process, and price. Both the quality of the performance and that of the recording are discussed. Only one recording of each work has been chosen.

Libbey, Ted. *The NPR Guide to Building a Classical CD Collection.* Workman Publishing, 1994. 498p. illus. index.   LC 92-50292   1-56305-051-X $15.95 paper

> When the Schwann catalog, *Schwann Opus* (Schwann, quarterly), lists eighty-six versions of Beethoven's Fifth Symphony and eighty-one of Vivaldi's *The Four Seasons,* where is the classical music fan to turn for help in locating the best versions? To this guide, of course! The author is a critic for the *New York Times* and host of the NPR "Basic Record Library." All of the choices are personal, of course, but Libbey is knowledgeable and gives a wealth of detail on each choice and its whys and wherefores. This is a good choice for all collections.

Weisbard, Eric and Craig Marks, eds. SPIN *Alternative Record Guide.* Vintage, 1995. 460p. photogs. index.   LC 95-15753   0-679-75574-8 $20 paper

> Sixty-four contributors have contributed lengthy, solid reviews, each of which includes a complete group discography and is rated from one to ten. The "Top One Hundred Alternative Albums" at the time of publication are listed. The writing is geared to those in the know.

Popular Music

Gregory, Hugh. *Soul Music A-Z.* Rev. ed. Da Capo, 1995. 384p. illus. 0-306-80643-6 $17.95

> "Soul" is broadly interpreted here (David Sanborn, L.L.Cool J, and the artist formerly known as Prince are included). One thousand biographical entries

include discographies. Sketches range from one paragraph to several columns for James Brown. Forty-six of the artists are represented by full-page photos.

★ Hardy, Phil and David Laing. *The Da Capo Companion to Twentieth-Century Popular Music*. Rev. ed. Da Capo, 1995. 1168p. index. LC 95-6677 0-306-80640-1 $29.95 paper

> Two thousand recording artists, including singers, band leaders, instrumentalists, vocal groups, and behind-the-scenes figures, are profiled with dates, birthplace, discography, and brief biographies. Two hundred entries are new to this edition. Popular music in this work includes pop, jazz, old time, rock and roll, easy listening, and so forth. One reviewer especially recommends this book for small libraries where "each music reference book must provide as much information as possible."

McAleer, Dave. *The All Music Book of Hit Singles*. Miller Freeman, 1994. 431p. illus. index. LC 94-11272 0-87930-330-1 $22.95 paper

> There's a lot of bang for the buck in this listing of forty years of pop music history, pictures, and trivia. Listings indicate platinum or gold titles and length of time on the pop charts. A good introduction tells how the book was compiled and what its sources were. Much parallel info is given for the United Kingdom, making this an especially valuable work for lovers of pop culture.

Country Music

Cackett, Alan. *The Harmony Illustrated Encyclopedia of Country Music*. 3d ed. Random House Value, 1994. 208p. illus. 0-517-17619-X $6.99 paper

> Although it doesn't qualify as a critical study, this useful work has five hundred biographies and selective discographies. The usual Harmony publication plethora of illustrations (about five hundred color photos) can be found here. Older singers have new material, and there are added entries for newer stars.

Carlin, Richard. *The Big Book of Country Music: A Biographical Encyclopedia*. Penguin, 1995. 526p. LC 94-39275 0-14-023509-4 $16.95

> With more than five hundred pages full of biographies, this covers the important artists and gives a selective discography for most of them. This book was in a *Library Journal* bibliography of "best books" in country music.

Carr, Patrick and *Country Music Magazine* Editors, eds. *The Illustrated History of Country Music*. Times Books/Random, 1996. 562p. photogs. index. LC 95-1468 0-8129-2455-X $25 paper

> This work, written by the editors of one of the most popular magazines in the field, traces the development of country music from the late 1800s to 1995.

★ McCloud, Barry. *Definite Country: The Ultimate Encyclopedia of Country Music and Its Performers.* Berkley/Perigee, 1995. 1200p. photogs. bibliog.   LC 94-28400 0-399-51890-8; 0-399-52144-5 $40; $20 paper

> Ten years in the making, this work consists mainly of biographies of country personalities with a few topic entries. Each entry gives vital statistics for the artist or group and follows with background information and a list of recommended albums. The invaluable end material includes such goodies as music award listings, gold and platinum lists, agents, managers, record companies, publishers, publicists, fan clubs, festivals, radio stations, and movies with country stars. Highly recommended, especially for this latter material.

Millard, Bob. *Country Music: Seventy Years of America's Favorite Music.* HarperCollins, 1993. 416p. photogs. index.   LC 92-56276   0-06-273244-7 $20 paper

> The most important records, debut artists, awards (Grammys, Country Music Association Awards), and many other benchmarks in the history of country music are recorded here. The author is a regular contributor to *Country Music Magazine.* This is a handy reference tool for country music of the twentieth century.

Richards, Tad and Melvin B. Shestack. *The New Country Music Encyclopedia.* Simon & Schuster, 1993. 270p. photogs. discog. index.   0-671-88294-5 $25

> Each entry in this book is found under a subject heading such as style, memorable songs, awards, and so forth. The discography, "101 Album Country Library," alone is worth the price.

Jazz

Case, Brian and Stan Britt. *The Harmony Illustrated Encyclopedia of Jazz.* 3d rev. ed. Crown, 1987. 208p. illus. index.   0-517-56443-2 $13.95 paper

> This book consists of 450 entries for jazz musicians and various jazz topics with lots of photos and album covers. A bit breezy to be a first-line source, it does give informed assessments of many musical greats.

Chilton, John. *Who's Who of Jazz: Storyville to Swing Street.* 4th ed. Da Capo, 1985. 362p. illus.   LC 84-20062   0-306-76271-4; 0-306-80243-0 $29.50; $12.95 paper

> One thousand jazz greats who were born prior to 1920 are discussed in biographies of up to two pages in length.

★ Erlewine, Michael, Vladimir Bogdanov, Chris Woodstra and Scott Yanow. *All Music Guide to Jazz.* 3d ed. All Music Guide Series. Miller Freeman, 1998. 1400p. index.   0-87930-530-4 $29.95 paper

> In this second edition, the number of musicians covered has been raised from 1,150 to 1,440; and the number of recordings has gone from 9,000 to 13,200. Each artistic biography has a selective discography with scorings for each recording. There is a history of jazz, a discussion of styles, and charts showing the historical development of jazz instruments. Highly recommended.

Feather, Leonard G. *Encyclopedia of Jazz*. Da Capo, 1984. 572p. illus.   0-306-80214-7
$19.95 paper

> Brief biographies, articles, and polls on jazz, organizations, schools, and so
> forth. For those libraries that serve jazz lovers, this book is followed by two
> supplements:
>
>> Feather, Leonard G. *Encyclopedia of Jazz in the 60s*. Da Capo, 1986.
>> 312p.   0-306-80263-5 $14.95 paper
>>
>> Feather, Leonard G. and Ira Gitler. *Encyclopedia of Jazz in the 70s*.
>> Da Capo, 1987. 393p.   0-306-80290-2 $16.95 paper

★ Kernfeld, Barry, ed. *The New Grove Dictionary of Jazz*. St. Martin's Press, 1994.
1358p. illus.   0-312-11357-9 $50

> This one-volume reprint of a two-volume (and $350!) 1988 work is a great
> bargain as well as an excellent reference work. There are some changes,
> such as death dates, and some corrections. The forty-five hundred entries
> are comprehensive in their coverage, and the contributors are internation-
> ally known.

Rock Music

Frame, Pete. *Harmony Illustrated Encyclopedia of Rock*. 7th ed. Crown, 1992. illus.
index.   LC 92-13813   0-517-59078-6 $19 paper

> Well written and well illustrated, with hundreds of color photos and album
> covers, the only "shortcoming" of this book is a British bias.

Heatley, Michael, ed. *The Ultimate Encyclopedia of Rock: The World's Most
Comprehensive Illustrated Rock Reference*. HarperPerennial/HarperCollins, 1993.
352p. illus. index.   0-06-271576-3; 0-06-273247-1 $40; $20 paper

> As one reviewer put it, this is not an encyclopedia, nor does it strictly deal
> with rock—it is, however, a good purchase for collections where information
> on rock musicians is in demand. Aside from rock, it deals with soul, rap,
> metal, R & B, and world music. Eight sections of biographies, each in a dif-
> ferent category, make up the largest part of this work. Twenty two-page es-
> says cover the careers of such legends as Elvis and Madonna. There is a time
> line of events from 1955 to 1992, and the book is full of good photographs.

Helander, Brock. *The Rock Who's Who*. 2d ed. Schirmer/Macmillan, 1996. 849p.
photogs. bibliog. index.   LC 96-28307   0-02-871031-2 $75

> In this biographical dictionary of rock stars, the author makes very selective
> choices, and only "the most innovative, avant-garde, and influential indi-
> viduals" make the cut. Entries are well written, and there is a discography
> for each artist. Good for all libraries that can afford the rather steep price.

Jancik, Wayne and Tad Lathrop. *Cult Rockers*. Fireside/Simon & Schuster, 1995.
352p. photogs.   0-684-81112-X $14 paper

"Long after commercial success or even life had abandoned them," many rock stars could claim a sizable cult following. From The Grateful Dead to less-well-known fringe groups, this book offers explanations for the cult status of various artists and groups. An inexpensive addition to biographical material on rock stars.

★ Pareles, John, ed. *The New* Rolling Stone *Encyclopedia of Rock and Roll.* Rev. ed. Simon & Schuster, 1995. 1184p. photogs. 0-684-81044-1 $25 paper

Twenty-two hundred well-researched entries give information on rock artists and bands, with years and dates, instruments, a discography, and an essay. Essays range from one hundred words to four pages (Elvis Presley). Some info is given on genres. A major flaw is lack of bibliography, but if a basic reference book on rock artists is needed, this is a good one.

Rees, Dafydd and Luke Crampton. *DK Encyclopedia of Rock Stars.* Dorling Kindersley, 1996. 952p. photogs. 0-614-2039-3-X $29.95 paper

Reviewers have questioned some of the exclusions and inclusions in this title, but the consensus seems to be that it is a good, well-researched book that gives chronological accounts of the careers of famous rock stars from both sides of the Atlantic.

Sumrall, Harry. *Pioneers of Rock and Roll: One Hundred Artists Who Changed the Face of Rock.* Billboard Books/Watson-Guptill, 1994. 320p. illus. index. LC 93-44847 0-8230-7628-8 $21.95 paper

Artists chosen for this work are arranged in alphabetical order, and each entry includes a list of songs and albums, with record label, year of release, and peak chart position. For each artist, a discussion of that person's career and an analysis of his or her music explains the artist's inclusion in this volume. An inexpensive source about musicians who had "commercial or aesthetic impact" on the field of rock and roll.

Songs

★ Bronson, Fred. *The Billboard Book of Number One Hits.* 3d ed., rev. and enlarged. Billboard Publications/Watson-Guptill, 1993. 848p. illus. index. LC 92-20318 0-8230-8298-9 $21.95 paper

These 650 one-page lists of the weekly hits from 1955 on include writers, performers, and stories about the songs. There are title and artist indexes.

Elrod, Bruce C. and T. Schultheiss, eds. *Your Hit Parade and American Top Ten Hits: A Week-by-Week Guide to the Nation's Favorite Music, 1935–1994.* Popular Culture, 1994. 672p. illus. index. 1-56075-037-5 $80

With origins in the radio and TV show of the same name, this "Hit Parade" book brings back a score of memories (Snooky Lanson?). Entries are week-by-week in chronological order with the top ten (or fifteen) hits. For each title, the entry also gives the top-selling recording. Quizzes are added occasionally, and there are lots of black-and-white photos. Tables show the top hits each year in various categories, even classical.

★ Ewen, David. *American Popular Songs from the Revolutionary War to the Present*. Random, 1966.   0-394-41705-4 $19.95

> The date, the composer, the lyricist, and the show (if any) are given for more than thirty-six hundred songs. This is a great source for the older material it includes.

★ Ferguson, Gary Lynn, comp. *Song Finder: A Title Index to Thirty-two Thousand Popular Songs in Collections, 1854–1992*. Greenwood, 1995. 344p. bibliog. index. LC 95-9936   0-313-29470-4 $79.50

> This work indexes 621 song collections and covers popular, children's, folk, religious, African American, and world music. Only the titles are indexed. More than one-third of these songs have not been listed elsewhere. The OCLC number is given for each collection to make interloaning easier.

★ Goodfellow, William D. *SongCite: An Index to Popular Songs*. Garland, 1995. 433p.   LC 94-44768   0-8153-2059-0 $60

> If the world needs more of anything, it's song indexes, and this book indexes more than seven thousand popular songs, mostly published since 1988. All of the publications indexed include piano and vocal arrangements. An excellent source for recent "words-and-music" questions.

Whitburn, Joel. *Billboard's Top Ten Charts, 1958–1995*. Record Research, 1995. 726p. index.   0-89820-113-6 $49.95

> Essentially a reprinting of all of *Billboard*'s Top Ten lists for the given years, this turned one reviewer's car ride into "an adventure in trivia and singing." The weekly list chronicles winners in rock, disco, and rap. There is an index of song titles with some supplemental lists: number-one hits, top-ten hits, and so forth. Again, great for nostalgia and party planners.

★ Whitburn, Joel. *Joel Whitburn's Pop Hits, 1940–1954*. Hal Leonard, 1995. 416p. illus.   0-793550-14-9 $29.95

> Pop singles for this era are taken from *Billboard*'s Pop Singles chart. Half of the text is an alphabetical listing by artist giving the debut date of the song, peak chart position, number of weeks, record label, and number. The second section lists peak songs and their final year standing in order by year. There is a great portion of the book called "Special Sections," where one can find info on Christmas singles, top artists ranked, songs with the longest title, and a list of "America's Most Enduring Songs" from 1890 to 1954. Great fodder for high school or college reunion committees.

★ Whitburn, Joel. *Joel Whitburn's Top Country Singles, 1944–1993*. Hal Leonard, 1995. 624p.   0-793550-13-6 $39.95

> One of Whitburn's famous *Billboard* compilations, this is a real treat for country music fans. Info from the country singles charts is presented in an

easy-to-use format—alphabetically by artist's name with a song index. There is some biographical information about the artists with each entry. Symbols convey such details as whether the song was part of a two-sided hit, a comedy song, a Christmas song, a reissue, and so forth. A "Chart Facts and Feats" section has lists of "interesting and unusual chart accomplishments."

Whitburn, Joel. *Top Pop Singles CD Guide, 1955–1979*. Compiled by Jerry Reuss. Record Research, 1995. 270p.   0-89820-107-1 $24.95

> More than ten thousand singles on compact disc are listed in this work mainly devoted to an artist-by-artist listing. Disc title, label, and number of the CD are given. A second section lists the song titles and gives the artist's name.

★ Whitburn, Joel. *Joel Whitburn's Top Pop Singles, 1955–1993*. Record Research, 1994. 893p. illus.   0-89820-104-7; 0-89820-105-5 $74.95; $64.95 paper

> This compilation of information from *Billboard*'s charts lists more than twenty thousand singles that made the charts between 1955 to 1993. Artists' biographies, information on song titles, and record prices are covered. The top five hundred artists are ranked in order of sales.

Whitburn, Joel, comp. *Rock Tracks*. Record Research, 1995. 250p. illus. index. 0-89820-114-4 $34.95

> Madame Audrey has probably missed a Joel Whitburn title somewhere, but by now you probably get the idea! *Billboard* began to keep track of album rock stations in 1981, and the charts are included in the first part of this book. In 1988, it began to track "modern" or "alternative" rock stations. These charts are covered in part 2. There is a song title index. Some of the career data here cannot be found elsewhere. Albums are covered from 1981 to 1995. This is a good addition to libraries where popular music questions are asked.

National Anthems

★ Reed, W. L. and M. J. Bristow, eds. *National Anthems of the World*. 8th rev. ed. Cassell/Sterling, 1993. 528p.   0-304-34218-1 $90

> In this edition of a classic reference work, each song is arranged with a single vocal line over piano accompaniment. Verses other than the first are printed after the music. The songs are revised up to January 1993 and include some new and restored anthems.

Musical Instruments

Dearling, Robert, ed. *The Illustrated Encyclopedia of Musical Instruments*. Schirmer Books, 1996.   LC 96-69152   0-02-864667-3 $75

A survey of the instruments of the world, this book gives us a look at each instrument, providing its characteristics, its uses, its place in musical history, and a list of major works written for it.

Diagram Group. *Musical Instruments of the World: An Illustrated Encyclopedia.* Facts on File, 1978. 320p. illus.   0-87196-320-5; 0-8160-1309-8 $37.50; 19.95 paper

Highly recommended for the layperson, this work contains more than four thousand drawings of musical instruments, with short information on each one.

Orchestral Music

Berger, Melvin. *The Anchor Guide to Orchestral Masterpieces.* Anchor/Doubleday, 1995. 384p.   LC 94-41050   0-385-47200-5 $14.95 paper

An accomplished musician and musical writer, Berger has attempted to provide a guide to helping others enjoy classical orchestral music to the fullest. Entries include a section on the creation of a composition, the form, and any anecdotes connected with it. This is recommended as a primary guide to classical music for all libraries.

Downes, Edward. *The New York Philharmonic Guide to the Symphony.* Walker, 1976. LC 76-13813   0-8027-0540-5 $65

Essays on 450 basic orchestral works, by composer, are the main feature in this quick reference work for the average classical music listener. Some excerpts from scores are included.

Amusement Parks

Norris, John and Joann Norris. *Amusement Parks: An American Guidebook.* 2d ed. McFarland, 1994. 168p. illus. index.   LC 93-27805   0-89950-789-1 $28.50

Because amusement park attendance exceeds 250 million in one year, it would behoove librarians to include information on these phenomena in their reference or, at least, their circulating collections. One hundred forty parks are arranged by state. A description of the park and its main attractions, hours, prices, addresses, and phone numbers are included in each entry. For some of the parks, other area attractions are listed.

Show Business

Franks, Don. *Entertainment Awards: A Music, Cinema, Theatre and Broadcasting Reference, 1928 through 1993.* McFarland, 1996. 560p. index.   LC 94-24192 0-7864-0031-5 $75

This is an expansion of *Tony, Grammy, Emmy, Country.* It now covers thirteen arts awards and is arranged chronologically. There is a name index, which should make it easy to locate persons who have been honored in more than one field.

Variety's Who's Who in Show Business. Rev. ed. Bowker, 1989. 412p.
0-8352-2665-4 $59.95

> This should be a first stop for brief biographical information about stars and their credits. People who died before June 30, 1988, are not included. This is older but still useful.

The Movies

Barson, Michael. *The Illustrated Who's Who of Hollywood Directors*. Vol. 1, *The Sound Era*. Noonday/Farrar, 1995. 480p. illus. index.   LC 94-40212   0-374-17452-0; 0-374-52428-9 $45.00; $27.50 paper

> This worthwhile, inexpensive addition to any library's collection on film covers the films of 197 directors whose work began before 1975. There are two- to eight-page essays on 153 people and brief biographies on 44 others. Some English directors and some low-budget specialists are included. Portraits and posters brighten the text.

Case, Christopher. *The Ultimate Movie Thesaurus: The Only Book You'll Ever Need to Find the Movie You Want*. Owl Books/Henry Holt, 1996. 704p.   0-8050-3496-X
$19.95 paper

> This book provides a subject approach to films and also includes such extras as a profitability grade and codes for nudity, violence, and gore. Well priced and useful, this will be a good addition to any film collection or any library where videos are popular.

★ Connors, Martin and Julia Furtaw, eds. *VideoHound's Golden Movie Retriever, 1997*. Visible Ink Press, 1996. 1600p. index.   0-7876-0780-0 $19.95 paper

> Claiming to be "the complete guide to movies on videocassette and laser disc," this lists twenty-two thousand films, with brief information on each one. Movies are rated, and ten indexes list cast members, directors, categories, and foreign films by country of production. This provides a good, cheap index with lots of features not found in more expensive video directories.

Doyle, Billy H. *The Ultimate Directory of the Silent Screen Performers: A Necrology of Births and Deaths and Essays on Fifty Lost Players*. Edited by Anthony Slide. Scarecrow, 1995. 368p. illus.   0-8108-2958-4 $49.50

> Birth and death dates are given for more than seventy-five hundred stars of the silent screen. Fifty longer essays on intriguing silent performers give background information and a filmography. Because silent films are often left out of other movie guides, this is a good place to find information. Unfortunately, the price may keep all but the larger libraries or the most dedicated from purchasing it.

Ebert, Roger. *Roger Ebert's Video Companion, 1998 Edition: With Pocket Video Guide*. Andrews and McMeel, 1997. 994p. index.   0-8362-3688-2 $17.95 paper

> Although Ebert is more generous in his compliments than some film critics, this need not be a fault for libraries whose readers (not film critics themselves) are looking for recommendations for video viewing. He reviews 1,250 movies with a one- to four-star rating system. Motion Picture Association of America ratings are also given. Updated annually.

Hardy, Phil, ed. *The Overlook Film Encyclopedia: Science Fiction*. Overlook Press, 1995. 478p. illus. index.   LC 93-24440   0-87951-626-7 $40 paper

> More than 1,450 science fiction films are arranged chronologically, up to 1990. Descriptions from one hundred to one thousand words in length have a plot synopsis and critical commentary.

Hardy, Phil, ed. *The Overlook Film Encyclopedia: The Western*. Overlook Press, 1994. 416p. illus. index.   LC 93-24439   0-87951-625-9 $40

> This and the science fiction volume (above) have lists of science fiction and western Oscar winners (the horror volume [below] does not) as well as critics' top tens and rental favorites. Fascinating bits of trivia are included in the critical commentary.

Juran, Robert A. *Old Familiar Faces: The Great Character Actors and Actresses of Hollywood's Golden Era*. Movie Memories Publishing, 1995. 320p. photogs. bibliog. index.   LC 95-76418   0-9646340-0-7 $24.95 paper

> Watch a lot of late-night or afternoon television? Do your patrons? If so, this book's one you'll find handy. Entries on eighty-nine character actors are supplemented by photos, filmographies, and three- or four-page biographies. Accurate and interesting for film fans.

Karney, Robyn and Gene Siskel. *Chronicle of the Cinema*. Dorling Kindersley, 1995. 912p. illus. index.   0-7894-0123-1 $59.95

> Although focusing primarily on the United States, this colorful book also includes some information on foreign cinema. Each decade in the film industry is highlighted with an essay, stills, posters, and commentary. Each year is begun with events in film, births and deaths, and Academy Award winners. An excellent index completes this entertaining history of film, with the emphasis on the industry and the eras, not on individual films and stars.

★ Katz, Ephraim. *The Film Encyclopedia*. 2d ed. HarperPerennial/HarperCollins, 1994. 1408p.   LC 93-43318   0-06-273089-4 $25 paper

> Two hundred thirty pages have been added to the previous edition in this work that covers actors, directors, screenwriters, composers, producers, cinematographers, editors, dance directors, and heads of studios. Full filmographies are given for directors and major stars. Both U.S. and foreign films are included, and there are definitions of film terms and descriptions of genres, styles, and schools. This should be owned by every library.

★ Maltin, Leonard, ed. *Leonard Maltin's Movie and Video Guide, 1997.* NAL
Dutton, 1996. 1580p. index.   0-452-27681-0 $19.95 paper

> For more than twenty-five years, this guide has provided brief plots and
> critical analysis of almost twenty thousand movies. Full production infor-
> mation is given, and a one- to four-star rating is used. Made-for-TV movies
> are included. Indexing is not as thorough as that in *VideoHound* (above),
> but either or both of these titles will serve libraries of all sizes well.

Maltin, Leonard, ed. *Leonard Maltin's Movie Encyclopedia: Career Profiles of More
Than Two Thousand Actors and Filmmakers, Past and Present.* NAL Dutton, 1995.
992p.   0-452-27058-8 $34.95

> Maltin is a film historian as well as a film correspondent, and, as such, he
> has written a highly usable encyclopedia of film targeted at the general
> reader. It includes bios of more than two thousand actors and filmmakers
> and is entertaining. For more scholarly reference use, readers will still want
> a copy of Katz (above).

Milne, Tom and Paul Willeman. *The Overlook Film Encyclopedia: Horror.* Edited by
Phil Hardy. Overlook Press, 1994. 496p. illus. index.   LC 93-23387   0-87951-624-0
$40 paper

> Revised and retitled, this book covers the horror genre from 1896 to 1992.
> Complete plot synopses and cast and production credits are given. The en-
> tries, written by film journalists, are arranged by year of production. Four
> hundred fifty black-and-white stills add to the text and give a picture of the
> history of the horror film and its trends. An essential purchase for libraries
> with horror fans.

Mowrey, Peter C. *Award Winning Films: A Viewer's Reference to Twenty-seven
Hundred Acclaimed Motion Pictures.* McFarland, 1994. 560p. index.   LC 92-56667
0-8995-0783-2 $35 paper

> Films from the silents to the 1990s are covered, with worldwide festivals
> and awards treated. Entries are arranged alphabetically with short produc-
> tion information and subject matter. Films do not have to be awarded a
> prize—movies with general critical acclaim are listed. Future editions may
> want to drop listings for films that received Oscars for makeup, costume,
> and so forth and had little else to recommend them. This, however, re-
> mains another valuable source for checking out a movie title.

Nowlan, Robert A. and Gwendolyn W. Nowlan. *Film Quotations: Eleven Thousand
Lines Spoken on Screen, Arranged by Subject and Indexed.* McFarland, 1994. 763p.
index.   LC 92-56673   0-89950-786-7 $75

> Nine hundred subject categories contain film quotes arranged chronologi-
> cally under each heading. Each entry gives the quotation, the context, the
> performer, the movie, the year, and the studio involved. There is an index of
> performers, so you have a chance to find out what that snappy line was even
> if you only remember that Kirk Douglas said it! This book will be useful if
> a book of film quotes is needed. It has one major flaw: there is no access

by the quote itself. If one knows the quote and wants to verify the movie or star, one must search through long listings for both and check each listing. For larger collections or for collections that answer movie questions.

Ogle, Patrick, comp. *Facets African-American Video Guide.* Facets Multimedia/Academy, 1994. 230p. illus. index.   0-89733-402-7 $12.95 paper

This inexpensive guide contains some errors and typos but will be useful in libraries that have film buffs. A wide range of videos and laser discs that deal with African-Americans are described and given some critical commentary. The major performer index is not adequate at the present time, because only 111 names are indexed. Documentary films on Africa, music, dance, and comedy are covered, as well as entertainment videos.

Osborne, Robert. *Sixty-five Years of the Oscar: The Official History of the Academy Awards.* Rev. ed. Abbeville Press, 1994. 352p. illus. index.   1-55859-715-8 $65

The book is arranged by decade and opens with the story of how and why the Academy came to be and came to offer awards. Full listings of nominees in all categories are given. Highlights and staging peculiarities of given years are also discussed. This well-illustrated volume makes the grade as a reference tool or coffee-table book.

Paietta, Ann C. and Jean L. Kauppila. *Animals on Screen and Radio: An Annotated Sourcebook.* Scarecrow, 1994. 385p. bibliog. index.   LC 94-29182   0-8108-2939-8 $42.50

A subject index provides access to this book that deals with animals in movies, television, and radio. There is also an index that lists actual and stage animal names. An annotated bibliography lists popular books and magazines. Despite some omissions, the work will be useful for trivia questions at any reference desk.

Sampson, Henry T. *Blacks in Black and White: A Source Book on Black Films.* 2d ed. Scarecrow, 1995. 735p. illus. index.   LC 93-1965   0-8108-2605-4 $89.50

With more than twice the information of the previous edition, this is an especially valuable guide to blacks in film. The author has assembled a large amount of information on all-black films that is not obtainable in other sources. There is a new chapter on whites in blackface and substantial material on actors, producers, and directors. The index is excellent, and the illustrations add to the value of the text. Expensive but good coverage of an important chapter of American entertainment.

★ Smith, Dave. *Disney A to Z: The Official Encyclopedia.* Hyperion/Little, Brown, 1996. 512p. photogs. bibliog.   0-7868-6223-8 $29.95

This book was especially compiled to help answer reference questions, such as release dates of films and names of cartoons in series. Both TV and movie releases are covered, along with key personnel, the amusement parks, and stores. Biographies provide only Disney-related info, no personal highlights. This will be useful in most libraries.

Vazzana, Eugene Michael. *Silent Film Necrology: Births and Deaths of Over Nine Thousand Performers, Directors, Producers and Other Filmmakers of the Silent Era, Through 1993.* McFarland, 1995. 381p. LC 95-14462 0-78640-132-X $55

> This biographical dictionary does an excellent job of covering the personalities of an era of entertainment that ended in the 1920s but still holds interest for film fans of today. Each entry gives birth and death date and place, given name, spouse(s), studio affiliation, and citations to sources of information. Names and addresses of fan clubs and newsletters are given.

★ Walker, John, ed. *Halliwell's Film and Video Guide 1998.* HarperCollins, 1997. 1312p. 0-06-273505-5 $22.50 paper

> Even with the tremendous amount of video and movie guides being published, *Halliwell's* remains one of the best. Each edition contains more than twenty thousand entries for individual movies, with dates, running times, synopses, critical comment, cast, director, and writer(s). Lists of four-star movies and notations of which soundtracks are on CD are also valuable. It is a bit more expensive than Maltin or *VideoHound* (above), but the detailed entries make it worthwhile. All three contain films the others do not, so purchase of at least two of the three is essential where film questions are asked frequently.

Radio

Brewer, Annie M. *Talk Shows and Hosts on Radio: A Directory Including Show Titles and Formats, Biographical Information on Hosts, and Topic/Subject Index.* 4th ed. Whiteford Press, 1996. 300p. index. 0-9632341-5-3 $40

> The United States, Guam, and Puerto Rico are covered in this geographic list of programs. Five hundred seventeen talk shows and 234 biographies have been added to this newest edition. Each entry contains call letters, name of the show, format, addresses and phone numbers, whether there are guests, and the host's name. Another section lists syndicated and network programs. This is the only current directory of its kind.

★ Lackmann, Ronald W. *Same Time . . . Same Station: An A-Z Guide to Radio from Jack Benny to Howard Stern.* Facts on File, 1995. 304p. photogs. bibliog. index. LC 95-5662 0-8160-2862-1 $45

> In one alphabetical order, the author provides show synopses, biographies, genre descriptions, a bibliography, and intriguing appendixes. We go back to "those thrilling days of yesteryear," when families actually played games, sewed, carved wood, or just sat and let their imaginations take over as they listened to . . . radio! (For fans of *Let's Pretend,* the great children's fairy-tale show, there is a wonderful picture of Miriam Wolfe, who always played the wicked queen. It doesn't disappoint!)

Swartz, Jon D. and Robert C. Reinehr. *Handbook of Old-Time Radio: A Comprehensive Guide to Golden Age Radio Listening and Collecting.* Scarecrow, 1993. 823p. bibliog. index. 0-8108-2590-2 $92.50

Tune in Yesterday, The Big Broadcast, and *Radio's Golden Years,* all reference classics, are now out-of-print, but the above three books do their best to supplement them. In short, if you have them, don't throw them away. If you don't have them, purchase one or two of the above titles. From 1926 to 1962, this volume covers networks and broadcasting and includes logs listing more than forty-five hundred programs by type and descriptions of best-known shows, with directory information about each.

Television

★ Brooks, Tim. *Complete Directory to Prime Time Network and Cable Television Shows, 1946 to the Present.* 6th ed. Ballantine, 1995. 1440p. index.   0-345-39736-3 $23 paper

> Included here is every TV show that aired for at least four weeks between the hours of 7 P.M. and 11 P.M. on any of the four networks (including Dumont). All pertinent information on the shows is given. It is indexed by personal name.

Brown, Les. *Les Brown's Encyclopedia of Television.* 3d ed. Visible Ink Press, 1991. 723p.   0-8103-8871-5; 0-8103-9420-0 $55.00; $22.95 paper

> This is the most inclusive source for TV history for the time period involved. Besides the expected information on the shows, there is some technical data aimed at the lay reader.

Davis, Jeffrey. *Children's Television, 1947–1990: Over Two Hundred Series, Game and Variety Shows, Cartoons, Educational Programs and Specials.* McFarland, 1995. 295p. illus. index.   LC 94-10808   0-89950-911-8 $42.50

> Remember Kukla, Fran, and Ollie? Howdy Doody? The Mickey Mouse Club? Well, this book will refresh your memory! Two hundred series are discussed in terms of history, casts, plots, times, and dates. The research is excellent, and this will be enjoyed by reference librarians, patrons, and those who just want to wallow in nostalgia. Series are placed in ten categories—action, cartoons, circus and magic, comedy, fun and games, informative, kindly hosts and hostesses, puppets, westerns, and specials. Great stuff!

Erickson, Hal. *Television Cartoon Shows: An Illustrated Encyclopedia, 1949 Through 1993.* McFarland, 1995. 669p. bibliog. index.   LC 94-23878   0-7864-0029-3 $75

> Erickson has written several other books on TV topics, and he has done exhaustive work on his topic here. A brief history and discussion of cartoon trends starts this work and is followed by an alphabetical listing of cartoon shows full of production information. A comprehensive and useful work.

Ward, Jack. *Television Guest Stars: An Illustrated Career Chronicle for 678 Performers of the Sixties and Seventies.* McFarland, 1993. 598p. illus. index. LC 92-51009   0-89950-807-3 $75

Although more costly than some works in this field, this book is a treasure trove of information of hundreds of actors who may never have had their own shows but won our hearts and piqued our interests on television. Each performer listed here had at least fifteen network guest prime-time appearances during the sixties and seventies. Because many of these performers went on to become celebrities, the book is a source of further information on many popular performers. Photos help the identification: "Oh *that's* who that was!" This is essential to any library where the patrons spent their formative years watching TV.

Performing Artists

Severson, Molly, ed. *Performing Artists.* Gale, 1995. 3 vols. 710p. illus. index. 0-8103-9868-0 $38

> What a great price for three volumes of information about artists of interest to young people! The volumes are attractive and readable, and the artists come from comedy, drama, film, television, and music. There is an address for user input in future editions. The range is broad, from Arnold Schwarzenegger to the Red Hot Chili Peppers, from Anthony Hopkins to Ice-T. This is fun for fans of any age.

Theater

Bordman, Gerald. *American Theatre: A Chronicle of Comedy and Drama, 1914–1930.* Oxford University Press, 1995. 832p. index.   LC 94-13842 0-19-509078-0 $49.95

> A year-by-year account of a particular period in American theatrical history, this text gives plot, critical reaction, and performance history of every New York production in that time. Because this time saw the works of O'Neill, Rice, Belasco, Shaw, LaGalliene, the Lunts, and other greats, it is rich in the historic foundations of today's theater. The book is not only complete and detailed, but very readable.

Brewer's Theater: A Phrase and Fable Dictionary. HarperCollins, 1994. 513p. LC 94-16436   0-06-270043-X $35

> Related terms are grouped under a common "head word" (e.g., "Lady" brings up "Lady Bountiful," "Lady Elizabeth's Men," and "Lady's Not for Burning"). All aspects of theater are included, such as plays, theaters, biographies, companies, and superstitions. Plot summaries are provided for many famous plays. A unique and rich theater reference.

Hartnoll, Phyllis, ed. *The Oxford Companion to the Theatre.* 4th ed. Oxford University Press, 1983. 934p. illus.   0-19-211546-4 $60

> This is the classic one-volume work on theater. Even though it is a bit old now, it gives the best coverage of the time period involved.

Leiter, Samuel L. *The Great Stage Directors: One Hundred Distinguished Careers of the Theater.* Facts on File, 1994. 340p. illus. index.   LC 93-33380   0-8160-2602-5 $35

> Beginning with the earliest directors and continuing till the present, this book presents us with international coverage and complete historical perspective. Entries contain biography, analysis of working methods, summaries of major productions, and bibliography. Not just a biographical dictionary, this work gives insights into the theater and how a director thinks and works.

★ Wilmeth, Don B. and Tice L. Miller, eds. *Cambridge Guide to American Theatre.* Cambridge University Press, 1996. 465p. bibliog. illus. index.   LC 92-35030 0-521-56444-1 $24.95 paper

> The heart of this book comes from the American entries in *Cambridge Guide to World Theatre* (Cambridge University Press, 1992). The entries have been revised, updated, and added to bring the work up-to-date. Not only is the editors' definition of "theatre" broad (circus, magic, vaudeville), there is also good material on Yiddish, gay and lesbian, African American, and other small theater worlds. The bibliography is excellent, and the biographical index leads the user to information about people in the body of the work. The material is written by eighty experts, and articles are signed.

Opera

Freeman, John W. *The Metropolitan Opera Stories of the Great Operas.* Norton, 1984. 565p. illus.   LC 84-8030   0-393-01888-1 $24.95

> Two main reasons for purchasing this title—many less familiar, "fringe" works are included and there is an excellent introduction to each opera, which covers source for the libretto, premiers, and a biography and portrait of each composer.

★ Harewood, Earl of, ed. *The Definitive Kobbe's Opera Book.* Rev. ed. Putnam, 1987. 1404p. illus. index.   0-399-13180-9 $40

> When you care enough to but the very best—opera plots, that is—buy *Kobbe's.* This is one of the finest of the genre. More than three hundred operas are included—supposedly those that the American or English operagoer would be likely to encounter.

Musicals

Hischak, Thomas S. *The American Musical Theatre Song Encyclopedia.* Greenwood, 1995. 568p. index.   LC 94-40853   0-313-20407-0 $59.95

> From "The Black Crook" to "Passion," this encyclopedia covers more than eighteen hundred songs from more than five hundred musicals. Author, original performers, dates of recordings, and a description are given for

each song. The indexes—song titles, shows, authors, and performers—are invaluable. Anything unique about a particular song is detailed. The listings of musicals in the back of the book include how many performances a show had.

Sports

★ Diagram Group Staff. *Rules of the Game: The Complete Illustrated Encyclopedia of All the Sports of the World.* St. Martin's Press, 1994.   0-312-11940-2 $15.95 paper

> Approximately 150 sports are covered, and each is given a detailed treatment as to objectives, playing area and equipment, rules, timing and scoring, number of participants, and officials. This is a necessary book for all libraries.

Hickok, Ralph. *A Who's Who of Sports Champions: Their Stories and Records.* Houghton Mifflin, 1995. 928p. bibliog. index.   LC 94-49144   0-395-73312-X $19.95 paper

> One of the best and most inclusive of its kind, this biographical dictionary includes more than two thousand sports personalities from the United States and Canada, representing more than fifty sports. Entries for each person emphasize his or her life in sports, although many personal details are mentioned.

Jacobs, Timothy. *One Hundred Athletes Who Shaped Sports History.* Bluewood Books, 1994. 112p. illus. index.   0-912517-13-1 $7.95 paper

> The athletes in this book cover the period from 558 B.C. through 1966. One-page entries are given to male and female multicultural athletes from all backgrounds. There is a map to show the birthplace and evidence in the biography of the athlete's unique talent. There is a time line cross-reference to each athlete. Compact and useful, this will be good in collections for middle school and up.

Porter, David L. *African-American Sports Greats: A Biographical Dictionary.* Greenwood, 1995. 480p. bibliog. index.   LC 95-7189   0-313-28987-5 $59.95

> This comprehensive listing arranges athletes by name, and each signed entry includes a bibliography. This is the best work of its kind available, covering 166 athletes of all types with baseball, basketball, and football predominating.

Porter, David L., ed. *Biographical Dictionary of American Sports: 1992–1995 Supplement for Baseball, Football, Basketball and Other Sports.* Greenwood, 1995. 848p. index.   LC 94-27941   0-313-28431-8 $89.50

> Articles in these dictionaries are two hundred to six hundred words in length, with bibliography. Not only are players included, but there are articles on coaches, managers, league administrators, broadcasters, and others. Baseball and football account for 383 of the 616 entries in this volume. Basketball has 58 entries. There is an index of all subjects and lists by sub-

ject's date of birth, women athletes by sport, sports halls of fame, and Olympic sites.

Sherrow, Victoria. *Encyclopedia of Women and Sports.* ABC-Clio, 1996. 400p. illus. bibliog. index.   LC 96-19600   0-87436-826-X $65

> With both subject and name entries, the author has put together an impressive array of biographical and issue-related material on women in sports. There are photographs, a time line, and a good bibliography. The sports range from track and field to bullfighting.

Sugar, Bert Randolph. *The One Hundred Greatest Athletes of All Time: A Sports Editor's Personal Ranking.* Citadel Press/Carol Publishing Group, 1995. 352p. illus. index.   0-8065-1614-3 $24.95

> Each listing of a great athlete is enhanced by a photograph and a good biography. The entries range from two to six pages. Twentieth-century sports figures from around the world make up the list, although most of them are from the United States. Because this was his personal choice, Sugar lists another 250 athletes who might have been included on someone else's list. A great gift for a sports fan and a useful addition to the reference collection.

Football

Neft, David S., Richard M. Cohen and Rick Korch. *Sports Encyclopedia of Pro Football.* 14th ed. St. Martin's Press, 1996. 768p. illus.   0-312-14424-5 $21.99 paper

> Even though, as an annual, this has to be replaced often, it is an inexpensive and comprehensive source on NFL football. The book is chock-full of info about team and player achievements, scores, rosters, and the Pro Football Hall of Fame. Small libraries can probably purchase this every other year.

Soccer

Henshaw, Richard and Michael L. LaBlanc. *The World Encyclopedia of Soccer.* Gale, 1993. 500p. illus. index.   0-8103-8995-9; 0-8103-9442-1 $42.00; $14.95 paper

> This handy book was designed to appeal to audiences of the World Cup, which was played in the United States for the first time in 1994. There is a spectator's guide to the World Cup and easily read explanations of rules and tactics. Lots of diagrams and a glossary help with the explanations. Eighty famous soccer players are covered.

Tennis

Collins, Bud and Zander Hollander, eds. *Bud Collins' Modern Encyclopedia of Tennis.* 2d ed. Visible Ink/Gale, 1993. 600p. illus. index.   0-8103-8988-6; 0-8103-9443-X $37.95; 14.95 paper

Finally revised from the 1980 edition, this is one of the most popular works on tennis facts and figures. Records, histories, rankings, hall of fame lists, and greatest players have been added in this update. A third of each edition is given over to great player profiles. Lots of photographs have been added.

Golf

Lane, James M. *The Complete Golfer's Almanac, 1996: A Compendium of Useful Golfing Facts and Information.* Berkley, 1996. 395p. index.   0-399-51992-0 $13.95

> Readability is a plus in this compilation of golf information. Brief biographies of famous golfers are included, as well as information on history, places, and schools. Summaries of golf are covered for countries, states, and courses. There is also a glossary, a list of associations, equipment sales data, and an index.

Baseball

Wolff, Rick, ed. *The Baseball Encyclopedia: The Complete and Official Record of Major League Baseball.* 10th ed. Macmillan, 1996. 2600p.   0-02-861435-6 $99

> Hailed as "the best and most complete record book . . . on any single game or sport," this book contains records, achievements, and rules, plus an introductory history of the game. You will also need these two:
>
> > *Baseball Encyclopedia Update 1995.* Macmillan, 1995.
> > 0-02-860089-4 $12 paper
> >
> > *Baseball Encyclopedia Update 1997.* Macmillan, 1997.
> > 224p   0-02-861512-3 $12 paper

Wright, Russell O. *The Best of Teams, the Worst of Teams: A Major League Baseball Statistical Reference, 1903–1994.* McFarland, 1995. 189p. index.   LC 95-15762 0-7864-0011-0 $29.95

> This compilation of baseball statistics is divided into five parts: "Winning and Losing," "Offensive Highs and Lows," "Defensive Highs and Lows," "Best Teams in Franchise History," and "Team Summaries." The book is set up so that the best and worst years a team has had in each category can be easily seen. Not just dry stats, there is a lot of narrative to add to the value of the book.

Camping

American Camping Association. *Guide to Accredited Camps, 1997–1998.* 41st ed. American Camping Association, 1997. illus.   0-87603-153-X $16.95 paper

> The purpose of this directory is to help parents select an American Camping Association–accredited summer camp for their little darlings. Entries

have been updated by camp owners as they renew their membership in the American Camping Association. Pages of essays help parents and campers by answering questions. Entries include information about the founding of the camp, the director, the operator, type of camp, capacity, ages, facilities, and times open. There is an activities index. Special camps (families, disadvantaged, special needs, and international) are listed separately.

Cook, Charles. *The Essential Guide to Wilderness Camping and Backpacking in the United States*. Michael Kesend Publishing/Talman, 1995. 324p. illus. maps. index. 0-935576-46-0 $24.95

> The basics of wilderness camping and backpacking are accompanied by a complete guide to U.S. parks and natural areas for camping and trails.

Fishing

Wood, Ian, ed. *The Dorling Kindersley Encyclopedia of Fishing*. Dorling Kindersley/Houghton, 1994. 288p. illus. index.   LC 93-28861   1-56458-492-5 $39.95

> Six chapters written in a clear, concise style cover tackle, bait, flies, fish species, techniques, and sites. Families of fish are discussed in terms of range and habits. There is information on fresh- and saltwater fishing. A good index rounds out the work, and, of course, there are tons of color photos.

800s
Literature

The literature section is a well-used part of most libraries. Many short-answer questions can be answered by glossaries of terms, books of literary allusion, and general encyclopedias of literature.

Writers at all levels need the help of books on grammar, style, and usage. Budding authors need guides to the profession to help them get started.

Nobody can be an expert in everything, and busy librarians are probably the biggest fans of the many fiction and genre guides to help them send patrons to good leisure-time reading selections. These books are also useful to librarians in planning displays, bibliographic bookmarks, programs, and lists of "good reads."

There is an old saying (and if there isn't, there ought to be) to the effect that no matter how many quotation books you have, the quote in question will not be in any of them. This is true of many types of reference questions, but the books listed here should get the small library off to a good start.

Books on the literatures of the world offer short answers to questions and are good beginnings to further research.

Literature

★ *Benet's Reader's Encyclopedia: The Classic and Only Encyclopedia of World Literature in a Single Volume.* 3d ed. HarperCollins, 1987. 1091p.   LC 87-45022 0-06-181088-6 $45

> Invaluable for those who enjoy looking up allusions they come across in their reading, *Benet's* covers biography, plot synopses, terms, characters, folklore, and literary movements. The scope is worldwide, and the time is ancient to the present. Readers have rejoiced at this, the first new edition since 1965. The more than nine thousand entries place more of an em-

phasis on twentieth-century and non-Western literature in this standard one-volume encyclopedia that belongs in all libraries.

Holman, C. Hugh and William Harmon. *A Handbook to Literature*. 7th ed. Macmillan, 1995. 624p. index.   LC 94-42741   0-87779-042-6 $30

> This book contains more than fifteen hundred words and phrases pertaining to things, people, and terms in American and English literature. The entries range from one to several pages in length. An abundance of cross-references and a list of the sources used in making up the definitions make this one of the classics in its field. Appendixes include lists of literary prizewinners.

★ *Merriam-Webster's Encyclopedia of Literature*. Merriam-Webster, 1995. 1236p. illus.   LC 94-42741   0-87779-042-6 $39.95

> With parents like the editorial departments of Merriam-Webster and the *Encyclopaedia Brittanica,* how can a kid go wrong? It couldn't, according to reviewers. The entries are brief but useful and cover writers and works, terms, characters, landmarks, folklore, scholars, illustrators, movements, and awards. There is good information on new authors, women authors, and multicultural writers. Pronunciation is given for most entries, and there are many illustrations and photographs. Entries on authors include biographical information and career info, plus a list of major writings. Because of its attempt to be more inclusive, some things are left out, which a North American reader might expect. Don't throw out your *Benet's Reader's Encyclopedia* (above), but use this new work as a more up-to-date and worldly complement.

Snodgrass, Mary Ellen. *The Encyclopedia of Utopian Literature*. Literary Companion Series. ABC-Clio, 1995. 644p. illus. bibliog. index.   0-87436-757-3 $65

> Fans of science fiction and fantasy as well as lovers of literature in general will want to look at this title. Well illustrated and full of details about hundreds of utopias, this book covers each site with details of plot, publishing history, and social context. Appendixes list primary sources, titles mentioned in the text, and a long bibliography.

Strouf, Judie L. *Literature Teacher's Book of Lists*. Center for Applied Research, 1997. 416p.   0-87628-554-X $29.50 paper

> With a stress on literature for young adults, this book is full of "useful, whimsical and necessary" info. Its many lists include terms, allusions, quotations, characters, and places involving literature. There are lists of juvenile books for all ages, middle-school lists, teen lists, lists of books for the college bound, and lists of genres, poems on various subjects, words that illustrate *onomatopoeia,* tips on how to give an oral book report or how to write one, careers in literature-related fields, and on and on and on. Fun for book lovers to browse and valuable for those working with young people of all ages.

Literary Terms

Abrams, M. H. *A Glossary of Literary Terms*. Harcourt Brace College Publishers, 1993. 434p.   0-03-054982-5 $19.50

> This indispensable aid to the study of literature includes short definitions of more traditional and relatively current terms.

Literary Allusions

Evans, Ivor. *Brewer's Dictionary of Phrase and Fable*. Edited by Adrian Room. 15th ed. Harper, 1995. 1321p.   0-06-270133-9 $45

> This one-volume work covers the areas of linguistics, literature, history, biography, and so forth. Entries are included for phrases, names, titles, quotes, proverbs, and genres.

Grote, David. *Common Knowledge: A Reader's Guide to Literary Allusions*. Greenwood, 1987. 420p.   LC 87-10710   0-313-25757-4 $65

> The three purposes of this book are (1) to identify characters that are part of our literary background, (2) to identify writers whose works we are likely to read, and (3) to give a good description of the characters and their sources. It is well organized and cross-referenced.

Writer's Markets

★ Bentley, Chantelle. *Poet's Market, 1998: Seventeen Hundred Places to Sell Your Poetry*. F & W Publications, 1997.   0-89879-796-9 $22.99

> This directory of publishers of poetry ranges from the major publishing houses and magazines to small presses and literary reviews. Contests, greeting-card companies, writing colonies, and so forth are listed. Almost two thousand entries help the budding or full-blown poet identify markets for his or her work. An alphabetical list of publishers gives type of market, what kind of work they accept, contact names, and submission and payment information. Lists of organizations, conferences, workshops, and writers' colonies are included along with interviews with editors and working poets.

★ Buening, Alice P., ed. *1997 Children's Writer's and Illustrator's Market*. F & W Publications, 1997. 378p.   0-89879-765-9 $22.99

> This, as with the other *Market* books, is full of good advice for hopeful authors of children's materials. Listings of individual publishers give directory info and how-to information on submitting a manuscript.

Burack, Sylvia K. *The Writer's Handbook: 1996 Edition*. The Writer, 1995. 900p. LC 36-028596   0-87116-179-6 $29.95

The business of writing for publication is covered in this work under such topics as children's materials, television, drama, poetry, and nonfiction. There are some listings of possible markets.

★ Holm, Kirsten. *Writer's Market, 1997.* F & W Publications, 1997. illus. 0-89879-792-6 $27.99

The main source for freelancers hoping to sell their written wares, this has more than four thousand listings, including names and addresses, payment information, contact persons, and writing tips. It is a useful list of many publishing markets for the novice and the experienced writer.

Style Manuals and Writer's Guides

The Chicago Manual of Style. 14th edition. The University of Chicago Press, 1993. 921p.   LC 92-37475   0-226-10389-7 $40

A long time ago, a proofreader jotted down a few simple rules of style to guide other proofreaders. The end result is this 921-page tome that many consider the last word in style and writing rules. This edition increases the number and variety of examples for each rule and includes more information on the use of computers. The documentation portion has been greatly revised and expanded. Among the included topics are the parts of a book, foreign languages in type, quotations, captions, rights and permissions, and abbreviations. This is invaluable for any library that serves writers or college students.

★ Gibaldi, Joseph and Phyllis Franklin. *MLA Handbook for Writers of Research Papers.* 4th ed. Modern Language Association of America, 1997. 300p. LC 97-014711   0-87352-572-8 $20 paper

Rules are covered in detail, and there are many examples of style and usage in this classic manual. Lists of abbreviations are included, and there are such topics as library research, spelling, and plagiarism. Suggestions for using word processors bring this old standard into the nineties.

Sutcliffe, Andrea J., ed. *The New York Public Library Writer's Guide to Style and Usage.* HarperCollins, 1994. 838p. illus. bibliog. maps. index.   LC 93-33255 0-06-270064-2 $35

A style manual that's almost fun to use! Who could ask for anything more? The book divides its information into sections including up-to-date information on usage, sexist language, grammar, capitalization, the editing process, and production and design. There is a good annotated bibliography of reference tools for writers.

★ Turabian, Kate L. *A Manual for Writers of Term Papers, Theses and Dissertations.* 6th ed. University of Chicago Press, 1996.   0-226-81627-3 $12.95

One of the standard guides for preparing formal papers, this has good information on computer use. There are good examples of actual page layouts for the beginning (or careful) writer.

Venolia, Jan. *Write Right! A Desktop Digest of Punctuation, Grammar and Style.*
3d ed. Ten Speed Press, 1995. 144p. illus. index.   0-89815-676-9 $6.95 paper

> This is a short, to-the-point treatment of the rules of punctuation and writ-
> ing for the layperson. The section on frequently misused words is all too
> useful. Finding a topic is simple. Under each chapter title, there are sub-
> headings in alphabetical order and clearly numbered rules for each item
> discussed. Cheap and handy!

Poetry

Brogan, T. V. F., ed. *The New Princeton Handbook of Poetic Terms.* Princeton University
Press, 1994. 339p.   LC 93-43944   0-691-03671-3; 0-691-03672-1 $47.50; $17.95 paper

> This book represents a handy, inexpensive compilation of information
> taken from *The New Princeton Encyclopedia of Poetry and Poetics* (Fine
> Communications, 1996). What remains are definitions of terms used in dis-
> cussing poetry, with substantial articles on major topics. Current bibliogra-
> phy is included with each entry.

Drury, John. *The Poetry Dictionary.* F & W Publications, 1995. 352p. index.
1-884910-04-1 $18.99

> Alphabetized terms in this dictionary are in boldface, and cross-referenced
> terms are in italics. All listed terms are in an index. Definitions of elements
> of poetry are handled clearly and concisely. The book can also double as an
> anthology of poetry, with many examples of poems of all poetics traditions.

★ Hazen, Edith P., ed. *The Columbia Granger's Index to Poetry: Indexing
Anthologies Published Through June 3, 1993.* 10th ed. Columbia University Press,
1993. 2078p.   LC 93-39161   0-231-08408-0 $225

> Although this is a bit over the cost of most of the books in this bibliogra-
> phy, *Granger's* should be one of the basic reference works in all but the
> smallest library. Four hundred anthologies are indexed, with 150 new an-
> thologies replacing 150 older titles. As a purchasing aid, the list of indexed
> titles is coded to indicate those titles most valuable for purchase by li-
> braries. As with older editions, the first section indexes titles and first lines
> of 79,000 poems. Newly included in this section are the last lines of the
> 12,500 most popular poems. Author and subject listings follow.

Monologues

Morris, Karen, ed. *The Smith and Kraus Monologue Index: A Guide to 1,778
Monologues from 1,074 Plays.* Smith and Kraus, 1995. 208p.   LC 94-48262
188-0399-75-X $14.95 paper

> This index to Smith and Kraus monologue collections will be useful as a
> searching tool for those collections and a purchasing guide to them. All

types of monologues are indexed, including male, female, dramatic, comic, and so forth. Useful for collections in areas where high school theater or forensics programs are popular.

Speeches

★ Safire, William, ed. *Lend Me Your Ears: Great Speeches in History.* 2d ed., expanded, rev. Norton, 1991. 1056p. index.   LC 96-43423   0-393-04005-4 $39.95

> Two hundred and twenty orations covering all times and places are included in this book of speeches that Safire thinks are "great." From Pope Urban to Colin Powell, the works cover a wide variety of topics and occasions.

Drama

★ Berney, K. A. and N. G. Templeton, eds. *Contemporary American Dramatists.* St. James Press, 1994. 771p. index.   LC 94-11448   1-55862-214-4 $40

> Two hundred playwrights, from Abbott to Zindel, are listed with a biography, a bibliography of writings, a list of critical studies, and a signed essay. There is a title index, and addresses are given for many authors. It contains much information not available in any other single volume.

Berney, K. A. and N. G. Templeton, eds. *Contemporary Women Dramatists.* St. James Press, 1994. 335p. index.   LC 94-13898   1-55862-212-8 $30

> The "best and most prominent" women playwrights of the twentieth century are covered here in entries that include brief biographies, literary agent's name, playwright's address, names of publications, comments made by the playwright, influences on her work, and a list of bibliographies and studies. One extremely valuable section is a compilation of essays on twenty-one important plays by women writers. There is a good historical overview and an index of plays.

★ Salem, James M. *Drury's Guide to Best Plays.* 4th ed. Scarecrow, 1987. 488p. LC 87-380   0-8108-1980-5 $39.50

> Plot summaries and cast information are given for more than fifteen hundred plays in this boon to community theaters and school drama departments. Plays from ancient Greece to 1985 are covered. The valuable cast indexes list plays containing from one to more than forty characters. Plays with all-male or all-female casts are also listed.

Quotations

Andrews, Robert. *The Columbia Dictionary of Quotations.* Columbia University Press, 1993. 1562p. index.   LC 93-27305   0-231-07194-9 $34.95

Of the eighteen thousand quotations in this current title, more than eleven thousand have not been included in quotation books before. Some of the "old familiars" are here, but the selection, even of historical writers, reflects 1990s issues. The book is arranged alphabetically by topic, for example, abortion, AIDS, aging, homosexuality, political correctness, and smoking. The source is fully identified and context for the quotations is given when necessary.

★ Bartlett, John. *Bartlett's Familiar Quotations*. 15th ed. Little, Brown, 1992. index. 0-316-08277-5 $45

> This is the classic quotation book with which most libraries will start their collections of such materials. It is arranged in chronological order by author with a keyword index to help find "just the right quote."

Berman, Louis A. with Daniel K. Berman. *Proverb Wit and Wisdom: A Treasury of Proverbs, Parodies, Quips, Quotes, Clichés, Catchwords, Epigrams and Aphorisms*. Perigee/Berkeley, 1997. 522p. bibliog. index.   LC 96-27373   0-399-52273-5 $16.95

> A great complement to *Bartlett's* and other more traditional books of quotations, this book groups "proverbs" under keywords, with more than ten thousand entries for variations and sayings from literary greats, the Bible, or more "obscure origins." There is also a section on contrasting proverbs. This may not be a necessity for the very small library, but it will charm lovers of words and language and will be a good addition to any collection of quotations books.

George, John and Laird Wilcox. *Be Reasonable: Selected Quotations for Inquiring Minds*. Prometheus Books, 1994. 361p. index.   LC 93-34704   0-87975-867-8 $32.95

> The quotation book for free thinkers, this book, according to the dust jacket, is full of quotes "meant to challenge tendencies toward censorship and suppression of ideas as well as the stifling effects of 'politically correct' behavior." There is a wide range of authors—from Mark Twain to the Ayatollah Khomeini—and quotations are in alphabetical order by author. Sources of quotes and birth and death dates are given.

Hyman, Robin, ed. *NTC's Dictionary of Quotations*. National Textbook, 1994. 520p. index.   0-8442-5753-2; 0-8442-5754-0 $19.95; $15.95 paper

> The criterion for inclusion in this book was the editor's idea of those quotations that would be known to general readers of English. Quotes are listed alphabetically by author with sources given. The nearly two-hundred-page index by keyword helps users access the main body of the text. *NTC's Dictionary of Quotations* is an extensive quotations dictionary at a good price.

King, Anita, ed. *Contemporary Quotations in Black*. Greenwood, 1997. 272p. photogs. index.   LC 96-47431   0-313-29122-5 $39.95

Most of these quotations are from periodicals and have not been anthologized previously. The more than one thousand phrases are taken from the words of musicians, politicians, athletes, physicians, and so forth. Entries are alphabetical by author, and the quotes are chronological within the entry. The index is by author and subject or keyword. Photographs of many of the persons quoted are included.

Maggio, Rosalie. *The New Beacon Book of Quotations by Women*. Beacon/Farrar, 1996. 800p. index. LC 96-19641 0-8070-6782-2 $35

> Almost tripling the coverage from *The Beacon Book of Quotations by Women,* the author once again makes quotes accessible by name, subject or keyword, or by subject headings. This is a good antidote to "normal" collections of quotations, which have still not caught up with the work of women.

★ Miner, Margaret and Hugh Rawson, eds. *American Heritage Dictionary of American Quotes*. Penguin Reference, 1997. 656p. index. LC 96-08046 0-670-10002-1 $29.95 paper

> Five thousand quotations are divided into five hundred topics. The sub-arrangement is chronological to trace attitudes about events in American life and history. This uniquely American book of quotations will be useful in most public libraries.

Partington, Angela. *Oxford Dictionary of Quotations*. 4th ed. Oxford University Press, 1996. 1044p. 0-19-866058-5 $39.95

> This classic book of quotations lists more than twenty thousand phrases from more than three thousand writers of all genres and all times.

Petras, Kathryn and Ross Petras, comps. and eds. *The Whole World Book of Quotations: Wisdom from Women and Men Around the Globe Throughout the Centuries*. Addison-Wesley Publishing, 1995. 576p. LC 94-12465 0-210-62258-0 $25

> Because most of the quotations in the standard quotation books are by "dead white men," it is refreshing to come across one that emphasizes "non-Westerners, nonwhites and women." The book is arranged by categories, and each quotation entry includes the author's name, dates, and the context or source of the quote. It will provide a good balance to older tools in this field.

Platt, Suzy, ed. *Respectfully Quoted: A Dictionary of Quotations from the Library of Congress*. Congressional Quarterly, 1992. index. 0-87187-687-6 $44.95

> First published in 1989, this quotation book is unusual in that it consists of quotes that were requested from the Congressional Research Service by members of Congress. Arranged by subject, accessible by author and keyword, two thousand quotes are listed, and information is given on the context of each. It includes quotes not found elsewhere. Who says government documents are dull?

Popular Fiction

Barron, Neil, ed. *Anatomy of Wonder: A Critical Guide to Science Fiction*. 4th rev. and updated ed. Bowker, 1994. 1000p. index.   0-8352-3288-3 $52

> This is an excellent survey of the various science fiction genres and an annotated bibliography of some of the world's best science fiction. It would be valuable for collection development, reader's advisory, and interloaning. More than twenty-one hundred books are evaluated, from the beginnings of science fiction to 1993. All aspects of the field are touched upon, as well as conventions, comics, magazines, and study guides.

Bodart, Joni Richards. *One Hundred World-Class Thin Books; or, What to Read When Your Book Report Is Due Tomorrow!* Libraries Unlimited, 1993. 206p. index. 0-87287-986-0 $27.50

> This delightful and highly useful volume divides its book-report candidates into three categories—"Thin," "Thinner," and "Thinnest." Each entry gives publishing information, categories and subjects, characters, a short book talk, major ideas, book-report ideas, and book-talk ideas. One almost gets the idea that one would not even have to read a *short* book! But seriously, folks, this is an excellent source for young adult librarians, for reader's advisory, and for teachers looking for books to assign that the whole class might read. Numerous indexes help find books by author, title, curriculum area, genre, readability, and subject. A gem!

DeAndrea, William L. *Encyclopedia Mysteriosa: A Comprehensive Guide to the Art of Detection in Print, Film, Radio and Television*. Prentice-Hall, 1994. 416p. 0-671-85025-3 $27.50

> This study of the mystery genre covers works in all media. Entries cover writers, actors, characters, novels, films, TV shows, and radio programs. There are lists of works, a glossary, organizations, awards, and listings for mystery bookstores.

Godin, Seth, ed. *Quick Lit: Plots, Theme, Characters and Sample Essays for the Most Assigned Books in English and Literature Courses—Written by Students for Students*. HarperCollins, 1992. 256p.   LC 92-52537   0-06-461041-1 $12 paper

> Thirty-five books are covered in this compilation of handy essays from which students can "borrow" when stumped in English class. There is information about the author, the key characters, ideas for essays on the work, the outline of essays, and a plot summary.

★ Goring, Rosemary, ed. *Larousse Dictionary of Literary Characters*. Larousse Kingfisher Chambers, 1996. 864p. index.   LC 94-75740   0-7523-0037-7 $17.95 paper

> The work of fifty contributors, this collection of sixty-five hundred personages from literature ranges from Tiny Tim to Pussy Galore. They are taken from "the Nobel prizewinner to the humble pedlar of formulaic thrillers."

Hartman, Donald K. and Gregg Sapp. *Historical Figures in Fiction*. Oryx, 1994. 368p. index.   LC 94-15105   0-89774-718-6 $45

This easy-to-use reference tool will fill the bill when students or casual readers are looking for historical fiction of a particular period. Forty-two hundred novels are listed in which more than fifteen hundred historical personages appear as major characters. The works are arranged alphabetically by person's last name, with dates and a brief biographical note for each person. All titles were published after the year 1940.

Henry, Laurie. *The Fiction Dictionary*. Story Press, 1995. 336p. index.   1-884910-05-X $18.99

Standard terms such as *plot, narrator,* and *legend* are defined in this work, as well as newer terms, such as *cyberpunk*. A concise definition is given and is followed by a discussion of each term. Fun to read and clearly written, this work contains many terms older dictionaries do not have.

★ Herald, Diana. *Genreflecting: A Guide to Reading Interests in Genre Fiction*. 4th ed. Libraries Unlimited, 1995. 367p. index.   LC 95-7633   1-56308-354-X $38

This tool for reader's advisory work or the selection of fiction analyzes westerns, thrillers, romance, science fiction, fantasy, and horror. Within each section, classics in the field are listed, and there are lists of biographies, bibliographies, encyclopedias, and so forth.

Hicken, Mandy and Ray Prytherch. *Now Read On: A Guide to Contemporary Popular Fiction*. 2d ed. Ashgate Publishing Co., 1994. 456p. index.   1-85928-008-0 $46.95

For librarians and readers wanting to open up new possibilities in fiction reading, this is an excellent place to start. Authors are listed under genres and were chosen from a sample of library users' favorites. A majority are British, but there is a good enough number of other English-speaking writers. Sixty new authors have been added since the first edition. Westerns, light romance, and "literary-styled" novels are excluded. Each entry includes a brief bio and comments on the style and content of each novel listed. It would be excellent for use in reader's advisory with veteran or newer readers of fiction.

Howes, Kelly King. *Characters in Twentieth-Century Literature, Book II*. Gale, 1995. 509p. bibliog. index.   LC 94-2687   0-8103-9203-8 $54.95

A continuation of *Characters in Twentieth-Century Literature, Book I* (Gale, 1989), this volume contains characters in contemporary novels, short stories, and plays not in the earlier volume. Each entry has a short plot summary and some critical commentary. The entries are well written and give a good deal of information on the book itself, not just the characters.

Husband, Janet and Jonathan F. Husband. *Sequels: An Annotated Guide to Novels in Series*. 3d ed. American Library Association, 1997. 688p.   LC 96-2729-6 0-8389-0696-6 $70

A buying guide for busy librarians who can't keep up with patron demands for "the book that comes after (blank) but before (blank)." Series books are popular, and this recent edition of *Sequels* covers one-third more authors than previous editions. Coverage of science fiction, fantasy, and thrillers is expanded to meet new demands.

Parker, Peter and Frank Kermode, eds. *A Reader's Guide to the Twentieth-Century Novel*. Oxford University Press, 1995. 784p.   0-19-521153-7 $40

> The emphasis in this compilation is on "literary" novels, and more than 750 of them are synopsized in this book. There is good coverage of minor novels, which makes this work valuable. As with many books of this sort, readers could argue all day about inclusions and exclusions, but it will fill a niche when answering questions about fiction.

Pringle, David, ed. *St. James Guide to Fantasy Writers*. Gale, 1995. 711p. index. 1-55862-205-5 $140

> Part 1 of a set of two (part 2 will be horror, ghost, and Gothic writers) stands alone as an essential purchase for libraries that serve fantasy fans. Each entry has a brief biography, a complete list of works, a signed critical essay, and (some) comments from the authors about their works. There are title and nationality indexes.

★ Salzman, Jack and Pamela Wilkinson, eds. *Major Characters in American Fiction*. Henry Holt, 1996. 960p.   LC 94-11460   0-8150-4564-3 $25 paper

> Sixteen hundred characters taken from American fiction are listed alphabetically and identified. Each entry also includes the title of the work, the author, the publishing date, and a short essay. More than twenty pages are devoted to narrators whose names are not given in the original work. There are some odd inclusions and exclusions, but this is a fine reference book and will be of interest to literary browsers.

★ Seymour-Smith, Martin, comp. *Dictionary of Fictional Characters*. Writer, 1992. LC 92-5025   0-87116-166-4 $18.95 paper

> A bargain at $18.95, this work has entries on more than twenty thousand character and five hundred authors over a period of six centuries.

American Literature

★ Andrews, William L., Francis S. Foster and Trudier Harris, eds. *The Oxford Companion to African American Literature*. Oxford University Press, 1997. 799p. index.   LC 96-41545   0-19-506510-7 $49.95

> Other works have focused on various aspects of African American writing, but this is the first one-volume book to cover all "the writers and writings that have made African American literature valuable and distinctive." Starting with a fifteen-page essay on the spread of the literature, entries include more than four hundred biographies, digests of works, fictional characters, and genres. This *Oxford Companion* is a great book that belongs in every school, academic, and public library.

★ Leininger, Phillip, ed. *Oxford Companion to American Literature*. 6th ed. Oxford University Press, 1995. 880p.   0-19-506548-4 $55

> This work, in dictionary format, contains short biographies, plot summaries, movements, background, social information, and some bibliography. The classic reference work on American literature, this is a must for all library collections.

Mark Twain

Rasmussen, R. Kent. *Mark Twain A to Z: The Essential Reference to His Life and Writings*. Facts on File; Oxford University Press, 1995; 1996. 552; 576p. photogs. LC 94-39156; LC 96-026826   0-8160-2845-1; 0-19511-028-5 $45.00; $21.50 paper

> This massive, unique work will be used in every library where Mark Twain is read. It is packed with information about his life and work, with every character, every associate, every riverboat, and every invention accounted for. Entries range from three lines to several pages, and they are packed full of information. Chapter synopses will be helpful to students or those trying to remember a plot point. A remarkable book, this was amazingly put together by a single author.

English Literature

Berney, K. A. and N. G. Templeton, eds. *Contemporary British Dramatists*. St. James Press, 1994. 886p. index.   LC 94-13899   1-55862-213-6 $40

> Two hundred ten playwrights from the United Kingdom and Ireland are covered in this work. Although it claims the title of "contemporary," the cut-off criteria is death in 1950, so Sean O'Casey, Noel Coward, T. S. Eliot, and Agatha Christie make the cut. Brief biographical information is followed by a complete list of published plays and books. There are also lists of bibliographies and critical studies. Although this and its companion volumes share many entries in common with *Contemporary Dramatists* (St. James Press, 1993), new to this volume is a section of in-depth essays on thirty-four contemporary plays.

★ Drabble, Margaret, ed. *The Oxford Companion to English Literature*. Rev. ed. Oxford University Press, 1995. 1171p.   0-19-866221-1 $55

> This work, according to present and past editors, is "a useful companion to ordinary everyday readers of English literature." Fifty-nine new authors have been added to this edition. A good place to turn for basic information on writers, major works, thinkers, national myth, and other topics important to intelligent readers.

★ Greenfield, John R., John Rogers and Arlyn Bruccoli, eds. *Dictionary of British Literary Characters: Twentieth-Century Novels*. Facts on File, 1994. 596p. index. LC 94-26620   0-8160-2180-5 $65

This dictionary is the most comprehensive source that covers British fiction. More than ten thousand characters in more than 686 British novels are identified. Characters are listed alphabetically by last name. Each entry gives the title, author, and identifying facts. There is a title index and an author index.

Hamilton, Ian, ed. *The Oxford Companion to Twentieth-Century Poetry in English.* Oxford University Press, 1994. 624p.   LC 93-1436   0-19-866147-9; 0-19-280042-6 $49.95; $16.95

Although it calls itself a "companion," this work is basically a biographical dictionary of fifteen hundred poets from English-speaking countries. It does have poetry-related topics but only one hundred entries. The information on the poets ranges from a paragraph to several pages, and some entries include information contributed by the writers themselves.

Ousby, Ian, ed. *The Cambridge Guide to Literature in English.* 2d ed. Cambridge University Press, 1993. 1061p. illus.   0-521-44086-6 $49.95

Updated and enlarged from the last edition, this work covers the whole English-speaking world. Writers, genres, titles, groups, theaters, movements, terms, magazines, and prizes are among the topics covered. In spite of the attempt to cover the world, the book includes many minor British authors at the expense of major American authors. The work is still useful for the information given.

Shakespeare

Lamb, G. F. *Larousse Shakespeare Quotations.* Larousse Kingfisher Chambers, 1994. 368p. index.   LC 94-75738   0-7523-5004-8 $10.95 paper

Two thousand quotations are arranged under 197 subjects, with the context, source, speaker, and person addressed noted. There is also a dictionary of characters, a section of quotes about Shakespeare, and a chronological list of the plays.

Marder, Louis, ed. *Speak the Speech: The Shakespeare Quotation Book.* HarperCollins, 1995. 496p. index.   LC 93-4842   0-06-272063-5 $15

Marder, the editor of *Shakespeare News,* has produced an easy-to-use resource. Each quote is followed by the speaker's name, the work, the act, the scene, the verse, and the line. A glossary with definitions of obscure words and Elizabethan idioms is included. Thirty-three hundred quotes are arranged in five hundred subject areas. All public and school libraries can use this volume.

★ *NTC's Shakespeare Dictionary.* National Textbook, 1994. 304p.   0-8442-5755-9 $27.95

The first three chapters of this work (biography, play production, and poetry) give encyclopedia information; and the fourth section, a bibliography, mentions more than 145 items. The last section offers identifying information on persons and places mentioned in the plays, plus actors, companies, theaters, and other Elizabethan figures. This is not a scholarly work on Shakespeare, but an accessible reference for students and general readers.

Quennel, Peter and Hamish Johnson. *Who's Who in Shakespeare*. Oxford University Press, 1995. 240p. 0-19-521081-6 $14.95 paper

> A reissue of the 1973 edition, this inexpensive paperback is still useful for all libraries where students study and people enjoy Shakespeare. All of Shakespeare's characters are included with a summary of the character's action and purpose. The pictures from the hardcover edition are missing, but this is still a valuable work. If you have the older edition in reference, this would be good for the circulating collection.

Sherlock Holmes

Bunson, Matthew E. *Encyclopedia Sherlockiana: An A to Z Guide to the World of the Great Detective*. Macmillan, 1994. 352p. illus. LC 94-10714 0-671-79826-X $25

> The game's afoot and all the clues are in this one-volume work that will delight Sherlockians in particular and mystery fans in general. Plot summaries, character descriptions, chronologies, Sherlock Holmes societies, films, and television are all given coverage.

Classical Literature

Howatson, M. C. *The Oxford Companion to Classical Literature*. 2d ed. Oxford University Press, 1989. 640p. maps. 0-19-866121-5 $55

> This work is useful for identifying geographical, historical, mythological, and political background relevant to the study of Greek and Roman literature.

French Literature

France, Peter, ed. *The New Oxford Companion to Literature in French*. Oxford University Press, 1995. 865p. 0-19-866125-8 $55

> A totally new work, this covers ten centuries of French-language literature. Topics go beyond the usual "literary" subjects and discuss philosophy, science, art, history, linguistics, and cinema. More than three thousand entries are written by 130 international experts. There is also a time line covering the authors listed, from 481–1993. Highly recommended.

Russian Literature

Terras, Victor, ed. *Handbook of Russian Literature*. 1985. Reprint, Yale University Press, 1990. 577p. 0-300-04868-8 $26 paper

> This valuable resource has entries on genres, authors, movements, and so forth. There are more than one thousand entries, with bibliographies for each one. The text is lucid and comprehensive. This is a good introduction to Russian literature for the serious reader.

900s
History and Geography

With changes taking place all around the world on a yearly, if not daily, basis, it is important for libraries of all sizes to have current tools to answer queries on geography and the "state of the nations." A 1989 atlas is no longer current, and even the smallest library must have recent atlases, gazetteers, and geographical dictionaries.

Questions on historical topics, which may be an end in themselves or stepping stones for further research, can be answered with a careful selection of chronologies, subject encyclopedias, and historical atlases. Be sure you have good material on the United States; then, add "Whole World" tools. Once this is accomplished, try to fill in gaps on other countries or regions with specific tools on those areas.

Biographic information is a highly requested type of information in most libraries. A selection of general biographic dictionaries (all times, all places) is an important part of the 900s in any library, with more-specific subject titles added as money and space permit. Author biographies are used by students writing book reports and by patrons simply interested in learning more about a favorite. Trivia about the presidents will always be in big demand, especially in phone reference!

They come into your library in droves, asking for help you can't give and materials you don't have. Who are they? Genealogists! Some of the materials here will help librarians and patrons with no background in genealogy get started in the search for their ancestors, and many give quite specific information on countries of origin.

American history and the history of the conflicts in which our countrymen and -women took part are perhaps the most important areas of the history section for small libraries to build up first. There is a good selection of books on the two world wars as well as information on later conflicts. American history books and books on Native Americans will be used by students and history buffs alike. A good selection will include atlases and historical encyclopedias.

World Data

★ Carruth, Gordon. *The Encyclopedia of World Facts and Dates*. HarperCollins, 1993. 992p. index.   LC 89-46521   0-06-270012-X $50

> This work offers events in the history, politics, culture, and religion of mankind from the time of the big bang to 1992. Despite some inaccuracies (especially in death dates of famous persons), this work is valuable as one of the most multicultural of world overviews.

World History

Chronicle of the World. Dorling Kindersley, 1996. 1175p. illus. index.   LC 96-14225 0-7894-1201-2 $59.95

> Political, social, technological, and natural events are arranged chronologically, with a column for each year. Events are described as though a contemporary journalist were covering them. The descriptions are objective and complemented by photos, usually in color. Students looking for report ideas and general readers will enjoy this book.

Derbyshire, Ian. *The Hutchinson Dictionary of World History*. ABC-Clio, 1994. 699p. maps.   0-87436-765-4 $49.50

> Any student or reader in need of a ready-reference resource on the history of the world will find this alphabetically arranged dictionary useful to have at hand. History is divided by period, nation, and topic, and there are good maps and chronologies. Definitions are short and to-the-point. The only flaw is the exclusion of biblical figures unless they were otherwise of historical interest. Science and technology are virtually ignored. With these reservations, this remains a handy source for short, concise answers about world history.

Grenville, J. A. *A History of the World in the Twentieth Century*. Belknap Press/Harvard University Press, 1994. 1024p. illus. maps. index.   LC 94-8591 0-674-39960-9 $39.95

> Politics is the dominant topic of this historical narrative, which is divided into eighteen sections. The sections themselves are arranged chronologically and geographically, from 1900 to 1994. Not really a reference book, this work has an extremely detailed index, which makes it easy to look up short-answer topics.

★ Grun, Bernard. *The Timetables of History*. Rev. ed. Simon & Schuster, 1991. 688p. 0-671-74271-X $20 paper

> This book consists of tables that show significant events in relation to contemporary happenings. Daily life is included as well as science, literature, historical events, and so forth. This would be a great source for students needing material or ideas for a history project.

★ Wetterau, Bruce. *World History: A Dictionary of Important People, Places and Events, from Ancient Times to the Present*. Henry Holt, 1995. 1198p.   LC 93-34819
0-8050-4241-5 $25 paper

> Political movements, cities, periods, documents, speeches, ships, philosophy, composers, battles, and languages are only a fraction of the things covered in this easy-to-use, readable dictionary. It includes 135 historical outlines, covers most countries of the world, and is geared to the average Western reader. Ten thousand entries make this a reference bargain for large and small libraries. It is an updated edition of *The Concise Dictionary of World History* but contains more material on social history than did that work.

Exploration

Saari, Peggy and Daniel B. Baker. *Explorers and Discoverers: From Alexander the Great to Sally Ride*. 4 vols. Gale, 1995. illus. maps. index.   0-8103-9787-8 $76

> With youngsters (and curious oldsters) in mind, the publishers of this set have put together an exciting collection of explorers, including women and non-Europeans, who are often left out of other collections. The lives of discoverers are summarized, with black-and-white photos, drawings, and portraits to illustrate. Each volume includes such listings as time lines, explorers by country, and indexes. The maps are spare but are easily read and supplement the other illustrations. Such topics as the influence of travelers and explorers on the worlds they visited (bubonic plague) prove fascinating reading for anyone with the slightest interest in history.

Waldman, Carl and Alan Wexler. *Who Was Who in World Exploration*. Facts on File, 1991. 720p. maps. bibliog.   0-8160-2172-4 $65

> Biographies of more than eight hundred explorers are included in this biographical dictionary. The text is enhanced by pictures and maps, and there is a good bibliography of related material. The explorers are indexed by the region of exploration, and there is a brief chronology. This work would be used by students and adults in any school or public library.

Battles

Morelock, J. D. Walter J. Boyne, ed. The Army Times *Book of Great Land Battles: From the Civil War to the Gulf War*. Berkley, 1994. 352p. illus. maps. index.
LC 94-8373   0-425-14371-6 $29.95

> Fourteen land battles are analyzed in terms of their historical and political importance. An account of the battle is followed by consequences and maps. There is an index. This book would be good for circulating and reference collections in school and public libraries.

Pirates

Marley, David F. *Pirates and Privateers of the Americas.* ABC-Clio, 1994. 458p. illus. maps. index.   LC 94-31348   0-87436-751-4 $62.50

> Individual pirates are covered in much greater detail here than in Rogozinski (below). Treatment is more scholarly and describes the events, people, places, and ships that have to do with the pirate life, especially in the seventeenth century. This is the best standard historical work dealing with American pirates.

Rogozinski, Jan. *Pirates! Brigands, Buccaneers, and Privateers in Fact, Fiction, and Legend.* Facts on File, 1996. 432p. illus. maps. index.   LC 94-12717   0-8160-2761-7; 0-8160-2773-0 $45.00; $19.95

> According to its review, the *American Reference Books Annual* went twenty-five years without treating a single book on pirates, and now, two wonderful titles pop up at approximately the same time! This book, aimed at a more popular audience than the Marley (above), deals not only with real-life brigands, but also covers their ilk in fiction, songs, movies, and so forth. A good choice for young adult or popular collections. Because there are so few books in this area, and the material does not "date," many libraries will want to add both.

Shipwrecks

Ritchie, David. *Shipwrecks: An Encyclopedia of the World's Worst Disasters at Sea.* Facts on File, 1996. 320p. illus. bibliog. index.   LC 95-15664   0-8160-3163-0 $40

> No work can list all shipwrecks, and the books you have will not list the shipwreck your patron wants—that's a law. However, this book lists several hundred such events, mainly from the years 1850 to 1940. Some entries give only the bare essentials, and other entries give longer coverage, with balanced information on controversies and colorful stories. This book will be a good addition to most public library collections.

Travel

Nwanna, Gladson I. *Americans Traveling Abroad: What You Should Know Before You Go.* 2d ed. World Travel Institute Press, 1996. 630p.   0-9623820-7-8 $39.99 paper

> Everything one needs to know is covered in this great guide to venturing out of the confines of the United States! Health problems, immunizations, visa information, dos and don'ts, insurance, customs, currencies, and more are covered, as well as traveling for the disabled, the elderly, and parents with small children. Guidelines for basic areas take up most of the work. This is affordable, reliable, and useful.

City Profiles USA, 1998: A Traveler's Guide to Major U.S. Cities. 3d ed. Omnigraphics, 1997. 700p.   0-78080-280-2 $95

> More than two hundred major cities are arranged alphabetically here, with two to four pages of facts on each one. Topics such as population, transportation, climate, lodging, shopping, media, colleges, attractions, and events are covered. There are lots of phone and fax numbers and lots of URLs. The info is short and concise and can easily be copied to be tucked in a purse or briefcase.

Geography

★ Merriam-Webster Editorial Staff. *Webster's New Geographical Dictionary.* Merriam-Webster, 1995. 1408p. illus. maps.   0-87779-446-4 $24.95

> This is a classic one-volume gazetteer that includes pronunciation. Entries range from a sentence or two to several paragraphs. Maps are included, but they are small and mostly show the location of a particular place. This is an essential purchase for all libraries.

Maps

Makower, Joel, ed. *The Map Catalog.* 3d ed. Random House, 1992. 364p. LC 92-5358   0-67974-257-3 $22 paper.

> With information about the many types of maps available, map products, and sources for purchase, this is a great place to check when looking for a map. Map skills are covered, and there are lists of maps organizations and state and federal map agencies.

Historical Atlases

★ Ferrell, Robert H. *Atlas of American History.* 4th ed. Facts on File, 1997. 192p. illus. maps. index.   0-8160-3702-7 $19.95

> Multicolored maps and photos are highlights of this updated version of a reference staple. Coverage is from 1492 (Christopher Columbus) to 1992 (Bill Clinton). Two hundred fifty maps cover such topics as population expansion, boundary changes, battles, railroad systems, voting patterns, and so forth. Forty-nine maps cover U.S. voting records by party. Maps of recent conflicts are particularly valuable.

Freeman-Grenville, G. S. P. *Historical Atlas of the Middle East.* Simon & Schuster, 1993. 144p. index. bibliog. maps.   LC 93-9294   0-13390-915-8 $65

> In this atlas for the general reader, the author has included 113 maps with text and commentary. There is a detailed table of contents, a good index, and a bibliography about the Middle East. Time covered is from early history to 1993.

★ Hammond Staff. *Hammond History Atlas*. Prentice-Hall, 1995. 72p. illus. maps. index.   0-13247-751-3 $9.26 paper

> With separate maps featuring topographic features and industrial, agricultural, and natural resources, this book gives a library its money's worth. State maps indicate counties with city and town locations. This historical atlas shows historical happenings and trends, and charts and graphs show immigration history, economic patterns, and trends in trade. There are pages of historic American flags and state flags.

★ National Geographic Society Staff. *Historical Atlas of the United States*. Rev. National Geographic Society, 1994. 298p. illus. maps. index.   LC 93-32201 0-87044-970-2 $79.95

> New maps, memorable photos, eye-catching diagrams, and fine text help to make a truly effective reference work. Land, people, economy, and transportation are only a few of the themes covered. An excellent work, this will be used in all libraries.

★ *The Times Atlas of European History*. HarperCollins, 1994. 208p. maps. index. 0-06-270101-0 $40

> With good, clear maps for each defined period of time, this is an essential purchase for most libraries. For each period of time, there is a two-page map of Europe showing the boundaries of the period. The next two pages have smaller maps that focus on particular events or places.

Atlases

Concise Atlas of the World. Oxford University Press, 1993. 3d ed. 256p. illus. maps. index.   LC 93-3811   0-19-521265-7 $35

> Although this is a "world" atlas, the primary market is the United States, and the first third of the book contains general, regional, and city maps of the United States. The United States is even represented by eleven pages in the world geography section. Thirty-five pages are given over to topical maps, and the printing is of generally good quality.

Fast, Timothy H. and Cathy Carroll Fast. *The Women's Atlas of the United States*. Rev. ed. Facts on File, 1995. 258p. bibliog. maps. index.   LC 94-29084   0-8160-2970-9 $75

> Sections on demographics, education, employment, family, health, crime, and politics are covered with good maps and plenty of helps for reading them. There are suggestions for further reading and an index.

★ Hammond Staff. *Hammond Road Atlas America 1996*. Hammond, 1996. 96p. maps.   0-8437-2717-9 $5.95 paper

> Colorful and appealing road atlases are a popular tool for home and library use. This small book (24 by 31 centimeters) is easier to store than some of the large-format atlases. Maps of Canada and Mexico are included, as well as maps of national parks and other recreation sites. The book contains many maps of larger cities, and there are handy mileage tables.

Hammond Staff. *Student Atlas of the World*. Hammond, 1995. 52p. maps. index. 0-8437-7926-8 $8.26

> Well put together and attractive, this small atlas has facts and figures on seas, canals, continents, islands, mountains, rivers, and lakes. The index is limited, but this is intended to be a flip-through atlas for students and casual users.

★ Mattson, Mark T. *Macmillan Color Atlas of the States*. Macmillan, 1996. 377p. illus. maps.   LC 96-10494   0-02-864659-2 $100

> This attractive book gives fact-filled profiles of the fifty states and the District of Columbia. Every state is given a seven-page section with a political map, smaller topical maps, and text on the state's history and present conditions. Although aimed at students in middle and high school, this will be useful for patrons of all ages.

★ Rand McNally Staff. *Cosmopolitan World Atlas*. Rand McNally, 1996. 304p. maps. index.   0-528-83809-1 $70

> This book is basically a reworking of *The New Cosmopolitan World Atlas* with numerous minor changes in boundaries and names. An essay entitled "The Real World" is the major new addition. This essay binds the book together with a "view" of our planet from space and comment on man's activities on the planet. The commentary covers terrain, climate, settlement, resources, economics, the environment, transportation, communication, people, and national boundaries. It is well illustrated and well written and covers many aspects of physical earth studies. The atlas itself is medium-sized and has a detailed name index. This is a useful general atlas.

Canada

Weihs, Jean. *Facts about Canada, Its Provinces and Territories*. H. W. Wilson, 1995. 246p. maps.   LC 94-23275   0-8242-0864-1 $35

> The 1991 census of Canada is used as a basis for facts about the United States' northern neighbor. Provinces and territories are listed separately with a map, location description, historical facts, name derivations, heraldry, holidays, climate, and on and on. There are literally zillions of facts with bibliography to add more information to the wealth that is already here.

The United States

Butcher, Devereux. *Exploring Our National Parks and Monuments*. Rev. by Russell D. Butcher. Roberts Rinehart, 1995. 478p. illus. index.   1-57098-025-X $16.95

> In the first revision of this 1985 work, a son has taken over for his father and included new information and topics. Geological and natural history aspects of each area take the emphasis. Some brief information on travel directions and facilities is given. The book is divided into national parks,

monuments, historical parks, preserves, sea- and lakeshores, rivers, recreational areas, and trails. Each entry answers the question, "Why has this area been preserved and protected?" Not a travel book but excellent for travelers.

★ Smith, Darren. *Business Phone Book U.S.A. 1997.* Omnigraphics, 1996.
0-780800-90-7 $135

Almost 150,000 listings of businesses, organizations, government offices, and institutions make this one of the most valuable books in any library. Fax and toll-free numbers are also included. The arrangement is both alphabetical and classified. Formerly *The National Directory of Addresses and Phone Numbers,* this handy book also lists e-mail addresses and web sites, where available.

★ *Washington Information Directory, 1996–1997.* Congressional Quarterly, 1996.
1100p.   LC 72-646321   0-871878-968 $105

This is useful for finding the "right" government agency for information on various topics. Many nongovernmental agencies are included as well.

General Biography

★ Air Staff. *Star Guide, 1998–1999.* Axiom Information Resources, 1998.
0-94321-328-2 $12.95

Although not a compendium of home addresses as many fans would like, this is a good listing of contact addresses for more than three thousand celebrities. Educators, businesspersons, authors, and astronauts are listed, as well as entertainers, sports figures, and politicians.

★ Bowman, John S., ed. *The Cambridge Dictionary of American Biography.*
Cambridge University Press, 1995. 941p. index.   0-521-40258-1 $44.95

Nine thousand notable denizens of the United States are profiled, many of whom are women or members of minority groups (note that this is not a repository of "dead white men"). Of this nine thousand, twenty-two hundred were alive at the time of publication. A few Canadians and Latin Americans are covered but not many. There is a forty-page name index and an occupational index. Most entries range from one hundred to two hundred words in length, but some are more than four hundred words long.

Garraty, John A. and Jerome L. Sternstein. *Encyclopedia of American Biographies.*
2d ed. HarperCollins, 1996. 1280p.   LC 96-76   0-06-270017-0 $50

More than one thousand individuals who made contributions to American history are covered in this work, which has been updated to include the last twenty years. The biographies are mainly from the political, business, and military milieu, but other fields are represented. The first section of each entry is a factual overview of a person's life and work, and the second part is evaluative.

Kranz, Rachel. *The Biographical Dictionary of Black Americans*. Facts on File, 1991. 192p. illus. bibliog.   0-8160-2324-7 $24.95

> There are two hundred entries in this biographical dictionary of African Americans, fifty with identifying photos or drawings. There is a subject guide to the biographees and suggestions for further reading.

★ Merriam-Webster Editorial Staff. *Merriam-Webster's Biographical Dictionary*. Rev. Merriam-Webster, 1995. 1184p.   LC 94-43025   0-87779-743-9 $27.95

> A revision of *Webster's New Biographical Dictionary,* this boasts forty more pages than the 1988 edition. Persons from all times and all places are covered in concise and informative entries, making this an excellent tool for identification or a jumping-off point for further research. This inexpensive title should be a part of any library's reference collection.

Nagel, Rob and Anne Commire, eds. *World Leaders: People Who Shaped the World*. Gale, 1994. 3 vols. illus. maps. index.   LC 94-20544   0-8103-9768-4 $62

> Entries on 120 leaders introduce young people to a wide range of the folks who have influenced the past four thousand years in history. Political, military, religious, and social figures dominate, and there are more Asians and Africans than is usual in works of this type. It should be noted, however, that the United States accounts for 30 of the 120 lives detailed here. The three volumes divide the leaders into geographic areas. A time line is provided, and all of the biographical subjects are placed on the time line. This is a good resource, mainly intended for school use.

★ Parry, Melanie, ed. *Larousse Dictionary of Women*. Larousse Kingfisher Chambers, 1996. 741p. photogs.   LC 95-082384   0-61420-411-9 $40

> This international dictionary covers famous women from the ancient world to present day. The more than three thousand entries are two or three paragraphs in length. They often are illustrated by a photo and contain quotations and a chronology of the subject's life.

Schraff, Anne. *Women of Peace: Nobel Peace Prize Winners*. Enslow Publishers, 1994. 112p. illus. index.   LC 93-37419   0-89490-493-0 $18.95

> As an inspiration to young women (and men!), the authors have written factual but dramatic essays about the nine women who have been awarded the Nobel Peace Prize. There is a short bibliography with each essay.

★ Stetler, Susan, ed. *Almanac of Famous People*. 6th ed. 3 vols. Gale, 1993. index. 0-8103-6988-5 $99

> Each entry gives the name, nickname or pseudonym, one-line description, occupation, dates, and citations to biographical dictionaries. It is an excellent source for small libraries and easy access for larger ones. There are also listings by place of birth and death, day of birth and death, and occupation. Another listing goes year by year, day by day, and lists the famous and infamous who were born or died each day.

Author Biography

Bailey, Brooke. *The Remarkable Lives of One Hundred Women Writers and Journalists*. Twentieth Century Women Series. Adams Publishing, 1994. 208p. 1-55850-423-0 $12

>A good introductory source, this inexpensive little volume presents readable biographies of one hundred American women writers. Entries average two pages in length and list sources for further reading. The 700- to 750-word essays on each author are written in a pleasant style and give critical and biographical information. Bibliography is included after each entry. Journalists, poets, novelists, screenwriters, and biographers are a few of the types of writers covered here. Because of a lack of indexing, this work is best suited to nonresearch libraries.

Goring, Rosemary, ed. *Larousse Dictionary of Writers*. Larousse Kingfisher Chambers, 1996. 1088p.   0-7523-0039-3 $18.95

>Thirty-six contributors have written six thousand entries on writers "from Cicero to Salinger." The articles feature brief biographical info plus critical commentary and a short bibliography. There is a British and American bias, but some balance is aimed for, and many countries and times are represented in the list of authors. There are some unusual inclusions and omissions that make this not necessarily a first resource, but a good "other place" to look for author information.

Magill, Frank N. *Great Women Writers: The Lives and Works of 135 of the World's Most Important Women Writers from Antiquity to the Present*. Holt, 1994. 672p. bibliog. index.   LC 93-47648   0-8050-2932-X $40

>Articles in this work are four to five pages long and cover the author's works, achievements, life, and criticism. There is a bibliography of the author's works and of criticism of her work. Eighty percent of the writers are from the twentieth century, and 50 percent were born in the United States.

★ Mote, Dave, ed. *Contemporary Popular Writers*. St. James Press, 1997. 528p. index.   LC 96-20634   1-55862-216-0 $130

>Living or dead, American or foreign, three hundred authors are covered in this useful work. The authors covered were active in the early sixties or later and remain "read" in the nineties. In truth, the authors are mostly American, British, and Canadian, but for libraries in the United States, that need not be a flaw. The entries are similar to those in *Contemporary Authors* (Gale, seven times per year), so if a smaller library has committed to purchasing that set, this book would not be a necessary purchase. Entries include a brief biography, a list of works, a list of criticisms, and a brief critical essay on the author's works. The work has three indexes—one for nationality, one for genre, and one by title. Articles on the contributors conclude the book.

★ Parker, Peter and Frank Kermode. *A Reader's Guide to Twentieth-Century Writers*. Oxford University Press, 1996. 825p.   0-19-521215-0 $40

More than one thousand authors are covered in this directory of poets, playwrights, and novelists. As with any volume of this type, there will be quibbles with omissions, but it is a good collection of author information that often includes more personal information than, for example, *Contemporary Authors*.

Shattock, Joanne. *The Oxford Guide to British Women Writers*. Oxford University Press, 1994. 512p.   LC 92-47232   0-19-214176-7; 0-19-280021-3 $35.00; $13.95

Alphabetical entries in this biographical dictionary include terms and schools as well as author biography. Selected bibliography on women writers is included. The biographical entries are approximately one or two pages in length and give a brief account of the author's life and works.

Presidential Lives

★ DeGregorio, William A. *The Complete Book of U.S. Presidents*. 4th ed. Random House Value Publishing, 1993. illus.   0-517-0824-46 $12.99

This handy reference tool adds to the bare facts found in Kane (below). Much of the Kane info is included plus portraits, personality sketches, and quotations. Cross-references help follow careers of persons who served under more than one president.

★ Kane, Joseph. *Facts about the Presidents*. H. W. Wilson, 1993. 432p. illus. LC 93-09207   0-82420-845-5 $55

A good first resource on the presidents, this belongs in every library. Aside from the biographical section on each president, there is a section of comparative information (how many children, physical characteristics, value of estates, and so forth) and a bibliography for each man.

Genealogy

Baxter, Angus. *In Search of Your Canadian Roots*. 2d ed. Genealogical Publishing, 1994. 350p. index.   LC 94-76789   0-8603-1448-6 $16.95 paper

Well organized, this title will give persons a good start in searching for Canadian ancestors. Research in individual provinces makes up the main portion of the book, which gives addresses for archives, libraries, churches, genealogical societies, records, and other data. There is also good information on working with the major institutions for such research—the National Archives of Canada and the Family History Library of the Church of Jesus Christ of Latter-day Saints.

Baxter, Angus. *In Search of Your European Roots: A Complete Guide to Tracing Your Ancestors in Every Country in Europe*. 2d ed. Genealogical Publishing, 1994. 292p. index.   LC 94-76791   0-8063-1446-X $16.95 paper

For the countries included, the author gives the location of archives, addresses, vital records locations, church records, censuses, wills, and emigration information. Material unique to some countries is also included, as is information on organizations that will do professional research in the former Soviet Union. This is convenient and user-friendly.

Baxter, Angus. *In Search of Your German Roots: A Complete Guide to Tracing Your Ancestors in the Germanic Areas of Europe*. 3d ed. Genealogical Publishing, 1994. 125p. index.   LC 94-76790   0-8063-1447-8 $11.95

> An addition to Baxter's other *In Search of* books, this deals with the tracing of ancestors in Austria, Belgium, Denmark, France, Italy, Liechtenstein, Poland, Germany, and any country that has significant German population. The book concentrates on records to be found in Germany and tells you costs and aspects of starting a search.

Bentley, Elizabeth Petty. *The Genealogist's Address Book*. 3d ed. Genealogical Publishing, 1995. 653p. index.   0-8063-1455-9 $34.95 paper

> The newest edition of this important work adds several hundred new entries and updates 80 percent of the old entries. It is an address book of "agencies, archives, libraries, publishers and publications, historical societies and other repositories and resources of genealogical and local history information or interest." Entries include the expected directory information and are arranged by national, state, ethnic, and religious types. There are some problems with the indexing, but this is a useful reference full of valuable information.

Colletta, John Philip. *Finding Italian Roots: The Complete Guide for Americans*. Genealogical Publishing, 1995. 128p. illus. maps.   LC 93-79083   0-8063-1393-5 $11.95 paper

> Chapters in this handy book for Italian Americans include preparation in the United States, civil record locations in Italy, religious records in Italy, libraries and resources in Italy, and ways to use these records. An eleven-page bibliography supplements this highly readable book. The text includes examples of Italian documents, passports, and census records.

Croom, Emily Anne. *The Genealogist's Companion and Sourcebook*. F & W Publications, 1994. 256p. index.   LC 93-46365   1-55870-331-4 $16.99 paper

> Mainly a list of genealogy resources for the amateur or expert, this book was put together by a librarian who is also a genealogist. It is a companion to an older book by Croom, *Unpuzzling Your Past* (F & W Publications, 1989), and fleshes out the information in that title. Listed are federal and state records, local records, special collections, libraries, immigration sources, and genealogical booksellers, societies, and papers that accept questions from readers.

★ Eichholz, Alice, ed. *Ancestry's Red Book: American State, County and Town Sources*. Rev. ed. Ancestry, 1991. 858p. maps. index.   0-916489-47-7 $49.95

Comprehensive and up-to-date, *Ancestry's Red Book* is the standard quick-reference work for genealogists. The arrangement is alphabetical by state, and there is information on where to obtain military, cemetery, land, vital, church, probate, and court records. Local history sources such as collections and newspapers are covered, and addresses are given for country courthouses. Information on African American and Native American genealogy is excellent.

★ Greenwood, Val D., ed. *The Researcher's Guide to American Genealogy.* 2d ed. Genealogical Publishing, 1992. 623p. index.   LC 89-81464   0-8063-1267-X $24.95

A good book for the serious family hunter who wants to learn the principles of genealogy, this low-priced work should be in every collection that supports genealogists. New material covers the use of personal computers in genealogical research.

Irvine, Sherry. *Your English Ancestry: A Guide for North Americans.* Ancestry, 1993. 196p. illus. maps. index.   LC 93-8461   0-916489-53-1 $12.95 paper

Because a large percentage of Americans have origins in the British Isles, how can they do genealogical research without actually going to England? Read this book! From the eighteenth century to the present, records from the Church of Jesus Christ of Latter-day Saints, records in genealogy libraries, records centrally located in England, and indexed records are covered. A lot of excellent, practical information is somewhat unbalanced by the sloppy editing. Good if you need the information on English genealogy.

★ Kemp, Thomas Jay. *International Vital Records Handbook.* 3d ed. Genealogical Publishing, 1994. 417p.   LC 94-77221   0-8063-1424-9 $29.95

What a bonanza for the armchair-bound genealogist! This collection of forms and instructions will help the researcher find documents relating to birth, death, marriage, divorce, or adoption in more than 225 countries of the world. Instructions are given for filing and using all the forms. Lots of addresses provide places to send for help in various countries. Readers are warned which countries have incomplete records.

McKenna, Erin. *A Student's Guide to Irish American Genealogy.* Oryx, 1996. 176p. photogs. index.   LC 96-26070   0-89774-976-6 $24.95

This fine handbook to Irish genealogy helps the beginner start the search, find his or her relatives, and write a family saga. Current resources are given, and there is a useful list of web sites on genealogy.

Stuart, Margaret. *Scottish Family History: A Guide to Works of Reference on the History and Genealogy of Scottish Families.* 1930. Reprint, Genealogical Publishing, 1994. 386p.   LC 77-90813   0-8063-0795-1 $25

All movie fans who would trace their history back to the William Wallaces of Scottish history can start with this title. A classic work in the field of Scottish genealogy, its main value consists of the sixty-five hundred family names in alphabetical order with a source in which each name is cited.

This will be of value to beginners or advanced genealogists, but readers should be warned that many of the sources listed will only be found in major research libraries or specialized genealogy collections.

Nicknames and Pseudonyms

★ Carty, T. J. *A Dictionary of Literary Pseudonyms in the English Language.* Fitzroy Dearborn Publishers, 1995. 750p.   1-88496-413-3 $75

> Authors are entered in the first section of this book by pseudonym and in the second section by real name. Birth and death dates, occupations, and significant works are listed. The work is fairly complete and covers early pseudonymous writers and current authors in fiction, romance, crime, fantasy, and science fiction. The only problem with this work is its cost.

Personal Names

Reaney, P. H. *A Dictionary of English Surnames.* 3d ed. rev. Revised by R. M. Wilson. Oxford University Press, 1997. 592p.   1-19-860092-5 $18.95 paper

> Although it will be of interest to genealogists, the main purpose of this work is to provide the meanings of surnames, not trace their history or give family information. More than four thousand names are added to those found in the second edition of this work. Users are directed to other works that are authoritative in the field of Irish, Welsh, and Scottish names. There are introductory essays on naming practices in various parts of the United Kingdom.

★ Robb, H. Amanda. *Encyclopedia of American Family Names.* HarperCollins, 1995. 768p.   LC 94-28719   0-06-270075-8 $45

> A must for all genealogical collections, this work had its origins in a newspaper column written by one of the author's grandparents. To expand on the information found there, the author went to the "Report of Distribution of Surnames in the Social Security Number File, September 1, 1984" (Department of Health and Human Services, 1985) and added names that showed a frequency greater than five thousand. Each name entry gives the name, the "root" name and variations, the Social Security ranking, the number of persons with the name as of 1980, the origin of the name, famous Americans of this name, and genealogies on this name.

State and National Symbols

★ Shearer, Benjamin F. and Barbara S. Shearer. *State Names, Seals, Flags, and Symbols: A Historical Guide.* Rev. ed. Greenwood, 1994. 440p. illus. index. LC 93-49552   0-313-28862-3 $49.95

> Nearly twice the size of the first edition, this book now contains information on U.S. districts and territories plus legal holidays, license plates, and

commemorative postage stamps. Color plates show the symbols in good-quality reproductions.

Mottoes and Slogans

Urdang, Laurence and Ceila Dame Robbins, eds. *Slogans*. Gale, 1984. index. 0-8103-1549-1 $82

> It's good to have a compilation of slogans of various types and times, but the librarian should beware that, contrary to the title, most of these slogans are of the commercial variety and most are of U.S. origin. The slogans here are organized into categories. There are two indexes: one for the slogan and the other for the source of the slogan.

Archaeology

Fagan, Brian M., ed. *The Oxford Companion to Archaeology*. Oxford University Press, 1996. 864p. maps. index.   LC 96-30792   0-19-507618-4 $55

> Seven hundred entries, written by experts in the field of archaeology, make up this authoritative work. It is the only recent book of its kind and fills a gap in history collections with its treatment of human fossils, historic sites, and digs and background on archaeology.

The Ancient World

★ Adkins, Lesley and Roy A. Adkins. *Handbook to Life in Ancient Rome*. Facts on File, 1993. 416p. illus. maps. index.   0-8160-2755-2 $40

> This unique handbook incorporates modern scholarship about ancient Rome and is useful for beginning Latin students and those pursuing advanced studies. Information is divided into "Republic and Empire," "Military Affairs," "Geography of the Roman World," "Towns and Countryside," "Travel and Trade," "Written Evidence," "Religion, Economy and Industry," and "Everyday Life." Use of the index is a must with the topical arrangement of the book. There is a gazetteer, which includes the ancient and modern names, biographical sketches of authors with information on their works, and a section on the numbering and makeup of the Roman Legions.

Bunson, Matthew. *Encyclopedia of the Roman Empire*. Facts on File, 1992. 512p. illus. maps index.   LC 91-38036   0-8160-2135-X $45

> Although the black-and-white line drawings are often lackluster, the information in this readable book on Rome is first-rate. It is written for general audiences and is interesting and colorful. The quality of the information on all aspects of the empire is good, and there are numerous chronologies, tables, and maps.

★ David, Rosalie. *Discovering Ancient Egypt*. Facts on File, 1994. 192p. illus. maps. index. LC 93-38601   0-8160-3105-3 $22.95

> The various sections of this book cover "Discoverers," "Sites," and "Outline History of Egypt." There is a good feeling for the tide of Egyptian history and three sections of color plates of monuments, reliefs, and artifacts. There are black-and-white pictures throughout the text. This is a good history for high schools and public libraries and will also be of interest to travelers.

★ Sacks, David. *Encyclopedia of the Ancient Greek World*. Facts on File, 1995. 320p. illus. bibliog. index.   LC 94-33229   0-8160-2323-9 $40

> Some encyclopedias of the classical world cover more items than does Sacks, but his "general topics" articles, such as those on women and homosexuality, give much insight into the life of the period. There are more than five hundred articles with cross-references and a detailed index. This is a good source of information on ancient Greece for the student, college researcher, and general reader.

Speake, Graham, ed. *A Dictionary of Ancient History*. Blackwell, 1994. 768p. maps. LC 93-1437   0-631-18069-9 $62.95

> Actually a dictionary of classical rather than ancient history, this is a good work for schools and smaller public libraries. There is no information on mythology, but people, places, and events are covered in articles that generally run from one to two paragraphs. The clear, concise articles are written with the lay reader in mind. As added bonuses, there are lists of members of various royal houses of the period and a 1,250-item list of books for further reference.

Visual Dictionary of Ancient Civilizations. Dorling Kindersley, 1994. 64p. illus. index.   LC 94-8395   1-56458-701-0 $15.95

> This book is a beautiful and sophisticated look at ancient peoples of the Mediterranean and the Far East. There are great pictures of daily life doings and parallel time lines that show the progress of civilization in five major land areas. A great starting place for history reports and ideas for same.

Jewish History

★ Castello, Elena Romero and Uriel Macias Kapon. *The Jews and Europe: Two Thousand Years of History*. Henry Holt, 1994. 239p. illus. bibliog. index. LC 94-16970   0-8050-3526-5 $50

> Jews have spent much of their history surviving in unfriendly lands, both Christian and Islamic. This fine book covers all aspects of that survival and places heavy emphasis on Jewish culture during this period, an emphasis that is helped by the more than 350 color illustrations. The authors, experts in the field of Jewish history, have included a glossary of Jewish terms and

phrases with meanings and explanations. There is a good bibliography and an index. This is a book for all public libraries.

Cohn-Sherbok, Dan. *Atlas of Jewish History*. Routledge, 1994. 224p. illus. bibliog. maps. index.   LC 93-15018   0-415-08684-1 $55

> Along with the 120 maps, extensive text is provided to illuminate them. The history of the Jewish people is covered from ancient times to the current century in this book written by a rabbi. It is geared to the general reader and has a good, detailed table of contents and a bibliography. Because of lack of detail in some maps, students of this topic may also want to consult Martin Gilbert's *Jewish History Atlas* (Macmillan, 1976), which has better maps but is not so current.

Comay, Joan. *Who's Who in Jewish History: After the Period of the Old Testament*. Rev. by Lavinia Cohn-Sherbok. 2d ed. Oxford University Press, 1995. 400p. index. 0-19-521079-4 $15.95 paper

> The introductory material in this book is rich in such features as a chronology, a glossary, and maps of journeys and areas famous in Jewish history. Entries range in length from a few sentences to a full page. Jews and non-Jews who have "contributed to Jewish life and culture" are discussed.

The Middle Ages

★ Bunson, Matthew E. *Encyclopedia of the Middle Ages*. Facts on File, 1995. 498p. illus. maps. index.   LC 94-33232   0-8160-2456-1 $45

> This inexpensive book is a must buy for any library. The text covers the years from 400 to 1500 and Europe and the Islamic countries. Entries range from a few words to several thousand. There are lots of chronologies, genealogies, lists of rulers, and maps to add to the excellent text. People, places, groups, ideas, laws, and institutions are defined and described.

Loyn, H. R. *The Middle Ages: A Concise Encyclopedia*. Thames & Hudson, 1991. 352p. illus.   LC 88-50254   0-500-27545-5 $24.95 paper

> For fast, easy reference on medieval topics, this work can't be beaten. It is well cross-referenced and has bibliographic citations. The illustrations are excellent and complement the text well. This is an excellent, inexpensive additional source on the Middle Ages.

The Great Wars

Ellis, John. *World War II: A Statistical Survey*. Facts on File, 1993. 315p. maps. LC 93-10627   0-8160-2971-7 $85

> The only work of its kind, this is a compilation of military data about all combatants. There is information on the command structures, orders of battle, tables of organization, equipment, strengths, casualties and losses, pro-

duction, and hardware. The differences in capability of the various fighting forces tells its own story of this war. An excellent source of facts.

★ Foot, M. R. and I. C. B. Dear, eds. *The Oxford Companion to World War II.* Oxford University Press, 1995. 1343p. illus. maps.   0-19-866225-4 $60

> Eighteen hundred entries give information on key figures, alliances, weapons, and events of the war. Nations involved get long entries (twenty to thirty pages). There are more than thirty-nine hundred illustrations, and the articles are signed by experts. Controversial subjects are given a well-balanced treatment. An excellent text that rises above the multitude of World War II books.

Gilbert, Martin. *Atlas of World War I.* 2d ed. Oxford University Press, 1994. 216p. maps. index.   0-19-521075-1; 0-19-521077-8 $19.95; $12.95 paper

> This book has been updated since its first edition and is well indexed. Battle maps are fairly general, but topical maps of such issues as food riots in Germany or British court-martial executions give a good picture of activity during the war. There is detailed economic and political coverage.

Keegan, John, ed. *Who's Who in World War II.* Routledge, 1995. 216p. 0-415-11889-1 $14.95 paper

> Edited by one of the world's most noted military historians, this book includes three hundred biographical sketches of persons on all sides and facets of the conflict. Each entry includes dates of birth and death and a chronological sketch. This is inexpensive and good for small libraries and history novices.

★ Livesey, Anthony. *The Historical Atlas of World War I.* Henry Holt, 1994. 192p. illus. maps. index.   LC 93-47649   0-8050-2651-7 $45

> Detailed military coverage with chronological maps is invaluable to students of the First World War. The text is easy-to-read and is aided by good full-color maps and "perspective strategic overview diagrams" that show how terrain affected the course of battle. Politics, battles, and personal experiences are covered in this excellent book on the war's progress.

Pope, Stephen and Elizabeth-Anne Wheal. *The Dictionary of the First World War.* Edited by Keith Robbins. St. Martin's Press, 1995. 561p. maps.   0-312-12931-9 $40

> The twelve hundred entries in this book range from single sentences to several pages. The entries are cross-referenced and cover weapons, tactics, commanders, and strategies. There is a chronology for easy reference to basic facts.

★ Venzon, Anne C., ed. *The United States in the First World War: An Encyclopedia.* Garland, 1995. 856p. maps. index.   LC 95-1782   0-8240-7055-0 $95

> Even though it only covers the American involvement in "The Great War," biography, economics, women's issues, foreign relations, battles, and armaments are covered in detail. Most articles are brief and include short bibliographies. Recommended for most libraries.

The Holocaust

Gilbert, Martin. *Atlas of the Holocaust*. William Morrow, 1993. 282p. illus. maps. index.   LC 92-33895   0-688-12364-3 $20

> This inexpensive atlas of the attempted extermination of European Jews tells the story in photographs, maps, and text. Maps tell of expulsions, deportations, massacres, and armed resistance. This is essentially a reprint of a 1982 work so the bibliography is dated, but the good price and good information will make it useful to public libraries.

★ Wigoder, Geoffrey, ed. *The Holocaust*. 4 vols. Grolier, 1997. photogs. bibliog. index.   LC 96-9566   0-7172-7637-6 $169

> Designed with a profusion of color and black-and-white photographs, this set was put together with middle- and high-school students in mind. The work was edited by an expert in Jewish studies, and he has included a thirteen-page bibliography to help interested readers with further study.

Great Britain

★ Palmer, Alan. *Dictionary of the British Empire and the Commonwealth*. John Murray/Trafalgar Square, 1996. 395p. maps. index.   0-7195-5650-3 $35

> All aspects of the British Empire are covered in an alphabetical format that has six hundred short entries. Covered are events, people, sports, topics, and more. Emphasis is on the last two hundred years of British history. Recommended.

Germany

Thompson, Wayne C., Susan L. Thompson and Juliet S. Thompson. *Historical Dictionary of Germany*. Scarecrow, 1994. 660p. illus. bibliog. maps.   LC 94-5673 0-8108-2869-3 $75

> From occupation by Rome to 1993, the history of Germany is covered through a chronology of events, a biographical dictionary, political parties, events, and terms. There is also a good bibliography. The main strength of the work is in its information on twentieth-century Germany.

Russia

Duffy, James P. and Vincent Ricci. *Czars: Russia's Rulers for More Than One Thousand Years*. Facts on File, 1995. 288p. illus. bibliog. index.   LC 94-44654 0-8160-2873-7 $29.95

Thorough and readable material on the rulers of Russia is full of interesting anecdotes that illuminate the history of that country. All of the czars are covered, warts and all, in this excellent basic survey.

Gilbert, Martin. *Atlas of Russian History*. 2d ed. Oxford University Press, 1993. 208p. maps. index.   LC 93-21920   0-19-521041-7 $19.95

This is the most complete English-language atlas of Russian maps available, and it is priced low enough for most libraries to purchase it. Reviewers note that the atlas is good at showing the rise of the revolutionary movement and the history of the Soviet Union. Charts show political, economic, cultural, and social developments.

The Cold War Era

Arms, Thomas S. *Encyclopedia of the Cold War*. Facts on File, 1994. 628p. illus. bibliog. index.   LC 90-26899   0-8160-1975-4 $70

Because the cold war dominated world history for almost fifty years, it is a complicated topic with many facets. This source covers them all, with seven hundred entries on people, places, and things involved in cold war history. There is a brief chronology of the war and a nine-page bibliography.

Dictionary of Twentieth Century Culture: Post-World War II America. Vol. 1. Gale, 1994. 352p. illus. index.   0-8103-8481-7 $90

In shorter entries ranging from several sentences to one thousand words, persons, places, events, and trends of this period are covered. All fields except science and technology are covered. The majority of the topics in this book for the general reader are biographical. A time line lists year-by-year activities and cultural occurrences from 1945 to 1993.

The Korean War

★ Sandler, Stanley, ed. *The Korean War: An Encyclopedia*. Garland, 1996. 456p. photogs. maps. bibliog. index.   LC 95-1932   0-8240-4445-2 $75

Compiled by a historian with the U.S. Army, this encyclopedia was written by sixty-three expert contributors and includes highly readable entries on people, places, battles, armed forces, weapons, and strategy. There is good coverage on such topics as brainwashing, airborne operations, and armistice negotiations. Good research and reading fare for students and general readers.

Summers, Harry G. *Korean War Almanac*. Facts on File, 1990. 352p. maps. photogs. bibliog.   0-8160-1737-9 $27.95

In this book, Summers provides us with a detailed treatment of the Korean conflict. A brief overview of the war is followed by a chronology and a "dictionary" section of war topics.

The Vietnam Conflict

★ Kutler, Stanley I. *Encyclopedia of the Vietnam War*. Prentice-Hall, 1996. 711p. illus. maps. index.   LC 95-20940   0-13-276932-8 $99

> A good purchase for any library, this work deals not only with the American experience in Vietnam, but with Vietnamese issues and participants. This outstanding one-volume historical and biographical encyclopedia is arranged in alphabetical order. There are ten authoritative essays on various aspects of the period, such as the antiwar movement, colonialism, and literature.

Olson, James S., ed. *Dictionary of the Vietnam War*. Greenwood, 1988. 593p. maps. bibliog. index.   0-313-24943-1 $79.95

> The nine hundred entries range from paragraphs to two pages. They cover persons, events, institutions, and so forth. Maps of Vietnam by military region and province are provided. A good supplement to the *Vietnam War Almanac* (below), it is longer and more comprehensive.

Summers, Harry G. *Vietnam War Almanac*. Facts on File, 1987. 416p. illus. maps. bibliog. index.   0-8160-1017-X $27.95

> This well-printed book gives a balanced discussion of the Vietnam War, with narrative, chronology, and an alphabetical dictionary of war topics and words. Summers provides an excellent overview of the conflict.

The Persian Gulf War

★ Hutchison, Kevin Don. *Operation Desert Shield/Desert Storm: Chronology and Fact Book*. Greenwood, 1995. 320p. illus. maps. index.   LC 95-21530 0-313-29606-5 $69.50

> Judged by some reviewers to be the best source on the Gulf War, this is mainly a day-by-day chronology of the war. There is information on movements, events, units, missions, equipment, and personnel. A glossary is included, as well as lists of coalition prisoners and casualties, lists of forces, and biographies of key personnel. Maps, charts, and photographs of weaponry add to the value of this great source of factual information.

Native Americans

★ Francis, Lee. *Native Time: A Historical Time Line of Native America*. St. Martin's Press, 1996. 356p. photogs.   LC 95-8027   0-312-13129-1 $35

> Recommended for all collections that deal with Native Americans, this time line was compiled by the director of Wordcraft Circle of Native Writers and Storytellers. It outlines the history of Native Americans in law and politics; literature, art, legend, and stories; heroes, leaders, and victims; and elder wisdom, philosophy, and songs.

★ Grinde, Donald A. *The Encyclopedia of Native American Biography: Six Hundred Life Stories of Important People.* Holt, 1996. 512p. illus. bibliog. LC 96-17113   0-8050-3270-3 $50

> Although this book repeats some of the biographies found in *Great North American Indians* (Van Nostrand Reinhold, 1977), *Who Was Who in Native American History* (Facts on File, 1990), and *Biographical Dictionary of Indians of the Americas* (American Indian Publishers, 1998), it contains many new biographies of contemporary Indians who are not found elsewhere. It is arranged alphabetically, and there are more than 150 illustrations.

★ Hoxie, Frederick E., ed. *Encyclopedia of North American Indians: Native American History, Culture, and Life from Paleo-Indians to the Present.* Houghton Mifflin, 1996. 837p. illus. maps. index.   0-395-66921-9 $45

> This highly readable resource contains four hundred excellent and accessible articles. It is a standout even in the large field of Native American reference. It contains more than one hundred biographies, information on one hundred tribes, cultural overviews, and terminology.

Klein, Barry T. *Reference Encyclopedia of the American Indian.* 7th ed. Todd, 1995. 890p. index.   0-915344-45-9; 0-915344-46-7 $125; $75 paper

> Two hundred more pages have been added to the seventh edition of this work. This is an excellent source of directory information on current Native Americans and Native American activities. Besides biographies, there are sections on Indian education programs, gambling sites, and Native American events. There is a wealth of directory information on Native American institutions and organizations.

Legay, Gilbert. *Atlas of Indians of North America.* Barron's Educational Series, 1995. 95p. illus. maps. index.   LC 95-13019   0-8120-6515-8 $16.95

> Colorful illustrations show the remarkable diversity of America's native peoples. Clear maps divide Indians into linguistic and cultural groupings. General historical locations of the various Indian nations are shown. The information is quick and brief but is well presented and will be valuable to students or anyone interested in native history and culture.

Native America: Portrait of a People. Visible Ink Press/Gale, 1994. 786p. illus. index. 0-8103-9452-9 $18.95 paper

> Nineteen chapters cover information on Indians, with an emphasis on contemporary Native Americans. Chapters contain information on activism, traditional culture areas, languages, religion, arts, and health. Biographies are also included. A good addition to the collections where material on modern Indians is needed.

Paterek, Josephine. *Encyclopedia of American Indian Costume.* Norton, 1996. 536p. illus. bibliog. maps. index.   LC 93-39337   0-393-31382-4 $19.95 paper

> Divided by traditional Native American culture areas, this book provides descriptions of both dress and ornamentation. There is a bibliography.

Black-and-white photos are the only drawback. Basic dress—including footwear, jewelry, hairstyles, and face and body embellishments—is covered, as well as the influence of European contact.

Tiller, Veronica E., ed. *Discover Indian Reservations U.S.A.: A Visitor's Welcome Guide*. Council Publications, 1992. 402p. maps. index.   0-9632580-0-1 $19.95 paper

In this unusual guide, all of the events, areas, and museums are owned or operated by Indians. It is basically a list of what to see and do in the Native American world, not including Alaska. The introductory material is good, and there are state maps and a list of reservations to help travelers.

American History

★ Carruth, Gordon. *Encyclopedia of American Facts and Dates*. 9th ed. HarperCollins, 1993. 1056p. index.   LC 92-54676   0-06-270045-6 $40

This quick-reference index is in chronological arrangement and lists concurrent events in American history in various fields of endeavor. This will be a first purchase for most libraries.

Dorling Kindersley Staff. *Chronicle of America*. Dorling Kindersley/Houghton, 1995. 984p. illus. index.   0-7894-0124-X $59.95

Modeled after a newspaper, with each historical event treated as an article, this massive book contains political, social, and cultural events, with many illustrations, including photos and art reproductions. Biographies of presidents and histories of the states are just two of the features in this work that covers history from the arrival of Asian tribes across the Bering Straits to the Oklahoma City bombing. Now *that's* history!

Doyle, Rodger. *Atlas of Contemporary America: A Portrait of the Nation: Politics, Economy, Environment, Ethnic and Religious Diversity*. Facts on File, 1994. 256p. maps. index.   LC 93-38380   0-8160-2545-2 $45

This work is divided into seven sections and is based on data from the 1990 census. The focus here is on ethnicity, linguistics, religion, environment and quality of life, politics, economics, and health. Most information is presented at a county level. The printing is of high quality, and the material accompanying each map adds to the value of the work, as do the bibliographic references.

Gordon, Lois and Alan Gordon. *The Columbia Chronicles of American Life, 1910–1992*. Columbia University Press, 1995. 837p. illus. index. 0-231-08100-6 $39.95

With this reasonable price, libraries can well afford to buy this excellent eight-hundred-page chronology that contains news items, facts, lists, quotes, and more than five hundred photographs. There is also great biographical material on people involved in all aspects of American life. The quotation section is excellent for its window on the minds of people involved in particular aspects of American history.

★ Kane, Joseph, Janet Podell and Steven Anzovin, eds. *Facts about the States.* 2d ed. H. W. Wilson, 1994. 624p. LC 93-30328 0-8242-0849-8 $60

Information about each state includes such data as demographics, economics, geography, climate, government, and history. Sections on the environment and "unusual facts" are new to this edition. Basic, "quick and dirty" information about each state of the union.

Kaspi, Andre, ed. *Great Dates in United States History.* Facts on File, 1994. 266p. maps. index. LC 93-42889 0-8160-2592-4 $25.95

Those interested in American history will be pleased with this inexpensive and user-friendly tool. Readers should be aware that nineteen of the thirty chapters cover twentieth-century topics, so coverage of earlier American history is less detailed. For modern American facts and dates, the book is accurate, brief, and will be appreciated by history teachers, students, and the general reader.

Stern, Jane and Michael Stern. *Jane and Michael Stern's Encyclopedia of Pop Culture.* HarperCollins, 1992. 640p. illus. index. 0-062715-23-2 $40

Want to know about Slim Whitman? The Super Bowl? Spandex? The Simpsons? Soul Train? 7-11? and Sinatra? They're all in this great, alphabetically arranged list of things that make America great! And that's only the *S*s!

Tuleja, Tad. *The New York Public Library Book of Popular Americana.* Macmillan, 1996. 0-02861-448-8 $14.95 paper

A good complement to the Stern title (above), this is another collection of people, events, things, and words that have become "cultural icons" among Americans. This lively, readable book contains more than four thousand entries on sports figures, cartoon characters, arts events, and so forth. This is great for browsing collections, as well as for reference. This is one of those great "Honey, listen to this" books with which to drive your relatives mad.

The Revolutionary War

★ Boatner, Mark M., III. *Encyclopedia of the American Revolution.* 3d ed. Stackpole Books, 1994. 1312p. maps. bibliog. index. 0-8117-0578-1 $32.95

Even though it is a valuable and inexpensive resource on the Revolutionary War, this book is essentially unchanged since the first edition, including the bibliography. It is still a comprehensive work on the war based on scholarship up to 1966. Given the fact that some of the other sources on the war are much more expensive, it is still an excellent choice for public libraries. There are entries on people, events, battles, and issues of the war, as well as maps. Just be aware that if you have the first or second edition, you do not have to replace it with this one.

Purcell, L. Edward. *Who Was Who in the American Revolution*. Facts on File, 1993. 548p. bibliog. index.   0-8160-2107-4 $60

> This book has fifteen hundred entries for a broad range of persons involved in both sides of the conflict in the American Revolution. There is a good index and a guide to further sources.

Symonds, Craig. *Battlefield Atlas of the American Revolution*. Nautical & Aviation Publishing, 1986. 112p. maps.   LC 86-63201   0-933852-53-3 $24.95

> Maps of the battles of the American Revolution can be used by students and history buffs alike. Symonds is known for writing and publishing in this area. This is a good title to add to material on colonial and revolutionary history.

The Civil War

★ Faust, Patricia, ed. Historical Times *Illustrated Encyclopedia of the Civil War*. HarperCollins, 1991. 1056p. illus. maps.   LC 94-16962   0-06-273116-5 $27.50

> The *American Reference Books Annual* reviewer calls this a "major achievement" and a "splendid reference book of lasting value." There are entries for battles, persons, places, and events.

★ McPherson, James M., ed. *The Atlas of the Civil War*. Macmillan/Simon & Schuster, 1994. 223p. illus. maps. index.   LC 94-16962   0-02-579050-1 $40

> A superb atlas prepared by nine historians, this is a combination of narrative, contemporary comment, two hundred black-and-white illustrations, and two hundred full-color maps. Each battle is covered in a two-page spread in a book divided into a section for each year of the conflict. A Pulitzer Prize–winning historian has compiled an essential purchase for most libraries.

Symonds, Craig L. *A Battlefield Atlas of the Civil War*. 3d ed. Nautical & Aviation Publishing, 1994. 115p. illus. maps.   1-877853-25-9 $24.95

> Forty-three maps detailing the major campaigns of the Civil War, each containing basic landmarks and troop movements, make up the main body of this book. For the price, an excellent title for small libraries to round out their Civil War material.

The American West

Beck, Warren A. and Ynez D. Haase. *Historical Atlas of the American West*. University of Oklahoma Press, 1992. 200p. maps. index.   LC 88-40540 0-8061-2456-3 $21.95

Every aspect of the West is covered in a series of excellent maps with a one-page essay on the events covered by the map. Not just a "cowboy" atlas, this covers such things as fur trappers' rendezvous and World War II prisoner-of-war camps.

Cusic, Don. *Cowboys and the Wild West: An A-Z Guide from the Chisholm Trail to the Silver Screen*. Facts on File, 1994. 356p. illus. bibliog. index.   LC 93-45584   0-8160-2783-8; 0-8160-3030-8 $40.00; $19.95

> Cowboy lingo, movies, TV, and songs and biographies of cowboys and western figures are just a few of the topics covered in this book that also includes information on Indian tribes, the Pony Express, Mormons, trappers, the Chisholm Trail, and so on. More than one hundred black-and-white illustrations complement the text, and there is a twelve-page double-columned bibliography.

Slatta, Richard W. *The Cowboy Encyclopedia*. Rev. ed. ABC-Clio, 1996. 474p. illus. index.   LC 94-19824   0-87436-738-7; 0-343-31473-1 $54; $17

> Focusing on the "equestrian cattle cultures of the Americas," thirteen hundred entries give information on cowboys of all types. Entries range from a brief definition to several pages. Information on cowboy history and culture also includes biography, dress, equipment, and music. There is material on Native American and African American cowboys. Appendixes give listings of films, periodicals, and museums.

Wexler, Alan. *Atlas of Westward Expansion*. Facts on File, 1995. 256p. illus. bibliog. maps. index.   LC 94-756   0-8160-2660-2; 0-8160-3206-8 $35.00; $19.95 paper

> A must buy for high-school and public libraries, this work concentrates on events that shaped the history of the western portion of our country. Chapters include text, maps, illustrations, and photographs. The writing is objective and straightforward. Sidebars and appendixes add interest to the text, and there is a long bibliography.

Author Index

Title Index

Audrey Lewis was formerly Library Services Coordinator at the White Pine Library Cooperative, where she also worked as a reference librarian. She is now director of the Thomas E. Fleschner Memorial Library in Birch Run, Michigan. Lewis is a graduate of Albion College and the University of Michigan. She is past chair of the Marketing and Public Relations Roundtable of the Michigan Library Association and has taught numerous reference workshops, including ten years with the Library of Michigan Beginning Certification Workshop. Lewis is married and has two grown children.